The Gourmet iOS Developer's Cookbook

The Gourmet iOS Developer's Cookbook

Even More Recipes for Better iOS App Development

Erica Sadun

✦✦ Addison-Wesley

New York • Boston • Indianapolis • San Francisco
Toronto • Montreal • London • Munich • Paris • Madrid
Cape Town • Sydney • Tokyo • Singapore • Mexico City

Editor-in-Chief
Mark Taub

Senior Acquisitions Editor
Trina MacDonald

Senior Development Editor
Chris Zahn

Managing Editor
Kristy Hart

Senior Project Editor
Betsy Gratner

Copy Editor
Kitty Wilson

Indexer
Tim Wright

Proofreader
Sarah Kearns

Technical Reviewers
Mark Granoff
Mike Greiner
Rich Wardwell

Editorial Assistant
Olivia Basegio

Cover Designer
Chuti Prasertsith

Compositor
Nonie Ratcliff

❖

Dedicated with great affection to Chris Zahn:
editor, enabler, and wonderful person.

❖

Contents

Preface   xiii

1 Media   1

Speech   1
Other Options   3
Delegate Callbacks   3
Dictation   5
Creating Barcodes   5
Filter Parameters   5
Building Codes   6
Reading Barcodes   8
Listening for Metadata Objects   10
Responding to Metadata   11
Extracting Bounds   13
Enhancing Recognition   14
Detecting Faces   14
Building AVFoundation Movies   14
Creating a Pixel Buffer   16
Drawing into the Pixel Buffer   17
Expressive Drawing   18
Building Movies from Frames   19
Adding Images to Movies   23
Wrap-up   24

2 Dynamic Typography   25

Type Size and User Needs   25
How Dynamic Type Works   25
Listening for Type Updates   28
Handling Dynamic Type with Attributes   31
Scanning for Text Style Ranges   32
Applying Text Style Ranges   34
Attribute-Ready Dynamic Elements   35
Custom Fonts Faces   36
Dynamic Text Views   37
Custom Sizing   38

Font Descriptors   39
 Descriptor Challenges   40
 Fonts with Multiple Variations   41
 Using String Attributes to Modify Fonts   42
Dynamic Type Gotchas   43
Wrap-up   43

3   Text Kit   45
Creating Complex Text Layouts   45
Glyphs   46
Text Storage   55
Layout Managers   56
Text Containers   56
 Adaptive Flow   58
 Insets   60
 Exclusion Paths   60
 Bounding Rectangles   62
Using Text Kit to Add Touch to Labels   63
 Establishing Text Kit   63
 Synchronizing   64
 Translating Coordinates   65
 Glyphs and Characters   66
 Checking for Links   67
 Adding Visual Feedback   67
Draggable Exclusion Zones   69
Building PDFs with Text Kit   71
Printing Text View Data   73
 Printing PDF Data   74
Wrap-up   74

4   Attributed Strings and Document Containers   75
Class Enhancements   75
 String Attachments   77
Building Attributed Strings from HTML   78
 Document Type Dictionaries   79
 Converting HTML Source to Attributed Strings   80

Converting Attributed Strings to Document
Representations   81

Generating HTML from Attributed Strings   82

Markup Initialization   83

RTF and RTFD   83

The RTFD Container   84

Initializing Attributed Strings from a File   84

Converting RTFD Text to Data   85

Writing RTFD Containers from Data   86

Inspecting Attributes   87

Establishing Document Attributes   89

Enhancing Attributed Strings   91

Returning Copies with New Attributes   92

Adjusting Attributes   93

Extending Mutable Attributed Strings   94

Text Ranges   95

Calculating Positions   95

Position Geometry   95

Updating Selection Points   97

Hardware Key Support   97

Wrap-up   99

5 Animation   101

Keyframe Animation   101

Building Physics with Keyframes   103

Blocking Animators   105

UIKit Spring-Based Animations   106

Practical Uses for Spring Animations   108

System Animations   109

Motion Effects   109

Building Planes   110

Shadow Effects   111

Custom Transition Animations   113

Delegation   114

Building Transitioning Objects   114

Implicit Animations   116
   Building an Animation-Ready Layer   116
   Building a View Around a Layer   118
   Timing   118
   Coordinating Animations   119
   Building Implicit Completion Blocks   120
   Animating Custom Properties   121
   Intercepting Updates   122
   Drawing Properties   123
Wrap-up   124

6   Dynamic Animators   125
Physics-Based Behaviors   125
   Building Dynamics   126
Detecting Pauses   127
   Creating a Frame-Watching Dynamic Behavior   131
Implementing Snap Zones   133
Leveraging Real-World Physics   135
   Connecting a Gravity Behavior to Device
   Acceleration   137
   Creating Boundaries   138
   Enhancing View Dynamics   138
Custom Behaviors   139
   Creating Custom Dynamic Items   139
   Subverting Dynamic Behaviors   141
   Better Custom Dynamic Behaviors   142
   Custom Secondary Behaviors   144
Collection Views and Dynamic Animators   147
   Custom Flow Layouts   147
   Returning Layout Attributes   148
   Updating Behaviors   149
Building a Dynamic Alert View   150
   Connecting Up the Jelly   150
   Drawing the View   152
   Deploying Jelly   154
Wrap-up   154

7 Presentations   155

Alerts   155

   Class Deprecations   155

   Building Alerts   156

   Enabling and Disabling Alert Buttons   161

   Adding Text Fields   162

Mask Views   164

   Shape Layer Masking   164

   Building Mask Views   166

Building Effect Views   169

   Building a Blur Effect   170

   Adding Vibrancy Effects   171

   Animating Effect Views   172

Building Popovers   175

   Supporting Bubbles   176

   Presenting Popovers   177

Wrap-up   177

8 Shape Magic   179

How to Shape a View   179

   Expanding Beyond Circles   180

   Resizing Bezier Paths   180

   Building a Bezier-Based Shape Image View   184

   Working with Unclosed Shapes   185

Adding Borders to Shaped Views   187

Building Shaped Buttons   190

Adding Attention-Grabbing Animations to Shaped
Views   193

Wrap-up   199

9 Adaptive Deployment   201

Traits   201

   Trait Properties   202

   Defining Traits   202

   Combining Trait Collections   203

   Designing for Traits   204

UIScreen Properties   205
  Coordinate Spaces   205
  Application Frame   206
  Screen Bounds   206
  Scale   207
Rotation   207
Size Classes and Assets   208
  Basic Deployment   208
  UIKit and Image Views   210
  The UIImageAsset Class   210
  Building Images from PDFs   211
Overriding Trait Collections   214
  Building Side-by-Side iPhone Split Views   215
  A Bit More About iOS 8 Split View Controllers   218
Wrap-up   219

10   Development Helpers   221
All the Lorems   221
  Placeholder Text   221
  Image Ipsums   223
  Generating Random User Data   225
  Bulk Names   225
  Generating Random Feeds   227
Random Everything   228
Directives   229
  Converting Comments to Warnings   229
  Warnings   231
  Testing for the Simulator   232
  Errors   232
  Testing for Inclusion   233
  Messages   234
  Wrapping Pragmas   234
  Overriding Diagnostics   235
  Unused Variable Warnings   235
  Marking Non-null and Nullable Items   236

Developer Tweaks   236

Saving Files from the Simulator   237

Tighter Logging   238

Wrap-up   238

11   A Taste of Swift   239

Swift Versus Objective-C   239

Building iOS Apps in Swift   240

Optionals   243

Inferred Types   244

The Optional Enumeration   245

Unwrapping Optionals   246

Assigning Values to Non-optionals   248

Cocoa Touch Patterns   248

Hybrid Language Development   251

Calling Objective-C from Swift   252

Accessing Classes   252

Calling Swift from Objective-C   253

Preparing Swift for Objective-C   254

Class Descent   255

Building the Basics   256

Watching Progress   257

Learning Swift   259

Wrap-up   260

Index   261

Preface

Developers can never have too many useful ideas to draw from, and this latest entry in the bestselling *Cookbook* series is filled with delicious possibilities. *The Gourmet iOS Developer's Cookbook* offers a curated selection of programming recipes to inspire your everyday iOS programming efforts. This volume serves up a new banquet of turnkey solutions for projects big and small. It offers a fresh collection of versatile solutions that promise to add spice to your code.

The goal here is simple. Each chapter should enable you to walk away with fresh ideas and master techniques off the beaten track. Whether you're reading about new takes on old technologies or completely fresh APIs, here's hoping you'll say, "Hey, I didn't know you could do that!" or "That's really cool."

The Gourmet iOS Developer's Cookbook offers a deep dive into the nonobvious. Its chapters cover techniques and technologies that skew away from the common and enable you to explore new development cuisines. It's not a book for those just learning how to cook apps. It offers tasty recipes for the iOS enthusiast who wants to builds fragrant, delicious, and exotic routines.

How This Book Is Organized

This book offers practical iOS development recipes. Here's a rundown of what you'll find in this book's chapters:

- **Chapter 1, "Media"**—This chapter explores advances that have made their way into AVFoundation over the past few years and shows how you can integrate these features into your own applications. In this chapter, you'll read about speech generation, barcode recognition (which enables you to leverage the device camera to recognize a wide range of barcode styles), and application of modern language features to AVFoundation movie creation.

- **Chapter 2, "Dynamic Typography"**—iOS's overhauled interface has shifted emphasis away from buttons and bars to a sparser and more text-centered experience, where text components have become even more critical parts of UI design. This chapter introduces ways your text can update itself automatically to match user preferences and expectations and discusses some critical lessons to be learned along the way.

- **Chapter 3, "Text Kit"**—Flexible text presentation is one of the most exciting and developing areas of iOS. With every new iOS release, these APIs have grown, matured, and expanded. Most UIKit interface classes now support rich text features. In the most modern iOS releases, that support has expanded to a suite of layout classes that continue to add mature type and frame settings to create flexible presentations.

- **Chapter 4, "Attributed Strings and Document Containers"**—Over the past few years, attributed strings have grown enormously in power and potential, and they now provide support for HTML and RTF rich text documents. Attributed strings provide seamless polymorphism between text presentation and representation. Text design now better migrates to the iOS screen and from iOS to other destinations. This chapter explores those expanded possibilities.

- **Chapter 5, "Animation"**—Of the technologies updated in the past couple years, iOS animation is one of the ones that has been most enhanced by new APIs. New dynamic styles enable your interfaces to integrate real-world physics for better and more exciting presentations and interactions. This chapter begins the discussion of animation features, introducing some of the profound updates that you'll use in your apps.

- **Chapter 6, "Dynamic Animators"**—Dynamic animators are some of the most exciting elements of iOS. Their physics-based view behaviors create lively and curious interfaces. At the same time, they can be difficult to work with. In this chapter, you'll learn how to incorporate these classes into your iOS apps for the best possible results and the fewest headaches.

- **Chapter 7, "Presentations"**—In the latest versions of iOS, user alerts are fully re-imagined and popovers are now universally available. Special effects highlight presentations to provide the greatest visual impact when you overlay content for modal interaction. This chapter gets you up to speed on these modern techniques.

- **Chapter 8, "Shape Magic"**—Non-rectangular views enable your apps to expand possibilities with fun and clever effects. For example, you might draw attention to a view by animating a halo behind it. Or you might use shapes to better stack buttons together for visual seamlessness. This chapter covers many advanced shape techniques you can use to add pizzazz to your user interfaces.

- **Chapter 9, "Adaptive Deployment"**—As the iOS family continues to grow, apps should automatically support all new displays, orientations, and screens. Although iOS targets are not nearly as splintered as Android's multitude, interfaces face numerous configurations for universal deployment. A truly adaptive app gracefully responds with a well-designed and engaging interface, ready for the user at any size. This chapter explores the basics of these new technologies and the APIs you need to learn for moving your apps forward.

- **Chapter 10, "Development Helpers"**—At times, it helps to have methods, functions, and techniques to help you through the development process. Together, the solutions in this chapter support you when building apps. They enable you to speed through your development day to better arrive at the app you're working on.

- **Chapter 11, "A Taste of Swift"**—Apple introduced the Swift programming language at the June 2014 WWDC Keynote. Swift offers a performance-tuned type-safe modern programming language. Today, many development fundamentals have coalesced, although the language and toolset have continued to evolve. This chapter surveys the base essentials of Swift development, providing a taste of this new technology. You won't learn the language in this chapter. Instead, you'll explore concepts and development issues that affect you as an iOS developer to get a sense of where this important technology is going.

About the Sample Code

This book follows the trend I started in my *iOS Developer's Cookbook* series. This book's sample code always starts off from a single `main.m` file, where you'll find the heart of the application powering the example. This is not how people normally develop iOS or Cocoa applications—nor how they should be developing them. It's hard to tell a story when readers must search through many files and try to find out what is relevant and what is not. Offering a single launching point concentrates the story, allowing access to an idea from a coherent starting point.

Getting the Sample Code

You'll find the source code for this book at https://github.com/erica/iOS-Gourmet-Cookbook on the open-source GitHub hosting site. There, you'll find a chapter-by-chapter collection of source code that provides examples of the material covered in this book.

Retrieve sample code either by using git tools to clone the repository or by clicking GitHub's Download button, which was at the right center of the page when I wrote this book. It enables you to retrieve the entire repository as a ZIP archive or tarball.

Contribute!

Sample code is never a fixed target. It continues to evolve as Apple updates its SDK and the Cocoa Touch libraries. Get involved. Pitch in by suggesting bug fixes and corrections and by expanding the code that's on offer. GitHub allows you to fork repositories and grow them with your own tweaks and features and then share them back to the main repository. If you come up with a new idea or approach, let me know.

Getting GitHub

GitHub (http://github.com) is the largest git-hosting site, with more than 150,000 public repositories. It provides both free hosting for public projects and paid options for private projects. With a custom web interface that includes wiki hosting, issue tracking, and an emphasis on social networking among project developers, it's a great place to find new code or collaborate on existing libraries. Sign up for a free account at the GitHub website, where you can then copy and modify this repository or create your own open-source iOS projects to share with others.

Contacting the Author

If you have any comments or questions about this book, please drop me an e-mail message at erica@ericasadun.com or stop by the GitHub repository and contact me there.

Acknowledgments

My sincere thanks go out to Trina MacDonald, Chris Zahn, and Olivia Basegio, along with the entire Addison-Wesley/Pearson production team—specifically Kristy Hart, Betsy Gratner, Kitty Wilson, Nonie Ratcliff, and Chuti Prasertsith—and my technical editors Rich Wardwell, Mark Granoff, and Mike Greiner.

My gratitude extends to everyone who helped read through early drafts and provide feedback. Specific thanks go out to Oliver Drobnik, Hamish Allan, Sebastian Celis, Maurice Sharp, Wess Cope, Jeremy Tregunna, Ken Lindsay, Cameron Banga, John Grosvenor, Matthias Neeracher, Chris Woodard, David Green, Alexander Kempgen, Chris Flesner, Remy "psy" Demarest, Ken Ferry, Mike Ash, Kevin Ballard, Phil Holland, August Joki, and everyone else who contributed to this effort. If I have omitted your name here, please accept my apologies.

Special thanks also go to my husband and kids. You are wonderful.

About the Author

Erica Sadun is the bestselling author, coauthor, and contributor to several dozen books on programming, digital video and photography, and web design, including the widely popular *The Core iOS 6 Developer's Cookbook*, fourth edition. She has blogged at TUAW.com, O'Reilly's Mac Devcenter, Lifehacker, and Ars Technica. In addition to being the author of dozens of iOS-native applications, Erica holds a Ph.D. in computer science from Georgia Tech's Graphics, Visualization and Usability Center. A geek, a programmer, and an author, she's never met a gadget she didn't love. When not writing, she and her geek husband parent three geeks-in-training, who regard their parents with restrained bemusement when they're not busy rewiring the house or plotting global domination.

Editor's Note: We Want to Hear from You!

As the reader of this book, you are our most important critic and commentator. We value your opinion and want to know what we're doing right, what we could do better, what areas you'd like to see us publish in, and any other words of wisdom you're willing to pass our way.

You can e-mail or write me directly to let me know what you did or didn't like about this book—as well as what we can do to make our books stronger.

Please note that I cannot help you with technical problems related to the topic of this book, and that due to the high volume of mail I receive, I might not be able to reply to every message.

When you write, please be sure to include this book's title and author as well as your name and phone or e-mail address. I will carefully review your comments and share them with the author and editors who worked on the book.

E-mail: trina.macdonald@pearson.com

Mail: Trina MacDonald
           Senior Acquisitions Editor
           Addison-Wesley/Pearson Education, Inc.
           75 Arlington St., Ste. 300
           Boston, MA 02116

1

Media

Each recent iOS iteration has delivered intriguing updates to the media capabilities of AVFoundation. This chapter explores some of the advances that have made their way into this framework over the past few years and shows you how you can integrate these features into your own applications. You will read about speech generation, the feature that exposes a text-to-speech API for developers; barcode recognition, which enables you to leverage the device camera to recognize a wide range of barcode styles; and block-based movie creation, which applies modern language features to a traditional AVFoundation task.

Speech

In iOS 7, Apple finally exposed a text-to-speech API for developers. Until that time, developers could either leverage license-heavy third-party libraries or develop in-house workarounds, often using App Store–unsafe routines that could not be sold as part of apps. With just a few AVFoundation APIs, synthesized speech became a reliable component, ready for general use and distribution.

Text-to-speech (TTS) transforms string snippets into localized audio, tuned to the accents of your users. TTS is highly useful for apps where the device screen may not be consulted or the user might not own an Apple watch. For example, when using exercise and navigation apps, an iOS device may be placed out of a user's line of sight. The unit might be set down next to a driver or stored in a pocket or backpack while the application is active and running. For these kinds of uses, audio cues act as a critical interface for communicating with users.

Listing 1-1 implements a barebones text-to-speech method. You pass a string to it, and it invokes TTS playback. This creates a single reference point for speech, enabling you to focus on application semantics instead of speech production. During execution, this function performs the following tasks:

- **Creating an utterance**—Utterances are the basic unit of iOS speech. Although you can pass quite a lot of text at once, each utterance should be short and contained— a simple word or phrase, as the class name suggests. For greatest fluency, don't try to split sentences down into word-by-word playback—it. will. sound. pretty. bad. Instead, let the synthesizer pick up on sentence structure and punctuation cues to create the most natural-sounding output.

- **Adjusting the playback rate**—At its default rate, speech is quite rapid. Consider lowering this to about 20%. The way the request is structured in Listing 1-1 enables you to choose a multiplier from 0.0 to 1.0. This ensures that the rate always falls between minimum and maximum levels.

- **(Optional) Selecting a voice**—Listing 1-1 retrieves the current language code and uses it to establish the spoken voice. If you do not supply a voice, the system default voice is used. You can query all available voices with the AVSpeechSynthesisVoice class speechVoices method. At this time, you cannot differentiate programmatically between male and female voices.

- **Speaking**—Listing 1-1 concludes by creating a speech synthesizer and requests that it speak the utterance.

Listing 1-1   **Speaking Text**

```
- (void) performSpeech: (NSString *) string
{
    // Establish a new utterance
    AVSpeechUtterance *utterance = [AVSpeechUtterance
        speechUtteranceWithString:string];

    // Slow down the rate.
    CGFloat rateRange = AVSpeechUtteranceMaximumSpeechRate -
        AVSpeechUtteranceMinimumSpeechRate;
    utterance.rate = AVSpeechUtteranceMinimumSpeechRate + rateRange * _rate;

    // Set the language
    NSString *languageCode = [[NSLocale currentLocale]
        objectForKey:NSLocaleLanguageCode] ? : @"en-us";
    utterance.voice = [AVSpeechSynthesisVoice voiceWithLanguage:languageCode];

    // Speak
    AVSpeechSynthesizer *synthesizer = [[AVSpeechSynthesizer alloc] init];
    synthesizer.delegate = self;
    [synthesizer speakUtterance:utterance];
}
```

Other Options

You optionally set an utterance's `pitchMultiplier`, which adjusts the playback voice's pitch without affecting its playback rate. Multipliers range from 0.5 (quite a low voice) to 2.0 (squeaky). This value cannot be adjusted after you submit the utterance to the synthesizer for playback. Whatever level you initially establish persists.

Although the class offers a `volume` property as well, the value you assign acts independently of the system volume. Tweak the volume to create sotto voce or emphasis. Users are still welcome to use the hardware toggle to fine-tune overall audio levels.

Delegate Callbacks

The `AVSpeechSynthesizer` class offers several delegate callbacks for catching when speech starts and ends. One method passes the range of characters currently being spoken, enabling you to follow along on a word-by-word basis during speech:

```
- (void) speechSynthesizer: (AVSpeechSynthesizer *)synthesizer
    willSpeakRangeOfSpeechString:(NSRange)characterRange
    utterance:(AVSpeechUtterance *)utterance
{
    NSString *substring = [utterance.speechString
        substringWithRange:characterRange];
    NSLog(@"Speaking: %@", substring);
}
```

At times, you want to delay performing actions until an entire utterance has finished. For example, you might start by disabling certain UI elements before speech and then re-enable them after. The following snippet offers an example of what this process might look like in your code:

```
self.navigationItem.rightBarButtonItem.enabled = NO;
 [SpeechHelper speakString:warningString withCompletion:^{
    self.navigationItem.rightBarButtonItem.enabled = YES;
}];
```

You can easily create a custom class that waits for speech to end and then executes an optional completion block. The built in speechSynthesizer:didFinishSpeechUtterance: delegate method enables you to catch the end of each speech sequence so you can perform post-speech sequences. Listing 1-2 shows the details of how you might approach this.

Listing 1-2   **Implementing Speech Completion Blocks**

```
typedef void (^SpeechCompletionBlock)();

@interface SpeechHelper () <AVSpeechSynthesizerDelegate>
@property (nonatomic, strong) SpeechCompletionBlock completion;
@end
```

```objc
@implementation SpeechHelper
- (void) speechSynthesizer:(AVSpeechSynthesizer *)synthesizer
    didFinishSpeechUtterance:(AVSpeechUtterance *)utterance
{
    if (_completion)
        _completion();
}

- (void) performSpeech: (NSString *) string
{
    // Establish a new utterance
    AVSpeechUtterance *utterance = [AVSpeechUtterance
        speechUtteranceWithString:string];

    // Slow down the rate
    CGFloat rateRange = AVSpeechUtteranceMaximumSpeechRate -
        AVSpeechUtteranceMinimumSpeechRate;
    utterance.rate = AVSpeechUtteranceMinimumSpeechRate +
        rateRange * _rate;

    // Set the language
    NSString *languageCode = [[NSLocale currentLocale]
        objectForKey:NSLocaleLanguageCode] ? : @"en-us";
    utterance.voice =
        [AVSpeechSynthesisVoice voiceWithLanguage:languageCode];

    // Speak
    AVSpeechSynthesizer *synthesizer = [[AVSpeechSynthesizer alloc] init];
    synthesizer.delegate = self;
    [synthesizer speakUtterance:utterance];
}

- (void) speakString: (NSString *) string
    withCompletion: (SpeechCompletionBlock) completion
{
    _completion = completion;
    [self performSpeech:string];
}

+ (void) speakString: (NSString *) string
    withCompletion: (SpeechCompletionBlock) completion
{
    [[self new] speakString:string withCompletion:completion];
}
@end
```

Dictation

iOS dictation APIs are the natural counterparts to text-to-speech elements. At the time of this writing, they remain fixed behind private API walls, which means they are *off-limits* to App Store merchandise. In an ideal future world, the private UIDictationController class would become a public part of UIKit.

Creating Barcodes

The Quick Response code standard, better known as QR codes, produces a two-dimensional barcode that visually represents text strings. A QR code uses a variety of square dots (aka "modules") to encode its information, conforming to the ISO/IEC 18004:2006 standard.

In iOS 7, Apple introduced the Core Image filter to generate QR code. With it, you build QR code images with almost no programming overhead. Before this filter, most developers relied on third-party libraries, which could be cumbersome both for development as well as licensing. Figure 1-1 shows a simple QR code, generated and presented in an iOS application using the Core Image filter.

Figure 1-1   Core Image's CIQRCodeGenerator filter enables you to roll your own QR codes with just a few lines of code.

Filter Parameters

The Core Image CIQRCodeGenerator filter uses two parameters. inputMessage consists of a data representation of a text string. inputCorrectionLevel controls the error correction format used in the encoding. Select from low ("L", 7%), medium, ("M", 15%), quartile

("Q", 25%), and high ("H", 30%) correction. Each percentage indicates a resilience level, which determines how well a barcode responds to localized damage.

For example, you might imagine someone accidentally ripping off the corner of a QR code or obscuring parts of it (as in Figure 1-2). Built-in Reed-Solomon error correction ensures that the high error-resistance representation used in this figure remains recognizable despite the damage applied to it.

Figure 1-2   This QR code remains readable even though the bottom-right corner is obscured.

Building Codes

Building a code takes just a few steps. You create a filter, set its correction level and input message, and retrieve the resulting image:

```
CIFilter *qrFilter = [CIFilter filterWithName:@"CIQRCodeGenerator"];
[qrFilter setValue:@"H" forKey:@"inputCorrectionLevel"];
NSData *stringData = [string dataUsingEncoding:NSUTF8StringEncoding];
[qrFilter setValue:stringData forKey:@"inputMessage"];
CIImage *result = [qrFilter valueForKey:@"outputImage"];
```

There's only one problem. The output image will be extremely small. The QR code generation filter creates an image that uses one point for each square module. For the image in Figure 1-1, that results in an image sized at 27 by 27 points:

```
<CIImage: 0x8f0b0a0 extent [0 0 27 27]>
```

You work around this by drawing the QR code into a larger context, and then you save the results to a new UIImage. However, there's one gotcha detail to be aware of, which you see in

Figure 1-3. Unless you disable interpolation, you'll run into blurry results instead of the clear ones you want to produce.

Figure 1-3   Blurry QR codes result from drawing small images into large canvases without disabling interpolation.

Listing 1-3 implements a custom `QRCodeGenerator` class that generates QR code images from a string and a size you supply. The implementation includes a line in its resizing method that disables interpolation by setting the interpolation quality to none, avoiding the issues you see in Figure 1-3 and instead returning the clear results shown in Figure 1-1.

Listing 1-3   **Creating QR Code Images**

```
+ (UIImage *) resizeImageWithoutInterpolation:(UIImage *)sourceImage
    size:(CGSize)size
{
    UIGraphicsBeginImageContextWithOptions(size, NO, 0);
    CGContextSetInterpolationQuality(UIGraphicsGetCurrentContext(),
        kCGInterpolationNone);
    [sourceImage drawInRect:(CGRect){.size = size}];
    UIImage *result = UIGraphicsGetImageFromCurrentImageContext();
    UIGraphicsEndImageContext();
    return result;
}

+ (UIImage *) imageWithCIImage: (CIImage *) aCIImage
    orientation: (UIImageOrientation) anOrientation
{
```

```
    if (!aCIImage) return nil;

    CGImageRef imageRef = [[CIContext contextWithOptions:nil]
        createCGImage:aCIImage fromRect:aCIImage.extent];
    UIImage *image = [UIImage imageWithCGImage:imageRef
        scale:1.0 orientation:anOrientation];
    CFRelease(imageRef);

    return image;
}

+ (UIImage *) qrImageWithString: (NSString *) string size: (CGSize) destSize
{
    // Create filter
    CIFilter *qrFilter = [CIFilter filterWithName:@"CIQRCodeGenerator"];
    if (!qrFilter)
    {
        NSLog(@"Error: Could not load filter");
        return nil;
    }

    // Set correction level
    [qrFilter setValue:@"H" forKey:@"inputCorrectionLevel"];

    // Set input text
    NSData *stringData = [string dataUsingEncoding:NSUTF8StringEncoding];
    [qrFilter setValue:stringData forKey:@"inputMessage"];

    // Retrieve output image
    CIImage *outputImage = [qrFilter valueForKey:@"outputImage"];
    UIImage *smallImage = [self imageWithCIImage:outputImage
        orientation: UIImageOrientationUp];

    // Resize and return
    return [self resizeImageWithoutInterpolation:smallImage size:destSize];
}
@end
```

Reading Barcodes

The AVFoundation framework enables you to scan barcodes using a device's built-in camera. iOS doesn't just support the QR codes discussed in the preceding section. It recognizes nearly every major barcode standard, providing a rich and powerful suite of recognizers. Supported formats include the following:

- **UPC-A and UPC-E**—The Universal Product Code (UPC) standard is widely used on trade products in the English-speaking world, particularly in the US, Canada, the UK, Australia, and New Zealand. The most common version, UPC-A, includes 12-digit identifiers. The UPC-E variation enables the use of UPC coding on smaller packages, where a full (12-digit) barcode might not quite fit. It omits leading and trailing digits. If you live in the US, you'll probably find this kind of code on the soda cans scattered around a typical developer's desk.

- **EAN-13 and EAN-8**—The International (formerly "European," hence the *E*) Article Number barcode is a proper superset of the UPC system. It consists of a 13-digit barcode that includes a 12-digit UPC-A identifier plus a 1-digit check number. The less common EAN-8 standard applies to smaller goods, such as candy. Although 2- and 5-digit versions of EAN exist, they are not supported on iOS at this time.

- **Code 39 and Code 39 mod 43**—Code 39 is a variable-length barcode system, with machine-readable sequences of arbitrary extent. The mod 43 version uses 43 characters including A–Z (uppercase), digits, and a few special characters (-, ., $, /, +, %, and a space character). Unlike EAN-13, Code 39 does not use check digits but is considered "self-checking" because a single error in printing or recognition can't generate a different valid character. Because it doesn't use check digits, you can basically print it out sequentially as a series of individual bar characters.

- **Code 93 and Code 128**—Code 93 enhances Code 39, adding greater data density, check characters, and custom start and stop characters. Code 128 can encode all 128 ASCII characters as well as Latin-1 characters (courtesy of a special extension character). Apparently, Code 128 is used mostly in shipping.

- **PDF417 code**—Used by the US Postal Service, the public domain (license-free) PDF417 standard produces stacked two-dimensional data, with user-specified dimensions. It has tons of nifty features, including symbol-to-symbol links.

- **QR code**—QR codes produce a two-dimensional error-resistant matrix barcode. Originally adopted by the auto industry, these popular barcodes are now widely used in many retail scenarios.

- **Aztec code**—This is another two-dimensional barcode encoding that appears superficially similar to QR code. It is especially space efficient. Although it is patented, Aztec has been released to the public domain.

In addition to recognition tasks, the latest releases of iOS Core Image include filters to support barcode generation for QR (`CIQRCodeGenerator`), Code 128 (`CICode128BarcodeGenerator`), Aztec (`CIAztecCodeGenerator`), and PDF417 (`CIPDF417BarcodeGenerator`) styles. Follow Listing 1-3 to build these styles but omit the input correction level parameter, which is a QR code–only key.

Listening for Metadata Objects

Metadata objects represent information about items embedded into an image. At this time, metadata is limited to information about faces and machine-readable barcodes. You enable iOS to automatically detect these items on your behalf by adding custom outputs to your `AVCaptureSession` instances.

Each capture session enables you to add inputs (typically onboard cameras) and outputs (whether a sampling buffer or a metadata detector) to process the data retrieved from onboard cameras. To get started, you query to find a particular device, such as the front-facing camera, like this:

```
+ (AVCaptureDevice *)frontCamera
{
    NSArray *videoDevices =
        [AVCaptureDevice devicesWithMediaType:AVMediaTypeVideo];
    for (AVCaptureDevice *device in videoDevices)
        if (device.position == AVCaptureDevicePositionFront)
            return device;

    return [AVCaptureDevice defaultDeviceWithMediaType:AVMediaTypeVideo];
}
```

You add that device to the current session. The following method uses a single input at any time, ensuring that all data being fed in is from a specific camera device:

```
- (void) useDevice: (AVCaptureDevice *) newDevice
{
    [_session beginConfiguration];

    // Remove existing inputs
    NSArray *inputs = _session.inputs;
    for (AVCaptureInput *input in inputs)
        [_session removeInput:input];

    AVCaptureDeviceInput *captureInput = [AVCaptureDeviceInput
        deviceInputWithDevice:newDevice error:nil];
    [_session addInput:captureInput];

    [_session commitConfiguration];
}
```

To work with barcode recognition, you must enable metadata output. This involves creating a new output, setting its processing delegate, and adding it to the session. The delegate declares the AVCaptureMetadataOutputObjectsDelegate protocol and implements a single callback to handle metadata output:

```
- (void) addMetaDataOutput
{
    [_session beginConfiguration];

    // Remove existing outputs
    NSArray *outputs = _session.outputs;
    for (AVCaptureOutput *output in outputs)
        [_session removeOutput:output];

    // Create capture output
    AVCaptureMetadataOutput *output = [[AVCaptureMetadataOutput alloc] init];
    [output setMetadataObjectsDelegate:self queue:dispatch_get_main_queue()];

    [_session addOutput:output];
    output.metadataObjectTypes = output.availableMetadataObjectTypes;
    [_session commitConfiguration];
}
```

Responding to Metadata

The AVCaptureMetadataOutputObjectsDelegate protocol consists of a single optional method, which you see in Listing 1-4. (It's pointless to declare the protocol and not actually listen for results, but you can do so if you really want to.) The output passes each pattern match to the delegate as an AVMetadataObject instance.

AVMetadataObject is an abstract class. It is so abstract, in fact, that the type of metadata it represents in its type property must be created in its concrete subclasses. At this time, there are two subclasses: one that recognizes barcodes and another that recognizes faces. As a rule, once you know the type you're working with, you need to cast the object to a specific subclass, such as AVMetadataMachineReadableCodeObject or AVMetadataFaceObject.

The barcode-specific subclass offers two properties: the string value of the barcode that's been read and the geometric corners (an array of CGPoint values) that define the geometric edges of the recognized item. In the sample project for this listing, these corners produce the visual overlay shown in Figure 1-4.

Figure 1-4   The line light overlaying the barcode is set using the detected metadata corners.

Listing 1-4   **Handling Metadata Recognition**

```
- (void)captureOutput:(AVCaptureOutput *)captureOutput
  didOutputMetadataObjects:(NSArray *)metadataObjects
  fromConnection:(AVCaptureConnection *)connection
{
    NSArray *barCodeTypes = @[AVMetadataObjectTypeUPCECode,
                              AVMetadataObjectTypeCode39Code,
                              AVMetadataObjectTypeCode39Mod43Code,
                              AVMetadataObjectTypeEAN13Code,
                              AVMetadataObjectTypeEAN8Code,
                              AVMetadataObjectTypeCode93Code,
                              AVMetadataObjectTypeCode128Code,
                              AVMetadataObjectTypePDF417Code,
                              AVMetadataObjectTypeQRCode,
                              AVMetadataObjectTypeAztecCode];

    for (AVMetadataObject *metadata in metadataObjects)
    {
        if ([barCodeTypes containsObject:metadata.type])
        {
            // Process Barcodes
            AVMetadataMachineReadableCodeObject *object =
```

```
              (AVMetadataMachineReadableCodeObject *) metadata;
          NSString *stringValue = object.stringValue;

          if (_metadataDelegate && [_metadataDelegate respondsToSelector:
                @selector(processBarcode:withType:withMetadata:)])
              [_metadataDelegate processBarcode:stringValue
                  withType:metadata.type withMetadata:object];
      }
      else if ([metadata.type isEqualToString:AVMetadataObjectTypeFace])
      {
          // Process face detection
          AVMetadataFaceObject *object = (AVMetadataFaceObject *)metadata;
          if (_metadataDelegate && [_metadataDelegate
              respondsToSelector:@selector(processFace:)])
              [_metadataDelegate processFace:object];
      }
      else
          NSLog(@"Captured unknown metadata object: %@", metadata.type);
  }
}
```

Extracting Bounds

In many situations, you want to coordinate recognition with some kind of visual display, as
shown in Figure 1-4. The bounds reported by extracted features are expressed as a rectangle
that ranges between (0, 0) and (1,1). To convert that rectangle into the visual coordinate space
of your preview layer, you need to call transformedMetadataObjectForMetadataObject, an
AVCaptureVideoPreviewLayer method, as is done in the following method:

```
- (void) processBarcode: (NSString *) barcode
    withType: (NSString *) codeType
    withMetadata: (AVMetadataMachineReadableCodeObject *) metadata
{
    AVCaptureVideoPreviewLayer *layer =
        [CameraHelper previewInView:previewView];
    AVMetadataMachineReadableCodeObject *codeObject =
        (AVMetadataMachineReadableCodeObject *)[layer
            transformedMetadataObjectForMetadataObject:metadata];
    overlay.frame = [self.view convertRect:codeObject.bounds
        fromView:previewView];
}
```

The transformedMetadataObjectForMetadataObject method returns an
AVMetadataObject with updated visual properties that match the receiver's
coordinate space. If you've rotated, mirrored, or applied a video gravity to your
preview layer, the method automatically takes these elements into account for you.

Enhancing Recognition

Although the iOS barcode recognition system is quite robust, you can greatly improve perfor-
mance with a simple trick introduced to me by developer Aaron Alexander. He pointed out that
zooming the video feed reduces the overall complexity of the scene and enhances detection
speed.

You accomplish this by tweaking the session's connections, the virtual bridge between a
session's inputs and outputs. The videoScaleAndCropFactor property enables you to apply a
digital zoom factor:

```
- (void) setVideoOutputScale: (CGFloat) scaleFactor
{
    [_session beginConfiguration];

    NSArray *outputs = _session.outputs;
    for (AVCaptureOutput *output in outputs)
        for (AVCaptureConnection *connection in output.connections)
            connection.videoScaleAndCropFactor = scaleFactor;

    [_session commitConfiguration];
}
```

The sample project for this section uses a zoom factor of 1.5, although you may want to experiment with even higher levels.

Detecting Faces

Listing 1-4 doesn't just handle barcode recognition. It implements face recognition as well.
When it encounters AVMetadataFaceObject instances, it passes them along to a custom,
optional delegate for handling. Just as a barcode object represents a single detected barcode,
each face object represents a single detected face.

Each item offers a unique faceID property, which is tracked as long as the same face remains
in-scene. Face identifiers are not reused. If a face leaves the preview and then re-enters, it is
assigned a new ID. This is analogous to touch handling, where a touch is tracked until it's
removed from the screen.

In addition to identifiers that track individual faces, each face object offers yaw and roll properties, enabling you to detect front-to-back face movement (yaw) and side-to-side head tilt (roll).

Building AVFoundation Movies

AVFoundation simplifies the process of making movies. When you have a series of images,
AVFoundation helps you stitch them together to create a QuickTime result to share with your
users. You use AVAssetWriter, a class that writes media to an audiovisual container. It enables

you to build H.264 movies with a minimum of code. You'll read about the code-level details a bit later in this section.

Although it's simple to create movies using AVFoundation, many developers seem to use this feature solely to combine screen shots or scrape camera feeds. As you're just feeding a pixel buffer into an asset writer, why not have a bit more fun than that? Enable your users to create and share videos that push boundaries further. For example, you might build movies that showcase the creation process of a drawing or enable users to build stick animations. Here's an example of a movie built using iOS Bezier paths: https://www.youtube.com/watch?v=zLMzlCDtfo0. As long as you can express individual frames, AVFoundation can help you stitch them together into a movie.

For the past few years, I've used a fairly basic moviemaker class. My class was based on old Apple sample code, and although I tweaked it a bit for efficiency, it was pretty barebones. This class enabled me to set up a movie file and feed it an image at a time. When I finalized the file, I had a brand-new movie ready to share with my users.

Two things inspired me to push the class a bit further. First was my work on my *iOS Drawing* book. In writing the book, I played a lot with UIKit drawing on top of older APIs — like the ones that power the pixel buffers used in movie creation. Pixel buffers store image data that the asset writer sends out to the movie file. Drawing into pixel buffers enables you to create custom drawings for movies instead of using photos or other presourced images that you didn't create.

The second thing was my experience with blocks, which have grown in importance over time both in Apple's APIs and in my personal expressiveness. They provide a way to encapsulate behavior into tangible objects, which can be passed as parameters to routines. Blocks play a huge role in day-to-day Swift development, where they are called *closures*.

I decided to combine these two elements to simplify the way I build movie frames. Instead of building an image and tossing it to the helper class, I now use UIKit drawing commands directly with the pixel buffer.

Before this modification, I'd perform image creation sequences over and over. In this approach, the image was never anything more than an intermediary for transferring data over to the pixel buffer. For example, the following code creates an iOS drawing destination, performs the drawing, retrieves an image, and passes it to the movie:

```
// Start drawing
UIGraphicsBeginImageContext(rect.size);
CGContextRef context = UIGraphicsGetCurrentContext();

// Fill the background with black
[[UIColor blackColor] set];
CGContextFillRect(context, rect);

// Draw a path in white
[[UIColor whiteColor] set];
[path fill];
```

```
// Fetch an image
UIImage *anImage = UIGraphicsGetImageFromCurrentImageContext();
UIGraphicsEndImageContext();

// Hand the image to a moviemaker helper
[myHelper addImageToMovie:anImage];
```

With blocks, I could draw directly to the pixel buffer. The following block contains drawing commands without using an intermediate image. This is a more appealing and parsimonious approach:

```
ContextDrawingBlock block = ^(CGContextRef context){
    // Fill the background with black
    [[UIColor blackColor] set];
    CGContextFillRect(context, rect);
    // Draw a path in white
    [[UIColor whiteColor] set];
    [path fill];
};
[myHelper addDrawingToMovie:block];
```

As this snippet demonstrates, passing a block enables you to skip intermediate storage and focus your creation task on the individual drawing steps needed for each frame.

> ### Note
>
> As a rule, you want to build videos on a device and not in the simulator. There are some simulator bugs that can cause artifacts in the rendered output.

Creating a Pixel Buffer

The key to a blocks-based approach for drawing movie frames lies in merging UIKit drawing with a Core Video pixel buffer. A pixel buffer is, as the name suggests, a wrapper for image data. You create a pixel buffer by calling CVPixelBufferCreate(). Pass it the width and height of the buffer and any options needed for compatibility. Once it is built, you draw into it and then append its contents to your movie:

```
- (BOOL) createPixelBuffer
{
    // Create Pixel Buffer
    NSDictionary *pixelBufferOptions =
    @{
        (id) kCVPixelBufferCGImageCompatibilityKey : @YES,
        (id) kCVPixelBufferCGBitmapContextCompatibilityKey : @YES,
    };
```

```
CVReturn status = CVPixelBufferCreate(
                    kCFAllocatorDefault,
                    width,
                    height,
                    kCVPixelFormatType_32ARGB,
                    (__bridge CFDictionaryRef) pixelBufferOptions,
                    &bufferRef);
if (status != kCVReturnSuccess)
{
    NSLog(@"Error creating pixel buffer");
    return NO;
}

return YES;
}
```

Drawing into the Pixel Buffer

The block example described in this section uses a custom type called `ContextDrawingBlock`. As a rule, it's easier to create block types than to add their raw declarations over and over. The following `ContextDrawingBlock` typedef declares one argument: the current drawing context:

```
typedef void (^ContextDrawingBlock)(CGContextRef context);
```

Although you can always grab the current context via `UIGraphicsGetCurrentContext()`, I have found that it's more convenient to provide that context for ready use.

The secret to direct block-based drawing lies in a pair of UIKit functions not many developers are familiar with. `UIGraphicsPushContext()` and `UIGraphicsPopContext()` enable you to add Quartz 2D contexts to the UIKit context stack and then remove them after drawing. These two functions add and remove drawing destinations in UIKit.

This approach creates a bridge between the Quartz and UIKit worlds, permitting you to use Objective-C UIKit-style calls (such as `[myColor set]`) in place of C-language Quartz calls (such as `CGContextSetFillColorWithColor(context, myColor.CGColor)`). In UIKit calls, the active context is inferred from the current stack, so you don't need to pass the context every time you update a setting or perform a drawing operation.

Listing 1-5 builds a Quartz context using the memory stored in the Core Video (CV) pixel buffer. It pushes this context onto the UIKit stack and executes its drawing block. It finishes by popping the stack, releasing the context, and unlocking the pixel buffer. By encapsulating all the pixel-level work in this method, the `ContextDrawingBlock` that's passed as an argument concerns itself only with actual drawing commands.

The lines that force a coordinate transform enable you to send all your block-based drawing commands using UIKit's coordinate system, which starts at the top-left corner and grows to the right and down. Native Quartz drawing uses a bottom-left origin, and the y axis grows upward. The transform applied by `CGContextConcatCTM()` in Listing 1-5 flips that Quartz system to the UIKit standard.

Listing 1-5 **Drawing to Pixel Buffers Using Blocks**

```
- (BOOL) drawToPixelBufferWithBlock:
    (ContextDrawingBlock) block __attribute__ ((nonnull))
{

    // Lock the buffer and fetch the base address
    CVPixelBufferLockBaseAddress(bufferRef, 0);
    void *pixelData = CVPixelBufferGetBaseAddress(bufferRef);

    // Establish color space
    CGColorSpaceRef RGBColorSpace = CGColorSpaceCreateDeviceRGB();
    if (RGBColorSpace == NULL) return NO;

    // Build a Quartz context using the pixel data from the pixel buffer
    CGContextRef context = CGBitmapContextCreate(pixelData, width, height,
        8, 4 * width, RGBColorSpace, (CGBitmapInfo) kCGImageAlphaNoneSkipFirst);
    if (!context)
    {
        CGColorSpaceRelease(RGBColorSpace);
        CVPixelBufferUnlockBaseAddress(bufferRef, 0);
        NSLog(@"Error creating bitmap context");
        return NO;
    }

    // Handle Quartz Coordinate System
    // This assumes all block calls will use the UIKit coordinate space
    CGAffineTransform transform = CGAffineTransformIdentity;
    transform = CGAffineTransformScale(transform, 1.0, -1.0);
    transform = CGAffineTransformTranslate(transform, 0.0, -height);
    CGContextConcatCTM(context, transform);

    // Perform drawing
    UIGraphicsPushContext(context);
    if (block) block(context);
    UIGraphicsPopContext();

    // Clean up
    CGColorSpaceRelease(RGBColorSpace);
    CGContextRelease(context);
    CVPixelBufferUnlockBaseAddress(bufferRef, 0);
    return YES;
}
```

Expressive Drawing

Any UIKit- or Quartz-compatible drawing API works with the moviemaker approach described in the previous section. You are not limited to Bezier paths and fill and stroke operations. If you can draw content to a standard UIKit view, those same operations will draw properly to the pixel buffer context. For example, you might want to combine image drawing with string rendering, as in the following snippet. Notice the simplicity of the implementation, even when creating and drawing attributed strings:

```
ContextDrawingBlock block = ^(CGContextRef context){
    // Fill background
    [[UIColor blackColor] set];
    CGContextFillRect(context, rect);

    // Draw image
    [frame drawInRect:insetRect];

    // Draw string
    NSAttributedString *s = [[NSAttributedString alloc]
        initWithString:title attributes:@{
            NSFontAttributeName:[UIFont fontWithName:@"Georgia" size:24],
            NSForegroundColorAttributeName:[UIColor whiteColor]}];
    [s drawAtPoint:CGPointMake(80, 80)];
};
```

Combining blocks with AVFoundation produces recognizable enhancements in clarity and simplicity with a minimum of code. In this implementation, blocks enable you to focus more on the content you're drawing than on the production of individual movie frames.

Building Movies from Frames

Listing 1-6 finishes the movie-building story by showing how each frame can be added to establish a standard movie file. You start by establishing AVAssetWriter, the class that's responsible for writing out media data. Listing 1-6 builds H.264 MPEG-4 QuickTime, which is specified in AVAssetWriterInput settings. The writer input, despite its name, is responsible for appending media samples to the asset writer. A pixel buffer adapter connects the CVPixelBuffer you draw into using Listing 1-5 to the writer input. This enables you to draw and then append each new frame to the asset writer's output file.

To add new frames, wait until the writer input is no longer busy, as shown in appendPixel-Buffer method. The class works asynchronously. You want to ensure that you don't trip over yourself by interrupting an ongoing writing operation. Then, append the current contents of the pixel buffer. You specify how long the frame should be displayed by establishing a presentation time. Listing 1-6 uses the CMTimeMake method to calculate that extent. Repeat until you've finished adding each frame.

You finalize the movie by setting an end time for the final frame and then cleaning up the helper classes you used to build the movie output.

Listing 1-6 **Movie Making**

```objc
// Build a new movie file
- (BOOL) createMovieAtPath: (NSString *) path
{
    NSError *error;

    // Create Movie URL
    NSURL *movieURL = [NSURL fileURLWithPath:path];
    if (!movieURL)
    {
        NSLog(@"Error creating URL from path (%@)", path);
        return NO;
    }

    // Create Asset Writer
    writer = [[AVAssetWriter alloc] initWithURL:movieURL
        fileType:AVFileTypeQuickTimeMovie error:&error];
    if (!writer)
    {
        NSLog(@"Error creating asset writer: %@",
            error.localizedDescription);
        return NO;
    }

    // Create H.264 Video output
    NSDictionary *videoSettings =
    @{
      AVVideoCodecKey : AVVideoCodecH264,
      AVVideoWidthKey : @(width),
      AVVideoHeightKey : @(height),
      };

    input = [AVAssetWriterInput
        assetWriterInputWithMediaType:AVMediaTypeVideo
        outputSettings:videoSettings];
    if (!input)
    {
        writer = nil;
        NSLog(@"Error creating asset writer input");
        return NO;
    }

    [writer addInput:input];

    // Build adapter
    adaptor = [[AVAssetWriterInputPixelBufferAdaptor alloc]
```

```
            initWithAssetWriterInput:input sourcePixelBufferAttributes:nil];
    if (!adaptor)
    {
        writer = nil;
        input = nil;
        NSLog(@"Error creating pixel adaptor");
        return NO;
    }

    [writer startWriting];
    [writer startSessionAtSourceTime:kCMTimeZero];

    return YES;
}


// Establish a new movie with a specified frame size and frame rate
// (fps is frames per second)
- (instancetype) initWithPath: (NSString *) path frameSize: (CGSize) size
    fps: (NSUInteger)  fps
{
    if (!(self = [super init])) return self;

    // Path must be nil
    if ([[NSFileManager defaultManager] fileExistsAtPath:path])
    {
        NSLog(@"Error: Attempting to overwrite existing file.");
        return nil;
    }

    if (!path)
    {
        NSLog(@"Error: Path must be non-nil");
        return nil;
    }

    // Sizes must be divisible by 16
    height - lrint(size.height),
    width = lrint(size.width);
    if (((height % 16) != 0) || ((width % 16) != 0))
    {
        NSLog(@"Error: Height and Width must be divisible by 16");
        return nil;
    }

    // Store fps
    framesPerSecond = fps;
    if (fps == 0)
```

```
    {
        NSLog(@"Error: Frames per second must be positive integer");
    }

    frameCount = 0;

    BOOL success = [self createMovieAtPath:path];
    if (!success) return nil;

    return self;
}

+ (instancetype) createMovieAtPath: (NSString *) moviePath
    frameSize: (CGSize) size
    fps: (NSUInteger) framesPerSecond __attribute__ ((nonnull (1)))
{
    return [[self alloc] initWithPath:moviePath
        frameSize:size fps:framesPerSecond];
}

- (BOOL) appendPixelBuffer
{
    // Append pixel buffer
    while (!input.isReadyForMoreMediaData);
    frameCount++; // this is a class instance variable that keeps track
    BOOL success = [adaptor appendPixelBuffer:bufferRef
        withPresentationTime:CMTimeMake(frameCount, (int32_t) framesPerSecond)];
    if (!success)
    {
        NSLog(@"Error writing frame %zd", frameCount);
        return NO;
    }
    return YES;

}

// Draw the next frame using the provided drawing block
- (BOOL) addDrawingToMovie: (ContextDrawingBlock) drawingBlock
{
    if (!drawingBlock) return NO;
    BOOL success = [self drawToPixelBufferWithBlock:drawingBlock];
    if (!success) return NO;
    return [self appendPixelBuffer];
}
```

```
- (void) finalizeMovie
{
    frameCount++;
    [input markAsFinished];
    [writer endSessionAtSourceTime:
        CMTimeMake(frameCount, (int32_t) framesPerSecond)];
    [writer finishWritingWithCompletionHandler:^{
        NSLog(@"Finished writing movie: %@", writer.outputURL.path);
        writer = nil;
        input = nil;
        adaptor = nil;
        CVPixelBufferRelease(bufferRef);
    }];
}
```

Adding Images to Movies

Listing 1-6 establishes a moviemaker class that supports block-based frame drawing. But what if all you really want to do is build a movie from screen shots or still frames? It's easy enough—expand the class to create image-based frames using the following method:

```
- (BOOL) addImageToMovie: (UIImage *) image __attribute__ ((nonnull))
{
    if (!image) return NO;

    // Draw image to pixel buffer
    ContextDrawingBlock imageBlock = ^(CGContextRef context)
    {
        CGRect rect = CGRectMake(0, 0, width, height);
        [[UIColor blackColor] set];
        UIRectFill(rect);
        [image drawInRect:rect];
    };

    BOOL success = [self drawToPixelBufferWithBlock:imageBlock];
    if (!success) return NO;

    return [self appendPixelBuffer];
}
```

This method uses the drawing-block approach to add a convenient still-image entry point. Call it with each image you wish to add, and you can essentially ignore the block-based approach that powers the class.

Wrap-up

Here are final points to wrap up what you've read in this chapter:

- iOS continues to grow in ways that enable users to interact with the world around them. Barcodes provide a flexible, easy-to-use way to connect with customers and patrons who may be frequenting physical sites. Incorporating recognition into your software provides access to real-world resources with a minimum of effort, which is why you see so many barcodes springing up at places ranging from retail spaces to public libraries and from parks to town centers.

- It's time to re-imagine interfaces. With built-in text-to-speech, your interactions can assume completely new screen-free models that rely on device sensors instead of user taps.

- The advances in AVFoundation enable you to expand application functionality without tying yourself to third-party libraries and licenses. Their built-in simplicity reduces your coding overhead and provides reliable and flexible tools that are ready for use.

- There's often a tendency to look at AVFoundation's C-like interface and forget to apply more modern language features like blocks and closures to leverage these APIs. If you ignore these features, you're missing out on powerful solutions that will simplify and enhance your code base.

2

Dynamic Typography

The major iOS 7 redesign in 2013 introduced an overhauled interface, shifting emphasis away from buttons and bars to a sparser and more text-centered experience. Text components became even more critical parts of UI design in this clean, white world. System additions such as Dynamic Type created a holistic text development system, one that deferred to user preferences and sensory limitations. In this chapter, you see how text display adjusts to user preferences and sensory limitations, letting content flow to match dynamically changing typography. Each app accommodates its user by adjusting text to match global system type preferences.

Type Size and User Needs

iOS serves the user. It creates a system of graceful deference to a user's preferences and needs. Dynamic Type (see Figure 2-1) exemplifies this philosophy. It enables users to globally adjust reading size across all applications. Younger users with strong eyes can dial back on font sizes, displaying more text on each screen. Older folk or those with visual impairments can push out bigger font requests with a simple drag. Apps that support this feature provide the kind of user-centered design that Apple promotes.

How Dynamic Type Works

Dynamic Type pushes notifications when text size preferences change. Conforming apps listen and adapt as users request bigger or smaller font sizes from the Settings app. By supporting Dynamic Type, apps can immediately update their layout to accommodate the new type levels, redrawing their screens to match the user-driven requests.

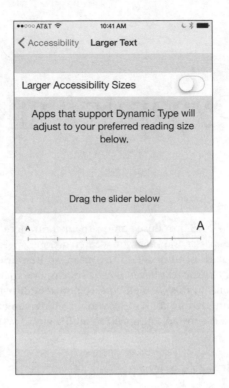

Figure 2-1 Text size settings (Settings > General > Accessibility > Larger Text) enable users to adjust their preferred reading fonts. For even larger sizes, enable the Larger Accessibility Sizes toggle. The default user setting for iOS corresponds to a "large" text category.

The way Dynamic Type works is indirect and clever. It requires you as a developer to take a step away from exact font sizes. Instead of implementing a fixed design with carefully selected typography, you transition your development to *styles*. A style describes the way text is used, such as in a headline or as body text. You base your layout around the following semantic descriptions:

- *Headlines* (UIFontTextStyleHeadline, bold, 14–20 points) provide the titles for your content. They are the largest and the most prominent style.

- *Subheadlines* (UIFontTextStyleSubheadline, 12–18 points) offer a second-order heading for document organization.

- *Body* (UIFontTextStyleBody, 14–20 points) fonts are used to present the primary text content on the screen.

- *Footnotes* (UIFontTextStyleFootnote, 12–16 points), *large captions* (UIFontTextStyleCaption1, 11–15 points), and *small captions* (UIFontTextStyleCaption2, 11–14 points) provide text for references, explanations, and comments.

The `UIFont` class translates text styles to fonts on your behalf. In the most basic use case, you place a request, such as "Please give me a body font." The class checks the current Dynamic Type settings, selects an appropriately sized font, and returns it to you. The user-specified sizes range from small to large and are enumerated into the following standard size categories:

- `UIContentSizeCategoryExtraSmall`
- `UIContentSizeCategorySmall`
- `UIContentSizeCategoryMedium`
- `UIContentSizeCategoryLarge`
- `UIContentSizeCategoryExtraLarge`
- `UIContentSizeCategoryExtraExtraLarge`
- `UIContentSizeCategoryExtraExtraExtraLarge`

The scaling from category to category isn't linear. For example, the Caption 2 font is 11 points for all four smaller size categories (extra small to large). Starting with the extra large size category, it grows to 12 points, then 13 and 14 points for the remaining categories. For this reason, you don't want to approximate the fonts on your own. Instead, allow the `UIFont` class to produce a curated font for the current Dynamic Type settings, as shown in Listing 2-1.

In addition to these seven categories, you may encounter five more accessibility-controlled extra large font size categories that users set in General > Accessibility > Larger Type. These items enable you to push fonts further for better visibility for users with limited vision:

- `UIContentSizeCategoryAccessibilityMedium`
- `UIContentSizeCategoryAccessibilityLarge`
- `UIContentSizeCategoryAccessibilityExtraLarge`
- `UIContentSizeCategoryAccessibilityExtraExtraLarge`
- `UIContentSizeCategoryAccessibilityExtraExtraExtraLarge`

The accessibility version of the medium font is slightly larger than the extra extra extra large version of the normal font.

Note

Each Apple-supplied item is built around a standard system font at a variety of sizes. However, Apple-supplied styles don't necessarily differ *only* by font size. For example, the headline font is boldface, unlike the other five styles.

Listing 2-1   **Building Fonts from Text Styles**

```
@implementation UIFont (BuiltInStyles)
+ (UIFont *) headlineFont
{
    return [UIFont preferredFontForTextStyle:
        UIFontTextStyleHeadline];
}

+ (UIFont *) subheadlineFont
{
    return [UIFont preferredFontForTextStyle:
        UIFontTextStyleSubheadline];
}

+ (UIFont *) bodyFont
{
    return [UIFont preferredFontForTextStyle:
        UIFontTextStyleBody];
}

+ (UIFont *) footnoteFont
{
    return [UIFont preferredFontForTextStyle:
        UIFontTextStyleFootnote];
}

+ (UIFont *) caption1Font
{
    return [UIFont preferredFontForTextStyle:
        UIFontTextStyleCaption1];
}

+ (UIFont *) caption2Font
{
    return [UIFont preferredFontForTextStyle:
        UIFontTextStyleCaption2];
}
@end
```

Listening for Type Updates

Font size categories don't change on their own. If a user hops out and adjusts settings, your application updates its views when the user returns. Enable your app to respond to updates by subscribing to content size change notifications. Upon detecting a notification, adjust any views that use text to reflect new user sizes. Add a notification block like this one to respond to changes:

```
theObserver = [[NSNotificationCenter defaultCenter]
    addObserverForName:
        UIContentSizeCategoryDidChangeNotification
    object:nil
    queue:[NSOperationQueue mainQueue]
    usingBlock:^(NSNotification *note) {
      ...perform updates here...
      // ...re-display view (setNeedsDisplay) if needed here...
}];
```

Size updates may influence custom-drawn elements built around drawRect: or image contexts. More commonly, they impact system-supplied items such as labels, buttons, text fields, and text views. You can create responsive versions of these items via subclassing. Listing 2-2 establishes a minimal, size category–aware text label class to demonstrate a barebones approach. Instances use a single text style and store it to a private textStyle string property.

This single-style approach avoids mix-and-match issues with attributes, lending itself to a clean and sparse implementation. When an instance detects a content size change, it requests a new version of the styled font and applies it to the label. Figure 2-2 shows an instance of the DynamicLabel class as a user selects extra small (top), large (middle), and extra extra extra large (bottom) fonts.

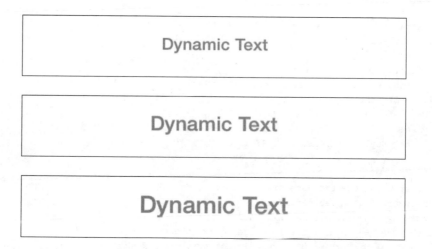

Figure 2-2 The Dynamic Type-aware DynamicLabel class responds to size category notifications by requesting a new copy of a stylized font.

Listing 2-2   **A Content Size Category–Powered Label**

```objc
#define DEFAULT_TEXT_STYLE  UIFontTextStyleHeadline

// This class supports only one style at a time
@interface DynamicLabel : UILabel
@property (nonatomic, strong) NSString *textStyle;
@property (nonatomic, strong) NSMutableArray *observers;
@end

@implementation DynamicLabel

// Disable attributed text to ensure the single style
- (void) setAttributedText:(NSAttributedString *)attributedText
{
    // no op here but this is addressed later in this chapter
}

- (instancetype) initWithTextStyle: (NSString *) textStyle
{
    if (!(self = [super initWithFrame:CGRectZero]))
        return self;

    // Establish the current style
    _textStyle = textStyle;

    // Initialize the font based on the style
    self.font = [UIFont preferredFontForTextStyle:_textStyle];
    if (!self.font)
    {
        self.font = [UIFont preferredFontForTextStyle:DEFAULT_TEXT_STYLE];
        _textStyle = DEFAULT_TEXT_STYLE;
    }

    // Listen for the category size notification
    _observers = [NSMutableArray array];
    __weak typeof(self) weakSelf = self;
    id observer = [[NSNotificationCenter defaultCenter]
        addObserverForName:UIContentSizeCategoryDidChangeNotification
        object:nil
        queue:[NSOperationQueue mainQueue]
        usingBlock:^(NSNotification *note) {
            __strong typeof(self) strongSelf = weakSelf;
            strongSelf.font =
                [UIFont preferredFontForTextStyle:strongSelf.textStyle];
    }];
    [_observers addObject:observer];
```

```objc
        return self;
}


// Any initWithFrame: calls use the default text style
- (id)initWithFrame:(CGRect)frame
{
    return [self initWithTextStyle:nil];
}


// Preferred entry point for creating dynamic labels
+ (instancetype) labelWithTextStyle: (NSString *) textStyle
{
    DynamicLabel *instance =
        [[self alloc] initWithTextStyle:textStyle];
    return instance;
}


- (void) dealloc
{
    for (id observer in _observers)
        [[NSNotificationCenter defaultCenter]
            removeObserver:observer];
}
@end
```

Handling Dynamic Type with Attributes

Dynamic Type grows complicated when you integrate its features with NSAttributedString, a common building block for modern iOS views. As you mix Dynamic Type with attributes, consider how each type element works within that string. In the most basic case, when your text is relatively static, as in Figure 2-3, you can simply rebuild it whenever you receive a content size notification. The following method establishes a string with static, predefined content:

```objc
- (void) loadAttributedString
{
    NSMutableAttributedString *attributedString =
        [NSMutableAttributedString string];

    NSAttributedString *baseString;

    // Build the headline
    baseString = [[NSAttributedString alloc]
        initWithString:@"Headline\n"
        attributes:@{NSFontAttributeName : [UIFont headlineFont]}];
    [attributedString appendAttributedString:baseString];
```

```
// Build the content
baseString = [[NSAttributedString alloc]
    initWithString:@"This is the body text"
    attributes:@{NSFontAttributeName : [UIFont bodyFont],
        NSForegroundColorAttributeName : [UIColor darkGrayColor]}];
[attributedString appendAttributedString:baseString];

textView.attributedText = attributedString;
}
```

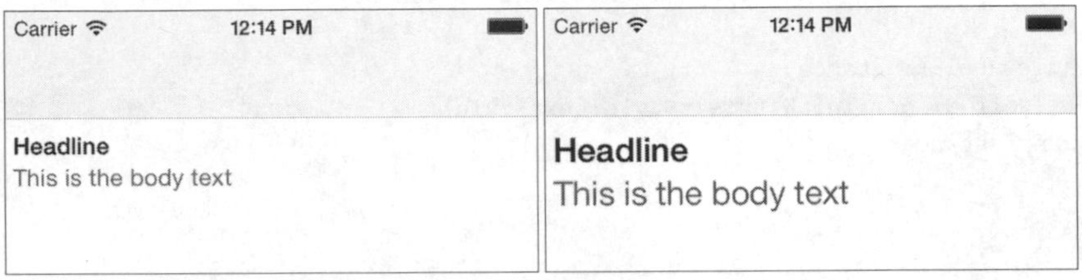

Figure 2-3   Each element in an attributed text string may need to be updated when a content size change is detected.

This approach isn't a very good one. It is unusable for large, complex content and user-created content that blends custom text and attributes—the most common use case. Fortunately, you can easily automate Dynamic Type updates for complex attributed strings.

Scanning for Text Style Ranges

There's a much simpler solution for integrating complex attributed strings with Dynamic Type. Instead of rebuilding strings from first principles at each update, you scan attributed strings to find where each style applies and store that information in a dictionary of ranges.

The scan is inexpensive to run. Enumerate the string's attributes and find the places where system fonts are used. Then store a style name. Don't store the actual font, as it will be invalid when the Dynamic Type system updates. Using the text style name ensures that when you revisit font attributes, you create updated elements that match current Dynamic Types. Listing 2-3 shows how you might create a range dictionary for an attributed string.

Listing 2-3 goes beyond system-supplied elements. For each attribute run that mentions a font, the TextStyleRangeDictionary() function tests whether the font uses a system-supplied text style. If so, it stores the name of that style. If not, it stores the style that most closely matches the font in point size. You use this style as a baseline for re-creating a dynamic version of a given font. A multiplier reflects the ratio between the custom font's current point size, and the system version ensures that custom fonts are not just rounded up or down to static levels.

Listing 2-3   Scanning Attributed Strings for System-Supplied Fonts

```objc
// Built in fonts and styles
#define BUILTIN_FONTS @[[UIFont headlineFont], \
    [UIFont subheadlineFont], [UIFont bodyFont], \
    [UIFont footnoteFont], [UIFont caption1Font], \
    [UIFont caption2Font]]
#define BUILTIN_TEXT_STYLES @[UIFontTextStyleHeadline,\
    UIFontTextStyleSubheadline, UIFontTextStyleBody, \
    UIFontTextStyleFootnote, UIFontTextStyleCaption1, \
    UIFontTextStyleCaption2]

// Return the closest system style to a given font
NSString *ClosestSystemStyle(UIFont *font)
{
    CGFloat minimumDistance = MAXFLOAT;
    NSInteger selectedIndex = -1;
    NSInteger index = 0;

    for (UIFont *candidate in BUILTIN_FONTS)
    {
        CGFloat distance = fabsf(font.pointSize - candidate.pointSize);
        if (distance < minimumDistance)
        {
            selectedIndex = index;
            minimumDistance = distance;
        }
        index++;
    }

    return BUILTIN_TEXT_STYLES[selectedIndex];
}

// Build the style range dictionary
NSDictionary *TextStyleRangeDictionary(
    NSAttributedString *attributedString)
{
    NSMutableDictionary *dict = [NSMutableDictionary dictionary];

    [attributedString
        enumerateAttributesInRange:
            NSMakeRange(0, attributedString.length) options:0
        usingBlock:^(NSDictionary *attrs, NSRange range, BOOL *stop) {

        // Test if font attribute is mentioned
        UIFont *font = attrs[NSFontAttributeName];
        if (font)
```

```
    {
        // Is it a system font?
        NSInteger index = [BUILTIN_FONTS indexOfObject:font];
        if (index != NSNotFound)
        {
            // If so, store the style for the range
            NSString *textStyle = BUILTIN_TEXT_STYLES[index];
            dict[[NSValue valueWithRange:range]] = @[textStyle];
        }
        else
        {
            // Otherwise store:
            //    closest style, face, multiplier
            NSString *closestMatch = ClosestSystemStyle(font);
            UIFont *closestSystemFont =
                [UIFont preferredFontForTextStyle:closestMatch];
            if (closestSystemFont)
            {
                CGFloat multiplier = font.pointSize /
                    closestSystemFont.pointSize;
                dict[[NSValue valueWithRange:range]] =
                    @[closestMatch, font.fontName, @(multiplier)];
            }
        }
    }
}];

    return dict;
}
```

Applying Text Style Ranges

Once you've stored text style ranges using Listing 2-3, it's a simple matter to update an attributed string. On receiving a content size notification, iterate through the range dictionary and create new font attributes based on the stored styles. Listing 2-4 presents the ApplyTextStylesToAttributedString function, which applies the information stored in the range dictionary to create a new attributed string that reflects current Dynamic Type settings.

Listing 2-4 **Updating System-Supplied Fonts via a Range Dictionary**

```
// Return an updated attributed string
NSAttributedString *ApplyTextStylesToAttributedString(
    NSAttributedString *sourceString,
    NSDictionary *styleDictionary)
{
    NSMutableAttributedString *attributedString =
```

```
        [[NSMutableAttributedString alloc]
            initWithAttributedString:sourceString];

    for (NSValue *value in styleDictionary.allKeys)
    {
        NSRange range = value.rangeValue;
        NSArray *array = styleDictionary[value];
        if (array.count == 0) continue;
        UIFont *font;

        NSString *textStyle = array[0];
        if (array.count == 1) // system-supplied
        {
            font = [UIFont preferredFontForTextStyle:textStyle];
        }
        else if (array.count == 3) // custom font
        {
            NSString *face = array[1];
            UIFont *sysFont =
                [UIFont preferredFontForTextStyle:textStyle];
            NSNumber *multiplier = array[2];
            font = [UIFont fontWithName:face
                size:sysFont.pointSize * multiplier.floatValue];
        }
        [attributedString addAttributes:@{NSFontAttributeName:font}
            range:range];
    }

    return attributedString;
}
```

Attribute-Ready Dynamic Elements

The six system-supplied text categories (headlines, body, captions, etc.) suit many layout needs. They are inspired by the kinds of styles used in web design. They focus on long-form reading and Twitter-style timelines where text is a primary actor in the interface.

For some developers, default fonts or font sizes may not match interface nuances created by a design team. In such cases, you can use the approaches in Listings 2-3 and 2-4 to store and update font style offsets rather than directly using system-supplied styles.

Earlier, Listing 2-2 introduced the UILabel subclass, which updates its font whenever a content size update is detected. It takes just a few steps to update that listing to incorporate the kinds of dynamic attributes used in Listings 2-3 and 2-4. First, the class needs to persistently store a dictionary that maps text attribute ranges to system-supplied styles:

```
@property (nonatomic, strong) NSDictionary *rangeDictionary;
```

You re-create this dictionary whenever you update the label's attributed text. Contrast the following method implementation to Listing 2-2, whose method was more or less stubbed out to enforce a "don't do this" approach. Here you scan as the attributed text is assigned:

```
- (void) setAttributedText:(NSAttributedString *)attributedText
{
    [super setAttributedText:attributedText];
    _rangeDictionary = TextStyleRangeDictionary(attributedText);
}
```

Redirect any updates that use `setText:` to the attributed handler. Take care when using a label's `text` attribute with attributed content as the two systems are no longer tightly coupled. Whereas iOS 7 automatically redirected any updates to the attributed handler, iOS 8 and later do not. Without the following method, iOS 8 `text` updates won't respond to type updates. You can see this behavior in the chapter's sample code by commenting out this method:

```
- (void) setText:(NSString *)text
{
    NSMutableAttributedString *attributedString =
        [[NSMutableAttributedString alloc] initWithString:text
            attributes:@{NSFontAttributeName:self.font}];
    [self setAttributedText:attributedString];
}
```

Another change that took place from iOS 7 to iOS 8 limited attributed text updates to the view. This change required a call to `setNeedsDisplay`. The `DynamicLabel` class sample code for this chapter includes this iOS 8-and-later adjustment. It also works with iOS 7 even though the extra call isn't needed.

In the notification block, respond to content size changes by applying the range dictionary to the label's attributed text:

```
NSAttributedString *updatedText = ApplyTextStylesToAttributedString(
    strongSelf.attributedText, strongSelf.rangeDictionary);
strongSelf.attributedText = updatedText;
```

Custom Fonts Faces

Figure 2-4 shows an updated label class that handles fully attributed text. These screen shots show the smallest and largest Dynamic Type settings. This label uses the Cochin font, and its middle word is colored using the application's default tint (which you can't actually see in this black-and-white book, but it's a medium blue). As the label's size updates, all font attributes scale smoothly, despite this text not using a system-supplied font.

You can base custom fonts on system styles. When you do, your custom font can grow and shrink in synchrony with Dynamic Text callbacks. A simple function like the following adapts a font face to a system style and returns an instance with matching size. In Figure 2-4, the smaller letters are based on the caption 1 style. The large initial capitals were designed to mimic the headline style:

```
UIFont *SystemSizeBasedFont(NSString *fontName, NSString *textStyle)
{
    if (!fontName || !textStyle) return nil;

    UIFont *font = [UIFont preferredFontForTextStyle:textStyle];
    return [UIFont fontWithName:fontName size:font.pointSize];
}
```

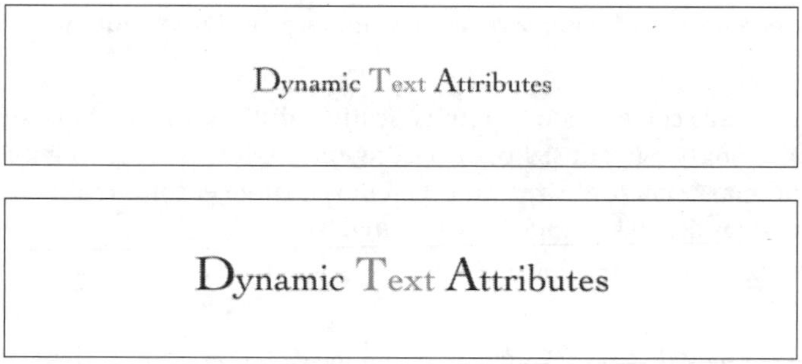

Dynamic Text Attributes

Dynamic Text Attributes

Figure 2-4   All the attributes of the string, including mixed fonts and colors, update at Dynamic Type notifications.

Dynamic Text Views

The same approach used to create dynamic labels can be used to update text view content whenever a content size category notification is encountered. The challenge for text views is keeping the content in sync with the range dictionary, especially when the text view is user editable.

Since you don't want to take away the delegation from any potential client, a dynamic text–aware text view should listen instead for notifications and respond to edits by updating the range dictionary:

```
// Listen for text edits
id observer = [[NSNotificationCenter defaultCenter]
    addObserverForName:UITextViewTextDidChangeNotification
    object:self
    queue:[NSOperationQueue mainQueue]
    usingBlock:^(NSNotification *note) {
        __strong typeof(self) strongSelf = weakSelf;
        strongSelf.rangeDictionary = TextStyleRangeDictionary(
                strongSelf.attributedText);
}];
```

This frees the `delegate` property for use by text view clients while allowing you to build a Dynamic Type–ready text view.

Custom Sizing

Apple's text style point sizes are non-linear. They do not grow in lock step from a minimum font to a maximum font, with stops along the way for each size category. When you implement your own sizing, follow Apple's example in this. You can do so in either of two ways. You can establish a fixed scaling ratio for multiplication between the default sizing and your fonts, as in Listings 2-3 and 2-4. Or you can use a curve-based algorithm, as in Listing 2-5. This listing leverages a cubic ease-in curve to move between minimum and maximum font sizes supplied to the function.

As Figure 2-5 shows, this curve produces results nearly indistinguishable from system-supplied items, freeing you from tying your sizing to existing font styles. With Listing 2-5, you choose the minimum and maximum font sizes, and the built-in curve ensures that your font grows or shrinks naturally in tandem with Apple's own sizing.

> **Note**
>
> Font sizes are not all the same. Two different font faces in size 12 can express very different heights, widths, and weights. Listing 2-5 focuses on relative size changes for a single font within the minimum and maximum extremes you set.

Listing 2-5   **Calculating Fonts from User-Preferred Size Categories**

```
#define TEXT_SIZE_CATEGORIES \
@{UIContentSizeCategoryExtraSmall:@0, \
UIContentSizeCategorySmall: @1, \
UIContentSizeCategoryMedium: @2, \
UIContentSizeCategoryLarge: @3, \
UIContentSizeCategoryExtraLarge: @4, \
UIContentSizeCategoryExtraExtraLarge: @5, \
UIContentSizeCategoryExtraExtraExtraLarge: @6, \
UIContentSizeCategoryAccessibilityMedium: @7, \
UIContentSizeCategoryAccessibilityLarge: @8, \
UIContentSizeCategoryAccessibilityExtraLarge: @9, \
UIContentSizeCategoryAccessibilityExtraExtraLarge: @10, \
UIContentSizeCategoryAccessibilityExtraExtraExtraLarge: @11}

UIFont *StylizedFont(NSString *fontName,
    CGFloat minimumFontSize, CGFloat maximumFontSize)
{
    // Retrieve user-selected size category
    NSString *preferredSize = [[UIApplication sharedApplication]
```

```
        preferredContentSizeCategory];
    NSInteger categoryCount = TEXT_SIZE_CATEGORIES.allKeys.count;
    NSInteger sizeIndex =
        [TEXT_SIZE_CATEGORIES[preferredSize] integerValue];
    CGFloat percent =
        (CGFloat) sizeIndex / (CGFloat) (categoryCount - 1);
    CGFloat targetFontSize = round(minimumFontSize +
        (maximumFontSize - minimumFontSize) * powf(percent, 3));

    return [UIFont fontWithName:fontName size:targetFontSize];
}
```

True Headline Font **Fake Headline Font** True Subheadline Font Fake Subheadline Font True Body Font Fake Body Font True Cap1 Font Fake Cap1 Font	**True Headline Font** **Fake Headline Font** True Subheadline Font Fake Subheadline Font True Body Font Fake Body Font True Cap1 Font Fake Cap1 Font

Figure 2-5   Size interpolation with an ease-in cubic function produces results close to Apple's own system-supplied items, even as users adjust Dynamic Type preferences.

Font Descriptors

Font variants present a challenge for anyone writing text-editing applications. UIKit's new font descriptor class helps automate the search for related items within a font family. For example, say that you create an AvenirNext font, as follows:

```
UIFont *font = [UIFont fontWithName:@"AvenirNext-Regular" size:12.0];
```

You request a bold variant of this font with a few simple steps. First, retrieve the font's descriptor. Next, add requests for a related font with a bold trait. Finish by creating a new version of the font sourced from the descriptor:

```
UIFontDescriptor *descriptor = font.fontDescriptor;
descriptor = [descriptor fontDescriptorWithFamily:font.familyName];
descriptor = [descriptor
    fontDescriptorWithSymbolicTraits: UIFontDescriptorTraitBold];
UIFont *boldFont = [UIFont fontWithDescriptor:descriptor size:12];
```

Running this code returns a new version of the font that expresses the bold attribute. Here is the original version, with the bold version produced via the font descriptor:

```
2014-11-28 09:50:14.619 Hello World[52353:70b] Font: <UICTFont: 0x8ea6fc0>
font-family: "AvenirNext-Regular"; font-weight: normal; font-style: normal;
font-size: 12.00pt
2014-11-28 09:50:14.626 Hello World[52353:70b] <UICTFont: 0x8c85340> font-family:
"AvenirNext-DemiBold"; font-weight: bold; font-style: normal; font-size: 12.00pt
```

Descriptor Challenges

UIFontDescriptor is a tricky class to use and a trickier one to use well. Consider Figure 2-6. The left screenshot shows a complex typographic result based on the ChalkboardSE family. The text presents a regular font along with bold, italicized, and bold-italic variations. There's one major challenge with this design goal. The right screen shot shows all three of the ChalkboardSE type variations available on iOS, and the font offers neither italic nor bold-italic variations.

Figure 2-6   The ChalkboardSE font does not offer italic variants.

When you run the following code:

```
UIFont *font = [UIFont instanceOfFontName:@"ChalkboardSE-Regular"];
UIFontDescriptor *descriptor = font.fontDescriptor;
descriptor = [descriptor fontDescriptorWithFamily:font.familyName];
descriptor = [descriptor fontDescriptorWithSymbolicTraits:
    UIFontDescriptorTraitBold | UIFontDescriptorTraitItalic];
UIFont *adjustedFont = [UIFont fontWithDescriptor:descriptor size:12];
```

and then look at the original and output fonts, you get this:

```
2014-11-28 10:07:56.530 Hello World[52595:70b] Font: <UICTFont: 0x8d33990>
font-family: "ChalkboardSE-Regular"; font-weight: normal; font-style: normal;
font-size: 12.00pt
2014-11-28 10:07:56.531 Hello World[52595:70b] <UICTFont: 0x8a28d80> font-family:
"Helvetica"; font-weight: normal; font-style: normal; font-size: 12.00pt
```

That is, you end up with Helvetica. To add insult to injury, the Helvetica font uses a normal weight, without applying the symbolic traits you requested. That's because the ChalkboardSE family provides only one custom trait, which is bold. The UIFont class cannot create an instance matching the requests in your descriptor, so it returns the default font instead:

```
ChalkboardSE-Light (San Serif) : <No Traits>
ChalkboardSE-Regular (San Serif) : <No Traits>
ChalkboardSE-Bold (San Serif) : Bold
```

Fonts with Multiple Variations

The problematic situation with descriptors remains even when you use a more expressive font family like AvenirNext. As you see in Figure 2-7, the family isn't hurting for variation. Here are the font members and the traits they express:

```
AvenirNext-MediumItalic: Italic
AvenirNext-Bold: Bold
AvenirNext-UltraLight: <No Traits>
AvenirNext-DemiBold: Bold
AvenirNext-HeavyItalic: Bold, Italic
AvenirNext-Heavy: Bold
AvenirNext-Medium: <No Traits>
AvenirNext-Italic: Italic
AvenirNext-UltraLightItalic: Italic
AvenirNext-BoldItalic: Bold, Italic
AvenirNext-Regular: <No Traits>
AvenirNext-DemiBoldItalic: Bold, Italic
```

Figure 2-7   AvenirNext offers many more font family faces than ChalkboardSE.

When you request a bold variant of AvenirNext-Regular, which variant should it offer: DemiBold, Bold, or Heavy? My tests returned instances of DemiBold. That's not because DemiBold is a more worthy bold variation than Bold or Heavy; it just happens to be the one randomly selected through the automated system.

Using String Attributes to Modify Fonts

The left screenshot in Figure 2-6, with its numerous font variations, doesn't use font descriptors. Instead, it leverages built-in string attributes for the NSMutableAttributedString class to tweak a font's presentation. iOS offers many attributes that enable you to modify how type is drawn. Commonly used attributes include color, underlining, strikethrough, shadows, and more.

Listing 2-6 details a category whose bold and italic toggles helped build the left Figure 2-6 screenshot. You apply these toggles by calling category methods, indicating whether you wish to apply or remove traits from the attributed string.

To bold items, the code adds a wider stroke attribute and offsets the font's baseline to accommodate the extra height produced. A negative stroking value ensures that the font is both filled and stroked. If you omit this, the font displays as an outline instead of being bolded.

The italic effect is created by adding an obliqueness attribute to the string, providing a custom slant. The default value of 0.0 produces output without skew. As you adjust the floating-point value, the text slants to the right for positive values and to the left for negative ones. This method uses a positive slant of 0.2 for a gentle italicized effect.

The three constants used in Listing 2-6 are arbitrary—specifically 2.5 and 12.0 for bolding and 0.2 for italics. I crowdsourced opinions in the #iphonedev chatroom on Freenode IRC, trying to find values that worked for a wide range of font faces and sizes. You may want to experiment further.

Listing 2-6   Adding Bold and Italic Attributes

```
@implementation NSMutableAttributedString (AttributedStringUtility)

// Toggle bolding on or off for the requested range
- (void) setBold:(BOOL) bold range:(NSRange) requestedRange
{
    CGFloat degree = bold ? 2.5 : 0.0;
    [self addAttribute:NSStrokeWidthAttributeName
        value:@(-degree) range:requestedRange];
    [self addAttribute:NSBaselineOffsetAttributeName
        value:@(-degree / 12.0) range:requestedRange];
}

// Toggle italics on or off for the requested range
- (void) setItalic:(BOOL) italic range:(NSRange) requestedRange
{
    [self addAttribute:NSObliquenessAttributeName
        value:@(italic ? 0.2 : 0.0) range:requestedRange];
}
@end
```

Dynamic Type Gotchas

Apple first introduced Dynamic Type APIs to the developer community back in iOS 7. Despite this relative longevity, adaptive types are not as widely used or recognized as one might hope. Many end users still do not mentally connect their settings for Apple-supplied engagement with third-party apps. As Figure 2-8 demonstrates, unless you provide in-app hints, users might entirely miss the point of user-controlled sizing.

Figure 2-8   iOS users are not generally trained to understand Dynamic Type.

Wrap-up

Here are a few final points to wrap up what you've read in this chapter:

- As an adaptive iOS citizen, text elements in your application should respond dynamically to user type settings, both for regular type and accessibility variations. A small investment in development time produces results that widen your pool of potential customers. Larger fonts are an essential feature for an older demographic, a customer base that averages more spending money per capita for app purchases. Money aside, creating more accessible applications is generally a karma-building effort, rewarding your spirit as well as your pocketbook.

- Integrating Dynamic Type into more complex elements such as text view content takes a bit of extra bookkeeping but is worth the overhead. Allowing complex elements to participate in Dynamic Type as fully as simple labels and buttons provides more holistic engagement with user preferences.

- Users may enable UI bolding through Settings > General > Accessibility > Bold Text. This toggle affects system-supplied fonts created through calls to `preferredFontForTextStyle:`, `systemFontOfSize:`, `boldSystemFontOfSize:`, and `italicSystemFontOfSize`. Other fonts you create remain unchanged, as they would have been with the toggle switched off. You cannot listen directly for this change as the phone reboots between toggles, but you can test for its effect by examining the base font reported by your `systemFontOfSize:` request.

- Downloadable fonts reduce system overhead, enabling your app to install fonts on an as-needed basis. While you'll never want to have your primary interface depend on a font that's not installed and that you don't ship with your app, these extra fonts play a role in user-driven content expansion.

- Although using `UIFontDescriptor` may sound like a terrific approach for finding related members within a font family, in practice you'll probably do better working around it than with it.

3

Text Kit

Flexible text presentation is one of the most exciting and developing areas of iOS. From as early as iOS 4, the move was on to migrate the Core Text C-based library into UIKit's Objective-C classes. With every new iOS release, these APIs have grown, matured, and expanded. By iOS 6, most UIKit interface classes supported rich text features. In the most modern iOS releases, that support has expanded to a suite of layout classes that continue to add mature type and frame settings to create flexible presentations onscreen, into images, and for PDF output.

Creating Complex Text Layouts

Text Kit offers a suite of classes that enable you to create rich, complex, and adaptable page design. Layout managers, text storage, and containers work together to create UIKit-based access to Apple's sophisticated Core Text technologies. Text Kit is, in Apple's words, a "fast, modern text layout and rendering engine," and it's built directly on top of the Core Text framework. While there are still a few bugs in the system, iterative updates continue to bring Text Kit closer and closer to Core Text's power.

Unlike Core Text, with its C-style design, Text Kit uses object-based APIs. Wrappers simplify memory management and provide better integration with UIKit classes. Figure 3-1 offers a quick rundown of some of the key terms you need to know when working with Text Kit:

- The heart of every Text Kit layout lies in its *text storage* that, as the name suggests, stores text. Text storage provides the content that Text Kit layout managers present. This material is an attributed string that stores the text and styles that should be shown onscreen. Changes to the text storage, which act as the model for Text Kit, automatically propagate to client layout managers, which draw the text into onscreen views.

- A Text Kit *layout manager* converts strings and their attributes into material that is ready for display. Managers convert stored characters to *glyphs*, the individual text drawings that represent those characters. Every layout manager draws the *same* content, each to its own set of containers. Adding more than one layout manager will clone content to different destinations. Unless you need to repeat text at more than one destination, use a single layout manager for your text storage.

- You assign one or more *containers* to each layout manager. A container sets the geometric size of the drawing destination. That content is broken into pieces, based on the available drawing space in each container.

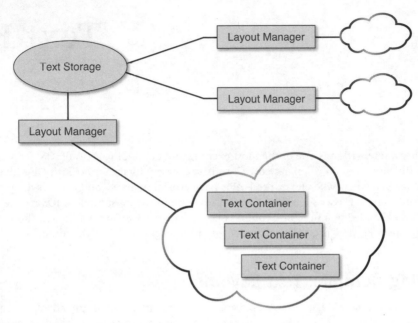

Figure 3-1   Text Kit overview.

The following sections discuss these concepts in greater detail, exploring how Text Kit is built from glyphs, containers, layout managers, and text storage.

Glyphs

Glyphs are individual character drawings. Each glyph represents one or more characters drawn to the screen or printed to the page. For example, the letter *a* is normally a single glyph. When using *ligatures*, a typesetting solution for reducing spaces between adjacent letters, two or more letters may combine to form a single glyph. You enable ligatures in attributed strings by adding the NSLigatureAttributeName attribute, as in this snippet:

```
[string addAttribute:NSLigatureAttributeName
    value:@(YES) range:string.fullRange];
```

Once NSLigatureAttributeName is added, iOS is smart enough to provide rendering support for ligature-enabled fonts like Hoefler Text and Zapfino.

The letters *fi* form the most commonly used English ligature. Normally, these characters produce two glyphs when rendered from an attributed string. Enabling ligatures returns the glyph sequence shown in Figure 3-2. In the third glyph of the word *refine*, the top of the *f* extends over and joins with the dot on the *i*. The two characters merge together into a single typographic item.

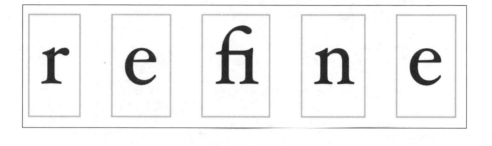

Figure 3-2   Top: The *f* and *i* letters are combined into a single glyph in this expanded view of the word *refine*. Bottom: Ligatures built into the Hoefler Text font.

Because of ligatures, you do not always experience a direct correspondence between an attributed string's characters and the underlying Core Text glyph-by-glyph layout. Each CGGlyph instance is an index, a reference to the internal glyph table for a given font. Figure 3-2 draws five glyphs, even though the word *refine* uses six characters. As you will discover, some APIs refer to glyphs and their ranges, while others work with characters. Be prepared to use both and prepare for some cross-framework discontinuities. Although Text Kit is built on top of Core Text, the two do not always match up exactly in their developer-facing terminology.

Listing 3-1 shows the code used to create Figure 3-2. This listing uses Core Text to pull out each glyph and draw it to the current context. This section of this chapter is the only one to use Core Text rather than Text Kit. It gives you a starting point to compare the complexities and approach of Core Text with other code throughout this chapter. Here you see plenty of old-style Core Text calls, with their C style interfaces and manual memory management. As you see in Listing 3-1, these C-based implementation details aren't a very big deal in Objective-C, but be warned. They can become unwieldy when moved to Swift.

Listing 3-1   Drawing Glyphs

```
// Test with refine, whiffle, flout, inflate, offal, hoofbeat,
// calfhood, fjarding, wolfkin, offbeat, offhand, tscheffkinite

- (UIImage *) drawGlyphs: (NSString *) initialString
{
```

```objc
// Establish a font
UIFont *theFont = [UIFont fontWithName:@"HoeflerText-Regular" size:60];

// Create the attributed string with ligatures enabled
NSMutableAttributedString *string =
    [[NSMutableAttributedString alloc] initWithString:initialString
        attributes:@{NSFontAttributeName:theFont,
            NSLigatureAttributeName:@(YES)}];

// Establish a drawing space
CGRect bounds = [string boundingRectWithSize:CGSizeMake(
        CGFLOAT_MAX, CGFLOAT_MAX)
    options:NSStringDrawingUsesLineFragmentOrigin context:nil];

// Inflate to allow spacing out
bounds.size.width *= 3;
bounds.size.height *= 3;

UIGraphicsBeginImageContextWithOptions(bounds.size, NO, 0);
CGContextRef context = UIGraphicsGetCurrentContext();

// White background
[[UIColor whiteColor] set];
CGContextFillRect(context, bounds);

// Flip for Quartz drawing coordinate system
[self prepareContextForCoreText:bounds.size];

// Point to start drawing
CGPoint point = CGPointMake(20, CGRectGetMidY(bounds));

// Draw each Core Text run
CTLineRef line = CTLineCreateWithAttributedString(
    (__bridge CFAttributedStringRef)string);
NSArray *runArray = (__bridge_transfer NSArray *) CTLineGetGlyphRuns(line);
for (id eachRun in runArray)
{
    CTRunRef run = (__bridge CTRunRef)eachRun;

    // Set the drawing font
    CFDictionaryRef attributes = CTRunGetAttributes(run);
    CTFontRef runFont = CFDictionaryGetValue(
        attributes, kCTFontAttributeName);
    CGFontRef cgFont = CTFontCopyGraphicsFont(runFont, NULL);
    CGContextSetFont(context, cgFont);
    CGContextSetFontSize(context, CTFontGetSize(runFont));
    CGFontRelease(cgFont);
```

```objc
// Iterate through each glyph in the run
for (CFIndex runGlyphIndex = 0;
    runGlyphIndex < CTRunGetGlyphCount(run); runGlyphIndex++)
{
    // Fetch the glyph based on its index in the run
    CGGlyph glyph;
    CFRange glyphRange = CFRangeMake(runGlyphIndex, 1);
    CTRunGetGlyphs(run, glyphRange, &glyph);

    // Calculate a surrounding rectangle
    CGFloat ascent, descent, leading;
    double glyphWidth = CTRunGetTypographicBounds(run,
        CFRangeMake(runGlyphIndex, 1), &ascent, &descent, &leading);
    CGRect destRect = CGRectMake(
        point.x, point.y - (ascent + descent) / 2.0,
        glyphWidth, ascent + descent);

    // Enable emoji support via font attributes
    NSDictionary *attributes =
        (__bridge NSDictionary *)CTRunGetAttributes(run);
    if (attributes[NSFontAttributeName] == theFont)
    {
        // Normal drawing
        [[UIColor blackColor] set];
        CGContextShowGlyphsAtPositions(context, &glyph,
            &destRect.origin, 1);
    }
    else
    {
        // Emoji
        UIFont *glyphFont = attributes[NSFontAttributeName];
        CTFontRef fontRef =
            CTFontCreateWithName((CFStringRef)glyphFont.fontName,
                glyphFont.pointSize, NULL);
        CTFontDrawGlyphs(fontRef, &glyph, &destRect.origin, 1, context);
        CFRelease(fontRef);
    }

    // Draw a rectangle in gray
    destRect = CGRectInset(destRect, -8, -8);
    destRect.origin.y -= descent;
    UIBezierPath *path = [UIBezierPath bezierPathWithRect:destRect];
    [[UIColor lightGrayColor] set];
    [path stroke];

    // Move to the right
    point.x += glyphWidth + 40;
```

```
        }
    }

    // Retrieve the image
    UIImage *image = UIGraphicsGetImageFromCurrentImageContext();
    UIGraphicsEndImageContext();

    return image;
}
```

Figure 3-3 shows the same *refine* text, using the Hoefler Text font from Figure 3-2 and displayed in a user-editable `UITextView`. A cursor appears centered over the *fi* ligature, midway between the *f* and the *i*. From a user's point of view, this word has six characters, not five glyphs. The UIKit representation mirrors the user experience, enabling the user to add and edit text without regard to rendering details. According to UIKit's TextKit queries, this string contains six glyphs.

Figure 3-3   UIKit's emphasis on user interaction can cause mismatches between underlying Core Text layout technology and UIKit APIs. Despite using ligatures, the cursor moves character-by-character to match a user's text entry.

UIKit APIs don't always match the values you expect from underlying rendering. The following calls return the number of glyphs stored in a text view and convert between glyph indices and character indices:

```
// Set the attributed string
[textView.textStorage setAttributedString:attributedString];

// Report the number of glyphs
NSLog(@"Number of glyphs in %@: %zd", attributedString.string,
    textView.layoutManager.numberOfGlyphs);

// If there is not a mismatch, return
if (textView.layoutManager.numberOfGlyphs != textView.textStorage.string.length)
    return;
// If there is, iterate through each item in the attributed string
// and report the indices and bounds
for (int index = 0; index < attributedString.string.length; index++)
{
    NSLog(@"Index: %zd glyph index for character: %zd", index,
        [textView.layoutManager glyphIndexForCharacterAtIndex:index]);
```

```
    NSLog(@"Index: %zd character index for glyph: %zd", index,
        [textView.layoutManager characterIndexForGlyphAtIndex:index]);
    NSLog(@"Index: %zd bounds: %@", index,
        NSStringFromCGRect([textView.layoutManager
            boundingRectForGlyphRange:NSMakeRange(index, 1)
        inTextContainer:textView.layoutManager.textContainers.firstObject]));
}
```

This sample uses Text Kit technologies such as text storage and a layout manager, which are explored in greater detail later in this chapter. But before diving into those topics, you first need this bit of base knowledge about glyphs.

A standard UIKit text view stores six glyphs for the attributed ligature-enabled Hoefler Text *refine* text from Figure 3-3. It reports a 1:1 correspondence for each of these characters and glyphs. In the following results output, notice that the bounds for characters 2 and 3 are identical, as they use a single ligature glyph:

```
Number of glyphs in refine: 6
Index: 0 glyph index for character: 0 // r
Index: 0 character index for glyph: 0
Index: 0 bounds: {{5, 0}, {22.32, 60}}
Index: 1 glyph index for character: 1 // e
Index: 1 character index for glyph: 1
Index: 1 bounds: {{27.32, 0}, {28.079999999999998, 60}}
Index: 2 glyph index for character: 2 // fi
Index: 2 character index for glyph: 2
Index: 2 bounds: {{55.399999999999999, 0}, {35.039999999999999, 60}}
Index: 3 glyph index for character: 3 // fi
Index: 3 character index for glyph: 3
Index: 3 bounds: {{55.399999999999999, 0}, {35.039999999999999, 60}}
Index: 4 glyph index for character: 4 // n
Index: 4 character index for glyph: 4
Index: 4 bounds: {{90.439999999999998, 0}, {32.879999999999995, 60}}
Index: 5 glyph index for character: 5 // e
Index: 5 character index for glyph: 5
Index: 5 bounds: {{123.31999999999999, 0}, {28.079999999999984, 60}}
```

The matter grows more complicated with complex characters like the emoji shown in Figure 3-4. In this example, the text view incorrectly reports 11 glyphs and characters due to the larger Unicode storage for the emoji items. There should be only 9 glyphs.

Listing 3-2 extends the NSLayoutManager class to retrieve a true glyph count. It iteratively compares adjacent bounding rects and merges identical items represented by a single glyph.

Figure 3-4   Emoji characters currently report incorrectly as 2 glyphs and 2 characters each.

Listing 3-2   **Counting Glyphs by Checking Drawing Bounds**

```objc
@interface NSLayoutManager (GeneralUtility)
@property (nonatomic, readonly) NSUInteger trueGlyphCount;
@end

@implementation NSLayoutManager (GeneralUtility)
- (NSUInteger) trueGlyphCount
{
    if (self.numberOfGlyphs < 2) return self.numberOfGlyphs;

    NSUInteger count = 0;
    for (NSTextContainer *container in self.textContainers)
    {
        NSRange glyphRange = [self glyphRangeForTextContainer:container];
        if (glyphRange.length < 2)
        {
            count += glyphRange.length;
            continue;
        }

        // First item
        CGRect bounds = [self boundingRectForGlyphRange:
            NSMakeRange(glyphRange.location, 1) inTextContainer:container];
        count += 1;

        // Remaining items
        for (NSUInteger index = 1; index < glyphRange.length; index++)
        {
            CGRect testBounds = [self boundingRectForGlyphRange:
                    NSMakeRange(glyphRange.location + index, 1)
                inTextContainer:container];
```

```
            if (CGRectEqualToRect(bounds, testBounds)) continue;
            bounds = testBounds;
            count += 1;
        }
    }

    return count;
}
@end
```

If you are curious about what glyphs and ligatures any iOS font provides, Listing 3-3 may help. It creates an exhaustive presentation, returned in the form of an attributed string, which you can either throw into a `UITextView` as in Figure 3-5 or export to a document, as discussed in Chapter 4, "Attributed Strings and Document Containers." This method works by querying the font for the number of glyphs it supports. It then iterates through those items, drawing each glyph and showing its associated glyph name.

Figure 3-5   Glyph list for the Hoefler Text font. This font contains nearly 1,200 individual glyphs.

Listing 3-3   **Reviewing Font Glyphs**

```
- (NSAttributedString *) generateFontInformation
{
    NSMutableAttributedString *string = [NSMutableAttributedString new];

    NSString *fontName = @"HoeflerText-Regular";
    CGFontRef fontRef = CGFontCreateWithFontName(
```

```objc
            (__bridge CFStringRef) fontName);
size_t count = CGFontGetNumberOfGlyphs(fontRef);

NSString *title = [NSString stringWithFormat:@"%@\n", fontName];
NSAttributedString *attributedTitle = [[NSAttributedString alloc]
    initWithString:title attributes:@{NSFontAttributeName:
        [UIFont fontWithName:@"Courier" size:32]}];
[string appendAttributedString:attributedTitle];

CGFloat side = 30;
CGRect rect = CGRectMake(0, 0, side, side);
CGPoint drawingPoint = CGPointMake(12, 12);
CGFloat fontSize = 12;

for (CGGlyph i = 0; i < count; i++ )
{
    // Fetch glyph name
    NSString *name  = (__bridge_transfer NSString *)
        CGFontCopyGlyphNameForGlyph(fontRef, i);
    NSString *identity =
        [NSString stringWithFormat:@" %3d: %@\n", i, name];

    // Draw a sample of the glyph
    UIGraphicsBeginImageContextWithOptions(rect.size, YES, 0);
    CGContextRef context = UIGraphicsGetCurrentContext();
    CGContextSetFont(context, fontRef);
    CGContextSetFontSize(context, fontSize);
    CGContextSetTextMatrix(context, CGAffineTransformIdentity);
    CGContextTranslateCTM(context, 0, side);
    CGContextScaleCTM(context, 1.0, -1.0); // flip the context

    // Fill and frame the sample
    [[UIColor whiteColor] set];
    UIRectFill(rect);
    [[UIColor blackColor] set];
    UIRectFrame(rect);

    // Draw glyph
    CGGlyph glyph = CGFontGetGlyphWithGlyphName(fontRef,
        (__bridge CFStringRef) name);
    CGContextShowGlyphsAtPositions(context, &glyph, &drawingPoint, 1);
    UIImage *image = UIGraphicsGetImageFromCurrentImageContext();
    UIGraphicsEndImageContext();

    // Attachments are discussed in Chapter 7
    NSTextAttachment *attachment = [[NSTextAttachment alloc] init];
    attachment.image = image;
```

```
        attachment.bounds = (CGRect){.size = image.size};
        NSAttributedString *s1 = [NSAttributedString
            attributedStringWithAttachment:attachment];

        NSAttributedString *s2 = [[NSAttributedString alloc]
            initWithString:identity
            attributes:@{
                NSFontAttributeName:[UIFont fontWithName:@"Courier" size:12],
                NSLigatureAttributeName:@(YES)}];
        [string appendAttributedString:s1];
        [string appendAttributedString:s2];
    }
    CFRelease(fontRef);

    return string;
}
```

Text Storage

Apple defines *text storage* as "the fundamental storage mechanism of the Text Kit's extended text-handling system." Text storage manages characters and their attributes, such as fonts, weights, and colors. If this sounds eerily reminiscent of attributed strings, it's not by accident. The NSTextStorage class is simply a subclass of NSMutableAttributedString.

Text storage moves beyond attributed strings by coordinating with layout manager objects, the classes that manage the way text elements are placed onscreen. It synchronizes its client layout managers whenever content updates. Text storage objects are active participants in the string-to-presentation pathway.

For example, say you have a text storage object whose contents are spread out between several text views:

```
// Replace the text shown in the client text views
[storage beginEditing];
[storage replaceCharactersInRange:
        NSMakeRange(0, storage.length)
    withAttributedString:newAttributedString];
[storage fixAttributesInRange:NSMakeRange(0, storage.length)];
[storage endEditing];
// All clients are now automatically updated
```

To update view contents, you simply modify the text storage. This change at the level of the attributed string automatically propagates out to the storage's view clients without further work on your part.

The `beginEditing` and `endEditing` methods consolidate changes you make to the text storage. Using them delays client notifications until you've finished your updates, lowering any redrawing overhead.

> **Note**
>
> When working with text storage, as with any mutable attributed strings, edits may introduce internal inconsistencies. The `NSMutableAttributedString` class offers several methods to fix attributes. As a rule, use `fixAttributesInRange:`. This is the most general of the repair methods. It ensures that all attributes are repaired—including errors with attachments, fonts, and paragraph styles—with a single API call.

Layout Managers

A Text Kit *layout manager* takes responsibility for converting strings and their attributes into material that is ready for display. Managers convert stored characters to the glyphs that represent them. They also apply attribute styles such as underline and strikethrough, which are not a native part of fonts. Layout managers implement paragraph styles, such as line-to-line spacing, indentation, alignment, tabbing, and so forth. They draw these items into their set of attached text *containers*, which in turn define geometric destinations for drawing that text.

In normal use, you create a single layout manager instance and add it to a text storage instance, as is done in the following code snippet:

```
storage = [[NSTextStorage alloc]
    initWithString:initialString attributes:attributeDictionary];
NSLayoutManager *layoutManager = [[NSLayoutManager alloc] init];
[storage addLayoutManager:layoutManager];
```

Text views ship with a built-in layout manager and do not need you to create one unless you need to build more complex layouts with text flowing from one text view to another. Retrieve the built-in instance from a `UITextView` by accessing its `layoutManager` property.

When you need the same text to be echoed in several places in a layout, you may connect additional layout managers. All layout managers attached to a single text storage object present the same text material. The left image in Figure 3-6 shows a single layout manager, which draws to several destinations. The right image in Figure 3-6 uses multiple layout managers. Each manager draws its content in parallel, producing mirrored results.

Text Containers

Each *text container* defines a geometric extent for Text Kit drawing. A container constrains text layout to a specific region. You may add a single container destination to a layout manager or, as in the case in Figure 3-6 (left), use multiple containers and enable the text to flow from one destination to the next.

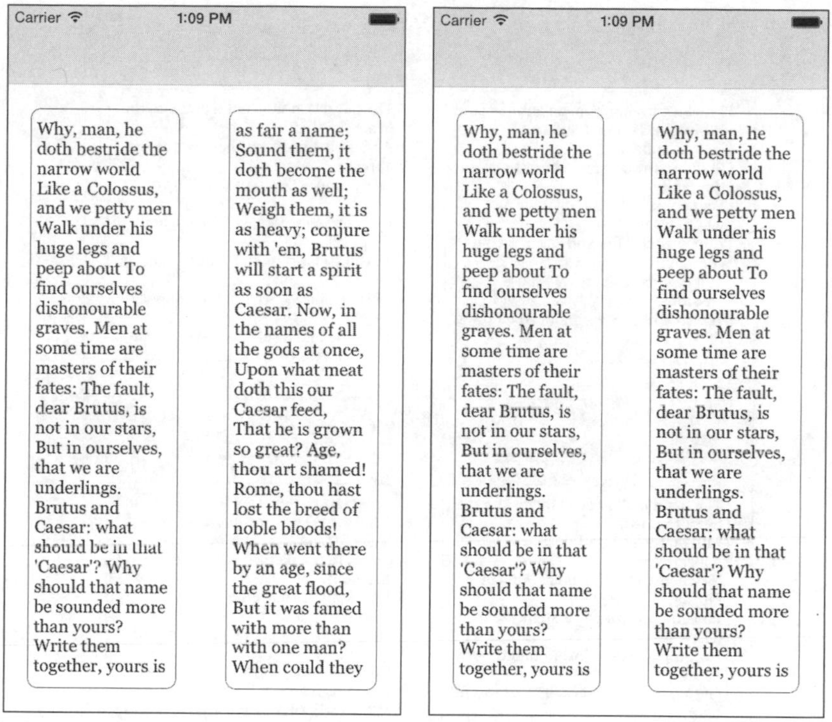

Figure 3-6   In the left image, a single layout manager flows its text from one text view container to the next. In the right image, two layout managers present identical text in parallel.

The order in which you add containers to your layout defines which area gets filled with text first. The top screen shot in Figure 3-7 was built by adding the left container and then the right one. The bottom screen shot in Figure 3-7 reverses that order. Text fills the right container before the left one because it was added to the layout manager first.

Here is the code that created the top screen shot. In it, the left container is added first, and then the right container:

```
NSTextContainer *textContainerLeft =
    [[NSTextContainer alloc] initWithSize:size];
NSTextContainer *textContainerRight =
    [[NSTextContainer alloc] initWithSize:size];
[layoutManager addTextContainer:textContainerLeft];
[layoutManager addTextContainer:textContainerRight];
```

The left and right qualities you see in Figure 3-7 arise from the layout of the two text views. There is nothing intrinsically "left" or "first" about the textContainerLeft instance other than the view it is attached to and the order in which it is added to the layout manager.

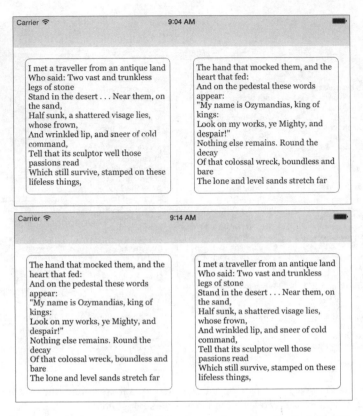

Figure 3-7   When you add these text containers in reverse order, the text fills the right container first.

Adaptive Flow

Containers define text extent, but they do not define specific geometric positions. That's because they establish sizes—not rectangles that mark out frames. A container is always subordinate to a layout manager. You leverage containers to create layouts that flow from one part of the screen to another, such as when working with columns. As a rule, it's easier to work with existing UIKit classes to create these layouts than to depend on custom views that must render their content. Text views make it easy to build adaptive material that adjusts itself to prevailing container geometries. Figure 3-8 shows an adaptive layout presenting two columns of text.

Figure 3-8   This layout reflows its text when bounds change due to device rotation.

To create this effect, use the built-in `UITextView` class with custom containers. The following code builds the text views shown in Figure 3-8:

```
// Build the text views
textViewLeft = [[UITextView alloc] initWithFrame:CGRectZero
    textContainer:[NSTextContainer new]];
textViewRight = [[UITextView alloc] initWithFrame:CGRectZero
    textContainer:[NSTextContainer new]];

// Disable scrolling and edits
textViewLeft.scrollEnabled = NO;
textViewRight.scrollEnabled = NO;
textViewLeft.editable = NO;
textViewRight.editable = NO;

// Create a new custom layout manager
layoutManager = [NSLayoutManager new];
layoutManager.allowsNonContiguousLayout = YES;

// Add the text containers from the text views
[layoutManager addTextContainer:textViewLeft.textContainer];
[layoutManager addTextContainer:textViewRight.textContainer];

// Connect the layout manager to the custom text storage
[textStorage addLayoutManager:layoutManager];
```

Consider a few key points about this approach:

- **Create custom containers for each text view in the interface.** Do not use the ones established by the standard initializers (`new`, `initWithFrame:`, `initWithCoder:`) as you cannot redirect those containers to a custom layout manager. The `initWithFrame:textContainer:` initializer pattern you see here avoids nasty crashes.

- **Disable scrolling.** Disabling scrolling enables the layout manager to flow the material properly from container to container.

- **Disable edits.** When using a custom layout manager, you bypass the text edit handlers built into `UITextView`.

- **Use Auto Layout to place your views.** Auto Layout ensures that the text views will automatically resize on bounds changes to the controller, updating their containers and causing the layout manager to reflow source text to accommodate the new geometries.

> **Note**
>
> If you want to track changes to a container's text view, make sure to enable its `heightTracksTextView` and `widthTracksTextView` properties.

Insets

Text containers enable you to adjust layout by adding insets or exclusion paths. As you see in Figure 3-9 (left), a container's `textContainerInset` property moves layout away from the edges. You add inset hints to a container by passing a `UIEdgeInsets` struct. This struct defines offsets from the top, left, bottom, and right of the container:

```
// Inset left text view
textViewLeft = [[UITextView alloc] initWithFrame:self.view.bounds
    textContainer:textContainerLeft];
[self.view addSubview:textViewLeft];

textViewLeft.textContainerInset = UIEdgeInsetsMake(50, 20, 50, 20);
```

Exclusion Paths

Exclusion zones prevent text from being drawn to parts of a container, typically where you want to insert an illustration embedded within the text. Created with Bezier paths, exclusion zones offer more flexibility than insets because you can theoretically use any shape, not just rectangles. Figure 3-9 (right) uses an exclusion path extending from the edges of a rectangle into an embedded oval. This zone consists an inverted oval Bezier path:

```
// Wrap text within oval exclusion zone
CGRect destination = CGRectInset(textViewRight.bounds, 20, 20);
UIBezierPath *exclusion = InversePathInRect(
```

```
    [UIBezierPath bezierPathWithOvalInRect:destination],
     textViewRight.bounds));
textViewRight.textContainer.exclusionPaths = @[exclusion];
```

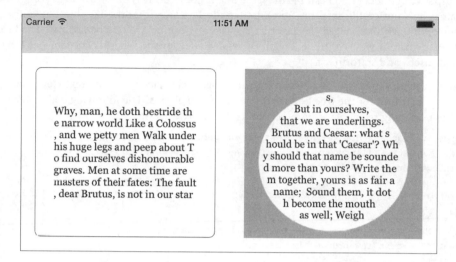

Figure 3-9   Insets (left) and exclusion zones (right) adjust output targets within a text container.

Notably, this zone inverts its path. It places the exclusion to the outside rather than the inside of the text. This shapes the text drawing, limiting it to the inner oval. Most commonly, you use exclusion zones to add embedded figures. The following inversion function use the odd/even fill rule for Bezier paths to create an inside-out effect for shaping text:

```
UIBezierPath *InversePathInRect(
    UIBezierPath *sourcePath, CGRect rect)
{
    UIBezierPath *path = [UIBezierPath bezierPath];
    [path appendPath:sourcePath];
    [path appendPath:[UIBezierPath bezierPathWithRect:rect]];
    path.usesEvenOddFillRule = YES;
    return path;
}
```

Be very careful in limiting an exclusion zone to the container bounds. In the current versions of iOS, zones extending outside the container can cause your apps to spiral into an infinite loop, never returning control to the user. Even zones carefully matched to container edges may produce unexpected artifacts. Text Kit is very good at simple rectangles, but it sometimes struggles with other geometries.

Bounding Rectangles

The text oval produced by the code you just saw should lie directly in the vertical center of
the output container. As you can see in Figure 3-9, it does not. It is offset from the top of the
container by a noticeable amount. Text Kit often displays layout quirks like this, especially
when working with text views—a class that displays any number of odd behaviors related to
whether the parent view controller enables extended edge layout, whether the view itself has
content insets, and so forth.

To adjust the gray area, which is drawn into an image view placed over the text view, query
the layout manager for the true bounds of the presented glyphs. The following code returns an
accurate bounding rectangle with respect to the parent text view:

```
NSRange fullRange = NSMakeRange(0, layoutManager.numberOfGlyphs);
CGRect trueRect = [layoutManager boundingRectForGlyphRange:fullRange
    inTextContainer:textContainerRight];
```

You often need to take note of the difference in size between the view's bounds and the text
container's size:

```
NSLayoutManager *layoutManager = textView.layoutManager;
CGFloat dY = textView.bounds.size.height
   - textContainer.size.height;
```

For example, when retrieving glyph outlines, you offset them by half the difference between
the two extents, as shown here:

```
for (int i = 0; i < layoutManager.numberOfGlyphs; i++)
{
    // Fetch glyph rect in container coordinates
    CGRect glyphRect = [layoutManager
        boundingRectForGlyphRange:NSMakeRange(i, 1)
        inTextContainer:textContainerRight];
    // Offset those to parent view coordinates
    UIView *v = [[UIView alloc] initWithFrame:
        CGRectOffset(glyphRect, 0, dY / 2)];
    [textViewRight addSubview:v];
    v.layer.borderColor = [[UIColor blackColor]
        colorWithAlphaComponent:0.5].CGColor;
    v.layer.borderWidth = 0.5;
}
```

Figure 3-10 shows the correctly outlined results.

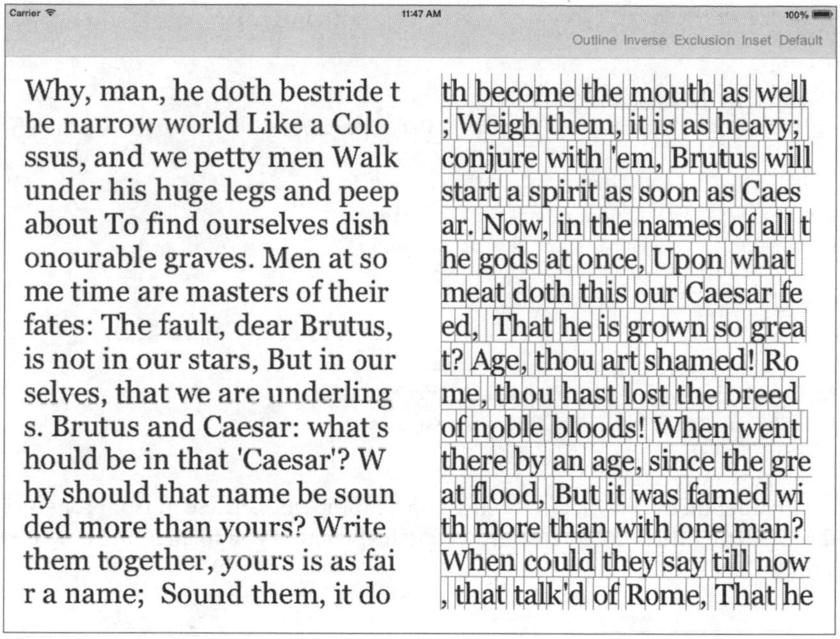

Figure 3-10 To properly outline these glyphs, you must take into account any difference between a text view's bounds and its container's size.

Using Text Kit to Add Touch to Labels

Although modern UIKit labels are fully Text Kit powered and attribute ready, they lack many conveniences included with the `UITextView` class. For example, you cannot initialize a label instance with a custom text container. UIKit has no APIs to directly integrate the two. It's relatively easy, however, to subclass `UILabel` to add more explicit Text Kit support.

So why would you subclass `UILabel`? URL handling offers one very good reason. Although a label instance will properly draw a URL, complete with underline and text hints, that link won't react to any touches. By integrating Text Kit into the label, you can create touch-to-glyph matching that allows you to find when a user has activated a hyperlink.

Establishing Text Kit

To get started with touch-enabled elements, establish Text Kit instances that act in synchrony with the label. This solution renders Text Kit text on top of views known to use Text Kit for layout so the two line up exactly. The following method builds new storage, a layout manager, and a container and stores these to local instance variables. These items are custom, mirroring the implementation already baked into the `UILabel`:

```
- (void) establishTextKitElements
{
    // Text storage
    textStorage = [[NSTextStorage alloc]
        initWithAttributedString:self.attributedText];

    // Layout manager
    layoutManager = [[NSLayoutManager alloc] init];
    [textStorage addLayoutManager:layoutManager];

    // Container
    container = [[NSTextContainer alloc] initWithSize:self.bounds.size];
    [layoutManager addTextContainer:container];
    container.maximumNumberOfLines = self.numberOfLines;
    container.lineBreakMode = self.lineBreakMode;
}
```

Each text container offers line break and line number properties. These mirror properties used for text labels. Setting them when creating a container enables you to align the new Text Kit elements to the label.

Synchronizing

Synchronizing Text Kit items with labels is critical in producing consistent lookups and accurate feedback. You must catch any updates that affect the string value, number of lines, or line break mode. The label's attributed text must always be matched to the custom text storage, and the lines and line break mode must be matched to the container. The following methods ensure that any label-level changes propagate to custom Text Kit elements:

```
- (void) setText:(NSString *)text
{
    if (!textStorage) [self establishTextKitElements];
    [super setText:text];
    [textStorage setAttributedString:self.attributedText];
}

- (void) setAttributedText:(NSAttributedString *)attributedText
{
    if (!textStorage) [self establishTextKitElements];
    [super setAttributedText:attributedText];
    [textStorage setAttributedString:self.attributedText];
}

- (void) setNumberOfLines:(NSInteger)numberOfLines
{
    if (!textStorage) [self establishTextKitElements];
    [super setNumberOfLines:numberOfLines];
```

```
    container.maximumNumberOfLines = numberOfLines;
}


- (void) setLineBreakMode:(NSLineBreakMode)lineBreakMode
{
    if (!textStorage) [self establishTextKitElements];
    [super setLineBreakMode:lineBreakMode];
    container.lineBreakMode = lineBreakMode;
}
```

Translating Coordinates

In addition to keeping the content synchronized, you must be able to translate points from
the view's coordinate system into the container's layout. The following methods retrieve the
bounding box for output glyphs and calculate vertical and horizontal offsets. By applying these
offsets, you can translate view touch points into glyph coordinates that enable you to match
characters to touches:

```
// Return unified bounds of all glyphs
- (CGRect) glyphBounds
{
    container.size = self.bounds.size;
    return [layoutManager boundingRectForGlyphRange:
            NSMakeRange(0, layoutManager.numberOfGlyphs)
        inTextContainer:container];
}


// Find half difference between view bounds and glyph bounds
// This assumes label vertical centering
- (CGFloat) verticalLayoutOffset
{
    CGRect glyphBounds = [self glyphBounds];
    return (self.bounds.size.height - glyphBounds.size.height) / 2;
}


- (CGFloat) horizontalLayoutOffset
{
    CGRect glyphBounds = [self glyphBounds];
    return -glyphBounds.origin.x;
}


// Adjust touch points to container
- (CGPoint) viewPointInLayoutCoordinates: (CGPoint) point
{
    CGRect glyphBounds = [self glyphBounds];
    CGFloat layoutOffset = [self verticalLayoutOffset];
```

```
    CGPoint adjustedPoint = CGPointMake(
        point.x + glyphBounds.origin.x, point.y - layoutOffset);
    return adjustedPoint;
}
```

Glyphs and Characters

As you read earlier in this chapter, glyphs and characters do not always match up. The next method leverages the touch point-to-glyph coordinate solution you just saw so you can find a glyph that corresponds to a user's touch:

```
// Search glyph-by-glyph for a match
- (NSUInteger) glyphIndexAtPoint: (CGPoint) point
{
    CGPoint adjustedPoint =
        [self viewPointInLayoutCoordinates:point];
    NSUInteger match = NSNotFound;
    for (int i = 0; i < layoutManager.numberOfGlyphs; i++)
    {
        // Test each glyph to see if it contains the point
        CGRect glyphRect = [layoutManager
            boundingRectForGlyphRange:NSMakeRange(i, 1)
            inTextContainer:container];
        if (CGRectContainsPoint(glyphRect, adjustedPoint))
        {
            match = i;
            break;
        }
    }
    return match;
}
```

Once you've found the glyph match, convert that glyph index into a character index. This enables you to look up that glyph in the label's attributed string and provides access to any attributes at that point:

```
// Find glyph and convert to character
- (NSUInteger) characterIndexAtPoint: (CGPoint) point
{
    NSUInteger glyphIndex = [self glyphIndexAtPoint:point];
    if (glyphIndex == NSNotFound)
        return NSNotFound;
    return [layoutManager characterIndexForGlyphAtIndex:glyphIndex];
}
```

Checking for Links

Use the character index to query the label's attributed string. The following method checks whether a link attribute is established at the given point. If so, it retrieves the attribute range (which corresponds to the Core Text "run" you read about earlier in the chapter) and returns the associated URL:

```
- (NSURL *) urlForPoint: (CGPoint) testPoint
    index: (NSUInteger *) index range: (NSRange *) range
{
    if (!textStorage) [self establishTextKitElements];

    // Find the character index at the touch point
    NSUInteger characterIndex = [self characterIndexAtPoint:testPoint];
    if (index) *index = characterIndex;
    if (characterIndex == NSNotFound) return nil;

    // Is there a URL?
    NSRange r;
    NSDictionary *attributeDictionary = [self.attributedText
        attributesAtIndex:characterIndex effectiveRange:&r];
    if (range) *range = r;
    return attributeDictionary[NSLinkAttributeName];
}
```

Adding Visual Feedback

A label implementation can present "active" URLs with a gray background highlight, as shown in Figure 3-11. A highlight appears as a touch enters a URL area and is dismissed when the touch strays from it. This feedback and its delayed action enable users to change their minds before lifting their finger from the screen, providing a better user experience.

The following method creates visual highlights. This code checks attributes at the string index passed to it. When there's a URL (and if it matches the reference URL established where the user first touched the screen), the code applies a background color attribute. The background color attribute is otherwise cleared from all other points in the string:

```
- (void) highlight: (BOOL) shouldHighlight forURL: (NSURL *) comparisonURL
    atIndex: (NSUInteger) index
{
    // Clear any existing highlights
    NSMutableAttributedString *string =
        self.attributedText.mutableCopy;
    [string addAttribute:NSBackgroundColorAttributeName
        value:[UIColor clearColor]
        range:NSMakeRange(0, string.length)];
```

```
// When the caller wants a highlight added, ensure
// the URL at the touched index matches the original
if (shouldHighlight)
{
    NSRange range;
    NSURL *url = [self.attributedText
        attribute:NSLinkAttributeName
        atIndex:index effectiveRange:&range];
    if ([url isEqual:comparisonURL])
        [string addAttribute:NSBackgroundColorAttributeName
        value:[[UIColor grayColor] colorWithAlphaComponent:0.3]
        range:range];
}

// Update the label's attributed string
self.attributedText = string;
}
```

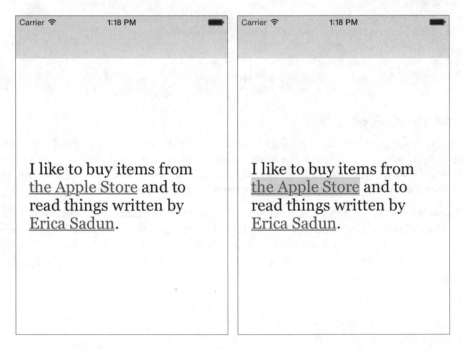

Figure 3-11   Attributed text backgrounds enable users to know when their touch will activate a URL.

This is where the Text Kit story ends. The remaining class implementation involves tracking touches and coordinating with a delegate, whose job it is to determine whether to give permission to highlight and open URLs. You can review them in the sample code for this chapter.

Draggable Exclusion Zones

Draggable exclusion zones are gimmicky. In text layout terms, they are unreliable except when using simple rectangles. Despite this, they are unaccountably popular as they update presentations in response to user interactions. Figure 3-12 shows a bunny shape, which can be moved around its parent text view. As it moves, the container's custom exclusion zone updates, allowing text to wrap around the shape.

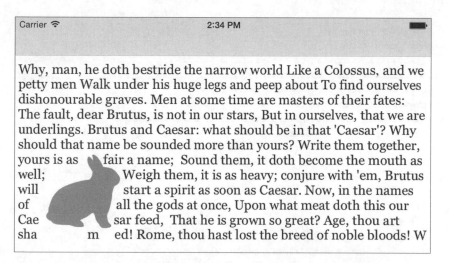

Figure 3-12   Exclusion zones enable text to wrap around shapes and images.

To create a text exclusion zone, build a draggable view using your favorite recipe. A `UIPanGestureRecognizer` offers a simple solution, but there are many other approaches available. The key to success lies in producing an exclusion path whose bounds match the floating view.

Listing 3-4 applies path translation through transforms. It creates a new safe copy of the original path and then translates it into position at each pan callback.

Large exclusion paths whose height or width exceeds that of the original text view may cause computation errors—specifically missing text under or to the right of the shape or drawing routines that never return. You may also find rendered glyphs overlapping each other in the final layout. I recommend filing bug reports with Apple when you encounter these.

Listing 3-4   **Updating Exclusion Paths with Drags**

```objc
@implementation DragView
{
    CGPoint previousLocation;
}

- (void) touchesBegan:(NSSet *)touches withEvent:(UIEvent *)event
{
    [self.superview bringSubviewToFront:self];
    previousLocation = self.center;
}

- (void) handlePan: (UIPanGestureRecognizer *) recognizer
{
    // Translate view
    CGPoint translation =
        [recognizer translationInView:self.superview];
    CGPoint destination = CGPointMake(
        previousLocation.x + translation.x,
        previousLocation.y + translation.y);
    if (CGRectContainsPoint(self.superview.bounds, destination))
        self.center = destination;

    // Update the exclusion to the new point
    if (_container && _shapePath)
    {
        // Update the path without altering original
        UIBezierPath *p = [UIBezierPath bezierPath];
        [p appendPath:_shapePath];
        [p applyTransform:CGAffineTransformMakeTranslation(
            destination.x - self.bounds.size.width / 2,
            destination.y - self.bounds.size.height / 2)];
        _container.exclusionPaths = @[p];
    }
}

- (void) setContainer:(NSTextContainer *)container
{
    _container = container;

    // Add in the exclusion zone if possible
    if (_container && _shapePath)
    {
        // Update path without altering original
        UIBezierPath *p = [UIBezierPath bezierPath];
        [p appendPath:_shapePath];
```

```objc
        _container.exclusionPaths = @[p];
    }
}

- (instancetype) initWithFrame:(CGRect)frame
{
    if (!(self = [super initWithFrame:frame])) return self;

    // Enable dragging through a gesture recognizer
    UIPanGestureRecognizer *recognizer =
        [[UIPanGestureRecognizer alloc] initWithTarget:self
            action:@selector(handlePan:)];
    [self addGestureRecognizer:recognizer];

    return self;
}

// Build instance with exclusion path
+ (instancetype) instanceWithFrame: (CGRect) frame
    path: (UIBezierPath *) path
{
    DragView *view = [[self alloc] initWithFrame:frame];
    view.shapePath = path;
    CAShapeLayer *maskLayer = [CAShapeLayer layer];
    maskLayer.path = path.CGPath;
    view.layer.mask = maskLayer;
    return view;
}
@end
```

Building PDFs with Text Kit

Text Kit simplifies PDF tasks enormously. Prior to Text Kit, I prepared PDF data using frame setters, the Core Text type that generates text layout frames. I was constantly converting coordinate systems between Quartz layout, where the origin is in the bottom-left corner, and UIKit, with its top-left origin. Keeping track of remaining fragments outside each container (that is, where the text material that was not consumed by each frame) was a nontrivial bookkeeping task. With Text Kit, the work shrinks to just a few easy-to-use lines. Elements like text attachments (images), borders, and other advanced Text Kit layouts are automatically handled for you. On the whole, things just work. That's a fabulous change from where things were before Text Kit debuted.

Nearly all the work involved in container-based layout can be expressed in the three boldfaced lines in Listing 3-5. The first of these lines calculates how many glyphs can fit into a container. This establishes an effective range for the items you want to draw. The second highlighted line performs the drawing, painting glyphs into the current context. The third highlighted line removes already-drawn glyphs from text storage, creating page after page until you've run out of material to add.

The rest of Listing 3-5 is bookkeeping. The remaining calls keep track of the consumed glyphs, excluding the material from each subsequent page. This method draws to a standard letter-sized PDF context, using a drawing rectangle inset an inch (72 points) on each side.

Listing 3-5   **Creating PDF Data from a `UITextView`**

```
+ (NSData *) PDFDataFromTextView: (UITextView *) textView
{
    // Define a standard US letter, one-inch margins
    CGSize pageSize = CGSizeMake(612, 792);
    CGRect drawingRect =
        CGRectInset((CGRect){.size = pageSize}, 72, 72);

    // Establish Text Kit representation
    NSTextStorage *storage = [[NSTextStorage alloc]
        initWithAttributedString:textView.textStorage];
    NSLayoutManager *manager = [[NSLayoutManager alloc] init];
    [storage addLayoutManager:manager];
    NSTextContainer *container = [[NSTextContainer alloc]
        initWithSize:drawingRect.size];
    [manager addTextContainer:container];

    // Build PDF data and start drawing
    NSMutableData *outputData = [NSMutableData data];
    UIGraphicsBeginPDFContextToData(outputData,
        (CGRect){.size = pageSize}, nil);

    // Keep drawing until the glyphs are entirely consumed
    while (storage.length > 0)
    {
        NSRange range;
        UIGraphicsBeginPDFPage();

        // Count the glyphs that fit into the container
        [manager textContainerForGlyphAtIndex:0
            effectiveRange:&range];

        // Draw those glyphs
        [manager drawGlyphsForGlyphRange:range
            atPoint:drawingRect.origin];

        // Remove already-drawn glyphs
        NSInteger endIndex =
```

```
        [manager characterIndexForGlyphAtIndex:range.length];
    NSRange clearRange = NSMakeRange(0, endIndex);
    [storage deleteCharactersInRange:clearRange];
}


// Finish the PDF drawing and return the results
UIGraphicsEndPDFContext();
return outputData;
}
```

Printing Text View Data

Some views offer a special formatter that enables you to transform view contents into printable representations. A viewPrintFormatter property is built into the UIView class, and some classes—including text views, map views, and web views—implement this property to create appropriate output for their content. In an adaptive world, the specifics of presentation geometry are disconnected from print or document preparation. They do not pay attention to whether a device is currently landscape or portrait or whether a view is experiencing other geometric limitations.

With text views, the focus remains on the stored attributed string. The output from the print method in Listing 3-6 ignores any current onscreen presentation details and queries the text view's view print formatter for the information it needs to build its print job.

Listing 3-6 **Printing Text Views**

```
- (void) print
{
    UIPrintInfo *printInfo = [UIPrintInfo printInfo];
    printInfo.outputType = UIPrintInfoOutputGeneral;
    printInfo.jobName = @"My Print Job";


    UIPrintInteractionController *printController =
        [UIPrintInteractionController sharedPrintController];
    printController.printInfo = printInfo;
    printController.showsPageRange = YES;
    printController.printFormatter = textView.viewPrintFormatter;

    [printController presentAnimated:YES completionHandler:
     ^(UIPrintInteractionController *controller,
       BOOL completed, NSError *error)
    {
        if (!completed)
        {
```

```
            NSLog(@"Printing error: %@", error.localizedDescription);
            return;
        }
    }];
}
```

Printing PDF Data

To adapt Listing 3-6 to print PDF data that's not associated with a particular view, you need only replace the print formatter assignment line with one that sets the printing item, as shown here:

```
printController.printingItem = data;
```

Here, you can pass a PDF NSData instance, such as the one produced by Listing 3-5, and it will print out that material without it having to be tied to a view. This is especially convenient for printing application-generated reports, annotated images, and other material that is not normally displayed to the user using the same layout applied to printed versions.

Wrap-up

Here are final points to wrap up what you've read in this chapter:

- There are many things Text Kit is *excellent* at. For example, it is perfect for simple text layout and column support. When Text Kit performs a job well, it's an absolutely invaluable tool. Its strengths lie in glyph/character/geometry coordination.

- There are many things that Text Kit is not very good at yet. Drawing to nonrectangular contexts with complex exclusion zones is not among its strengths. Despite its deployment time in the field, Text Kit still has rough edges. Where necessary, turn to Core Text. Core Text can be reliable for complex text layout tasks.

- Text Kit makes it insanely easy to produce PDF renderings of text view content. Its container-by-container layout features adapt perfectly to PDF page output.

- Don't forget that when working with columns and adaptive layouts, it's vital to limit text view scrolling. If you do not, your text will simply flow down the first of your text views and never continue to the next.

4

Attributed Strings and Document Containers

Attributed strings form the basis of some of the most portable and adaptive iOS elements. Over the past few years, this class has grown enormously in power and potential. New document support includes ways to encapsulate and transfer data. Attributed strings have grown to provide support for HTML and RTF rich text documents, providing seamless polymorphism between text presentation and representation. Text design now better migrates to the iOS screen and from iOS to other destinations. Image integration has become simple and effective. With Text Kit, attributed strings can now do a lot more than you might expect. This chapter explores some of those expanded possibilities.

Class Enhancements

Starting in iOS 6, Apple began introducing major revisions to its suite of UIKit text classes. Updates have enabled developers to use attributed strings in text views, in text fields, and in a variety of controls. These enhancements have extended control over fonts, coloring, and layouts to produce sophisticated and nuanced text output in common system-supplied classes, as shown in the text view in Figure 4-1.

NSParagraphStyle also debuted. It introduced ways to align and indent text in specific text regions, as well as control for paragraph-to-paragraph spacing, leading, and more. Later iOS updates added more features, like the tab stops that launched in iOS 7. These enabled developers to create tabular text, like that shown in Figure 4-2.

Figure 4-1   Attributed strings offer fine control over text formatting. This standard `UITextView` displays multiple fonts in a presentation of a single attributed string.

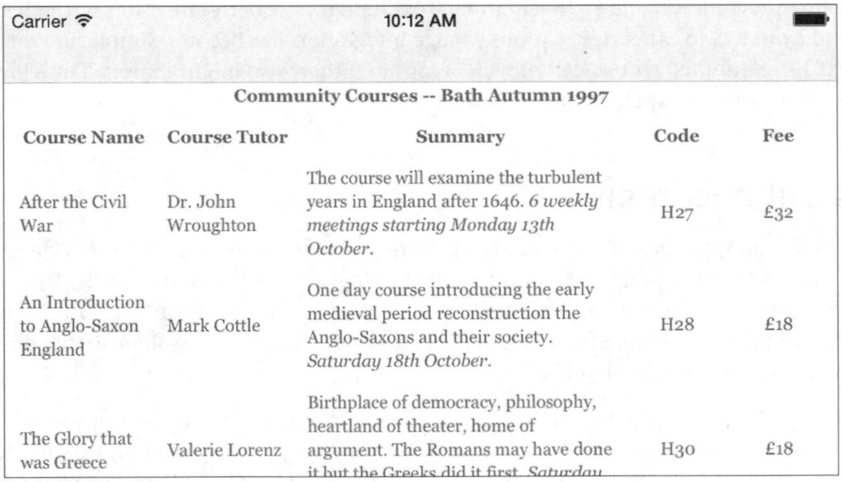

Figure 4-2   The attributed string in this text view uses tab stops to produce column-based output.

By iOS 7, Apple had also bumped up attributed strings to support document containers, offering HTML, RTF, and RTFD integration. The text view in Figure 4-3 shows content read in from an RTFD file container, complete with attached images. With these newer document types, it became ever simpler to build complex content with fine color, sizing, and alignment control.

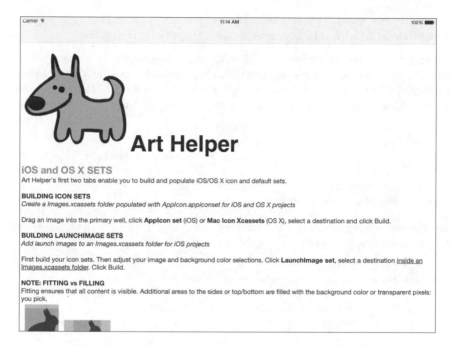

Figure 4-3   RTFD documents support embedded image attachments.

Instead of sourcing content from within an app, iOS has now opened itself up to importing material created using desktop editing suites. The text you present can now be as sophisticated and complex as you need it to be, without relying on web views.

String Attachments

Attachment attributes enable you to integrate images into your text storage. Attachments are markers that indicate which parts of a string are associated with an `NSTextAttachment` object. In the most manual approach, you create an attachment instance and apply it to the attributed string by using an `NSAttachmentAttributeName` attribute. It takes work to ensure that you've added a special attachment character and associated it with the proper attachment object. Fortunately, there's a much easier approach that leverages a built-in class method.

You build an attachment object by allocating a new `NSTextAttachment` instance. Many text attachments are images. For these, you build a new instance and assign a value to the built-in `image` property, as in the following snippet:

```
NSTextAttachment *attachment = [[NSTextAttachment alloc] init];
attachment.image = image;
attachment.bounds = (CGRect){.size = image.size};
```

The bounds property specifies the size associated with the attachment. Offset the origin of bounds to create an attachment that moves above or below the text baseline.

A special attachment character (NSAttachmentCharacter) denotes an attachment point. Although you can build your own string from this character and apply the attachment programmatically, you're better off using the built-in attributedStringWithAttachment: class method. This method returns a simple attachment string to insert into your text storage:

```
NSAttributedString *replacement = [NSAttributedString
    attributedStringWithAttachment:attachment];
// The range used here is a zero-length range where you want the
// attachment to be inserted
[textView.textStorage replaceCharactersInRange:range
    withAttributedString:replacement];
```

Without this convenience method, you populate a string with the special character, insert it into the attributed storage, and then apply the attachment attribute:

```
unichar c = NSAttachmentCharacter;
NSString *replacement = [NSString stringWithCharacters: &c length: 1];
[textView.textStorage replaceCharactersInRange:range withString:replacement];
[textView.textStorage addAttribute:NSAttachmentAttributeName
    value:attachment range:range];
```

Building Attributed Strings from HTML

With HTML import, attributed string creation is easier than ever. iOS can now automatically transform basic markup into view-ready attributes. Consider the following HTML string:

```
NSString *sourceString = @"<H1><font color=\"777777\">\
    This is a <i>Heading</i></font></H1>\
    <p>This is <b>body</b> text</p>";
```

This simple example consists of a header and body text, with a few integrated style tags. It takes very little work to convert HTML content into an NSAttributedString instance that is ready for display in a UITextView. This source produces the display shown in Figure 4-4, complete with the requested styles and colors.

The NSAttributedString class offers this easy transformation. With just a few simple calls, you can convert HTML and RTF text sources to their attributed string equivalents. To make this happen, call built-in initializing methods for the NSAttributedString class. These methods require a document type to enable the class to properly interpret whatever string or data has been passed to the initializer.

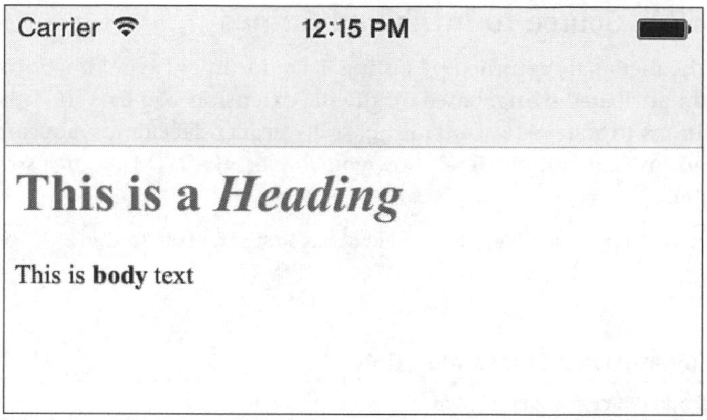

This is a *Heading*

This is **body** text

Figure 4-4   Simple markup produces text view–ready attributed strings.

Document Type Dictionaries

Listing 4-1 begins the process of transforming rich sources to attributed strings by establishing a document type dictionary. You need this dictionary to pass to NSAttributedString's various documentAttributes: parameters when converting data to and from these formats. The dictionary associates the NSDocumentTypeDocumentAttribute with a specific type, selected by looking up common file extensions. For HTML, pass either htm or html as a parameter. With just one key and one value, the dictionary built by Listing 4-1 is barebones. As you'll discover later in this chapter, you can add a lot more customization to a document dictionary. For now, however, this single key/value pair is enough to get you started with markup conversion.

Listing 4-1   **Creating a Document Type Dictionary**

```
NSDictionary *DocumentTypeDictionary(NSString *ext)
{
    NSDictionary *documentTypeDictionary =
    @{@"rtfd":NSRTFDTextDocumentType,
      @"rtf" :NSRTFTextDocumentType,
      @"html":NSHTMLTextDocumentType,
      @"htm" :NSHTMLTextDocumentType,
      @"txt" :NSPlainTextDocumentType};

    NSString *docType =
        documentTypeDictionary[ext.lowercaseString];
    return @{NSDocumentTypeDocumentAttribute :
            docType ? : NSPlainTextDocumentType};
}
```

Converting HTML Source to Attributed Strings

Listing 4-2 uses the dictionary returned by Listing 4-1's document type function to convert a source string to an attributed string, based on the file extension you pass in. This feature is part of the UIKit additions to NSAttributedString, so its header declaration appears in the UIKit framework and not in Foundation. Here's how you convert the HTML source string you just saw into an attributed version:

```
NSAttributedString *attributedVersion = AttributedStringWithString(
    sourceString, @"html");
```

Listing 4-2 **Using Attributed Strings with HTML**

```
// Create Attributed String from Data
NSAttributedString *AttributedStringWithData(
    NSData *data, NSString *ext)
{
    if (!data) return nil;
    if (!ext) return nil;

    NSDictionary *returnDict;
    NSError *error;
    NSDictionary *typeDictionary = DocumentTypeDictionary(ext);
    NSAttributedString *result = [[NSAttributedString alloc]
        initWithData: data
        options:typeDictionary
        documentAttributes:&returnDict
        error:&error];
    if (!result)
    {
        NSLog(@"Error initializing string with data (%@): %@",
            ext, error.localizedDescription);
    }

    return result;
}

// Create Attributed String from Stylized Source String
NSAttributedString *AttributedStringWithString(
    NSString *sourceString, NSString *ext)
{
    if (!sourceString) return nil;
    if (!ext) return nil;

    NSData *data = [sourceString
        dataUsingEncoding:NSUTF8StringEncoding];
```

```
        if (!data) return nil;
        return AttributedStringWithData(
            data, ext, nil);
}
```

Converting Attributed Strings to Document Representations

Listing 4-3 shows a parallel AttributedStringStringRepresentation() function that performs a reverse operation compared to the one in Listing 4-2. Starting with an existing attributed string, it produces string data. If you pass either html or htm, the string output is returned in HTML format. If you pass rtf, you create RTF results.

Listing 4-3 **Converting an Attributed String to a Document Representation**

```
NSData *AttributedStringDataRepresentation(
    NSAttributedString *string, NSString *ext)
{
    if (!string) return nil;
    if (!ext) return nil;

    NSError *error;
    NSDictionary *typeDictionary = DocumentTypeDictionary(ext);
    NSData *data =
        [string dataFromRange:NSMakeRange(0, string.length)
            documentAttributes:typeDictionary error:&error];
    if (!data)
    {
        NSLog(@"Error reading data from string (%@): %@",
            ext, error.localizedDescription);
        return nil;
    }
    return data;
}

// Passing nil to ext returns plain text
NSString *AttributedStringStringRepresentation(
    NSAttributedString *string, NSString *ext)
{
    if (!string) return nil;

    NSData *data =
        AttributedStringDataRepresentation(string, ext);
    NSString *result = [[NSString alloc]
        initWithData:data encoding:NSUTF8StringEncoding];
```

```
    if (result) return result;
    return string.string;
}
```

Generating HTML from Attributed Strings

As you've read, you can create attributed strings programmatically or import them from a document format like HTML or RTF. Once built, attributed strings are agnostic. They neither care what format they were initially created from nor force you to represent them using a particular standard. I've had quite a lot of fun exploring how far flat HTML data can represent more advanced elements such as those loaded from RTFD containers. (The answer is some, but it loses embedded images, although links still work.)

For example, here are the results produced when the attributed string displayed in Figure 4-4 is converted back to HTML. As you see in this dump, the output includes CSS styling and produces a more standards-compliant document than the minimal markup initially passed in:

```
<!DOCTYPE html PUBLIC "-//W3C//DTD HTML 4.01//EN" "http://www.w3.org/TR/html4/
strict.dtd">
<html>
<head>
<meta http-equiv="Content-Type" content="text/html; charset=UTF-8">
<meta http-equiv="Content-Style-Type" content="text/css">
<title></title>
<meta name="Generator" content="Cocoa HTML Writer">
<style type="text/css">
p.p2 {margin: 0.0px 12.0px 0.0px; font: 12.0px 'Times New Roman';
color: #000000; -webkit-text-stroke: #000000}
span.s1 {font-family: 'TimesNewRomanPS-BoldMT'; font-weight: bold;
font-style: normal; font-size: 24.00pt; font-kerning: none}
span.s2 {font-family: 'TimesNewRomanPS-BoldItalicMT';
font-weight: bold; font-style: italic; font-size: 24.00pt; font-kerning: none}
span.s3 {font-family: 'Times New Roman'; font-weight: normal;
font-style: normal; font-size: 12.00pt; font-kerning: none}
span.s4 {font-family: 'TimesNewRomanPS-BoldMT'; font-weight: bold;
font-style: normal; font-size: 12.00pt; font-kerning: none}
</style>
</head>
<body>
<h1 style="margin: 0.0px 16.1px 0.0px; font: 24.0px 'Times New Roman';
color: #777777; -webkit-text-stroke: #777777">
<span class="s1">This is a </span><span class="s2">Heading</span></h1>
<p class="p2"><span class="s3">This is </span><span class="s4">body</span>
<span class="s3"> text</span></p>
</body>
</html>
```

Markup Initialization

Apple documentation emphasizes that HTML initialization is meant only for lightweight use. When you need full HTML expression, you are better served by using web views instead of text views. What HTML offers in this case is a convenient way to build and store attributed text elements using a familiar markup system.

This approach is particularly suitable for anyone performing markup conversion. For example, say you have Markdown sources you wish to use in your application. Markdown (http://en.wikipedia.org/wiki/Markdown) is a simple formatting syntax for plain text that converts to HTML. The advantage of starting from a popular system like Markdown is its easy specification and inspection.

You might read in your .md sources and convert them to standard markup by using one of the many open source third-party libraries currently available. Once converted, iOS provides the final step from HTML to attributed strings, producing the content you need to populate your views.

RTF and RTFD

The attributed string conversion utilities you use with HTML also work for RTF and RTFD documents. RTF, aka Rich Text Format, is a proprietary format created by Microsoft in the 1980s. RTFD is a near cousin, and it offers in-text attachments to support images. Both RTF and RTFD are used extensively on OS X. In fact, their usage dates back to NeXTSTEP, the OS that preceded OS X.

You work with RTF as you work with HTML. The functions in Listings 4-2 and 4-3 support RTF as well as HTML. You pass `rtf` instead of `html`, but otherwise the calls are identical. Unlike HTML, however, RTF isn't exactly markup friendly. Here's the "This is a Heading" content from the previous example. As you can see, it offers neither readability nor easy tweaking in the fashion of HTML source:

```
\f0\b\fs48 \cf2 \expnd0\expndtw0\kerning0
\outl0\strokewidth0 \strokec2 This is a
\f1\i \cf2 \expnd0\expndtw0\kerning0
\outl0\strokewidth0 \strokec2 Heading
\f0\i0 \cf3 \expnd0\expndtw0\kerning0
\outl0\strokewidth0 \strokec3 \
\pard\pardeftab720\sa240\partightenfactor0
```

More typically, you work with files. You read in these files as strings or data and convert that material to the attributed string format. Alternatively, you allow users to create and edit material in a text view and then store the results out as RTF documents. In both cases, you omit details of the underlying RTF format—from both user and developer.

The RTFD Container

RTFD is the exception among iOS-supported text document types. The directory variant RTFD is not a flat file format. It uses a folder to store document attachments, typically images, as well as its text. For RTFD, you need a slightly different loading and extraction strategy than is used in Listings 4-2 and 4-3.

RTFD documents are containers. You examine them in OS X by selecting an RTFD item in the Finder. Control-click (or right-click) and choose Show Package Contents. Figure 4-5 shows the items stored in the RTFD file I used to create Figure 4-3. Here you find the source text (an RTF file) along with any files attached to the document. This example uses a number of images.

Figure 4-5   An RTFD bundle's package contents contains text and attachment files.

Initializing Attributed Strings from a File

Fortunately, there's a single unified approach for initializing any attributed string from a file. This approach works for every format that NSAttributedString natively supports, including RTFD containers, not just HTML and RTF. Listing 4-4 establishes an attributed string from any conforming file. The path's file extension sets the document type used to load the data.

The optional documentDictionary parameter returns information about the document you created. If you want to retrieve that information, establish a local variable and pass it by reference, as you would with NSError instances. Here are the dictionary results for the help.rtfd document shown in Figures 4-3 and 4-5:

```
2014-12-15 20:28:14.614 Hello World[29989:60b] {
    BottomMargin = 72;
    CocoaRTFVersion = "1265.18994140625";
    DefaultTabInterval = 0;
    DocumentType = NSRTFD;
    HyphenationFactor = 0;
    LeftMargin = 72;
    PaperMargin = "UIEdgeInsets: {72, 72, 72, 72}";
    PaperSize = "NSSize: {612, 792}";
```

```
    RightMargin = 72;
    TopMargin = 72;
    UTI = "com.apple.rtfd";
    ViewSize = "NSSize: {861, 635}";
}
```

Listing 4-4 **Reading Attributed Strings from Files and File Containers**

```
NSAttributedString *AttributedStringWithPath(
    NSString *path, NSDictionary **documentDictionary)
{
    if (!path) return nil;

    // Establish type dictionary
    NSDictionary *typeDictionary =
        DocumentTypeDictionary(path.pathExtension);

    // Initialize from file
    NSError *error;
    NSDictionary *returnDict;
    NSAttributedString *result =
        [[NSAttributedString alloc]
            initWithFileURL:[NSURL fileURLWithPath:path]
            options:typeDictionary
            documentAttributes:&returnDict error:&error];

    if (result && documentDictionary)
        *documentDictionary = returnDict;

    if (!result)
    {
        NSLog(@"Error reading from %@ into string: %@",
            path.lastPathComponent, error.localizedDescription);
        return nil;
    }

    return result;
}
```

Converting RTFD Text to Data

You cannot convert an RTFD-attributed string to a text-based representation without losing a great deal of formatting and attachment information. These elements don't come along for the ride as they are normally stored in separate files in a folder bundle. Instead, you convert them to data, a format that enables you to include both text and images. This is a form suitable for storing exact representations to the system pasteboard or writing to a flat file for future reference. Working with a data representation ensures that your material can be re-created in its entirety.

Listing 4-5 converts attributed strings to data representations. As with previous listings, this one creates data using the format you specify. Although you can use this listing's function to produce data for non-RTFD formats, its practical utility is almost exclusively limited to RTFD documents. Since the RTFD format interleaves text and resources from multiple files, the data representation provides a single element for saving and reading this material.

Keep size in mind. Data representations for plain text are quite small. RTFD output with embedded images can grow large. One further note: Creating HTML data from an RTFD source does not preserve images. If you want to use well-structured image and text material together in an attributed string, RTFD remains the go-to technology to use for the time being.

Here's an example of how you might start with an attributed string and then create an RTFD data representation of that instance. Any image attachments in that string *will* pass to the RTFD data representation:

```
NSData *data = AttributedStringDataRepresentation(string, @"rtfd");
```

Listing 4-5   Converting Attributed Strings to Data Representations

```
NSData *AttributedStringDataRepresentation(
    NSAttributedString *string, NSString *ext)
{
    if (!string) return nil;
    if (!ext) return nil;

    NSError *error;
    NSDictionary *typeDictionary = DocumentTypeDictionary(ext);
    NSData *data = [string
        dataFromRange:NSMakeRange(0, string.length)
        documentAttributes:typeDictionary error:&error];
    if (!data)
    {
        NSLog(@"Error reading data from string (%@): %@",
            ext, error.localizedDescription);
        return nil;
    }
    return data;
}
```

Writing RTFD Containers from Data

To move in the other direction—that is, to produce a folder of component RTFD files—build a file wrapper and initialize it with the serialized data representation. Point a file URL to the position where you want to create the folder and allow the wrapper to build the component files:

```
// Convert attributed string to RTFD data
NSData *data = AttributedStringDataRepresentation(string, @"rtfd");

// Create wrapper and initialize with serialized data
NSFileWrapper *wrapper = [[NSFileWrapper alloc]
    initWithSerializedRepresentation:data];

// Establish destination URL
NSString *path = [destinationPath stringByAppendingPathComponent:@"doc.rtfd"];
NSURL *fileURL = [NSURL fileURLWithPath:path];

// Write to wrapper
NSError *error;
if (![wrapper writeToURL:fileURL options:NSFileWrapperWritingWithNameUpdating
    originalContentsURL:nil error:&error])
    NSLog(@"Error writing to file wrapper: %@", error.localizedDescription);
```

Inspecting Attributes

At times, you might want to examine stored attributes, whether when working with strings you've created or when working with strings built by the attributed string import system. Listing 4-6 offers a simple reporting utility that iterates through a string's attributes, listing types and values range-by-range.

This is a handy utility to have on hand during debugging. However, its utility for deployed applications is limited.

Listing 4-6 **Enumerating Attributes**

```
void DumpStringAttributes(NSAttributedString *input)
{
    NSMutableString *string = [NSMutableString string];
    [string appendString:@"\n Loc Len  Text/Attributes\n"];
    [string appendString:  @" --- ---  --------------\n"];

    [input enumerateAttributesInRange:
        NSMakeRange(0, input.length)
        options:0 usingBlock:^(NSDictionary *attrs,
            NSRange range, BOOL *stop) {
        NSString *substring =
            [input.string substringWithRange:range];
        [string appendFormat:@"%4ld%4ld  \"%@\"\n",
            (long) range.location, (long) range.length, substring];
```

```
        int i = 1;
        for (NSString *key in attrs.allKeys)
            [string appendFormat:@"          %2d. %@: %@\n",
                i++, key, [(NSObject *)attrs[key] description]];
    }];

    printf("%s\n",  string.UTF8String);
}
```

This function uses the `enumerateAttributesInRange:options:usingBlock:` method to examine each typesetting run. The first line in Figure 4-4 was built around the words "This is a Heading." The HTML used to specify that output adds headline, color, and italic styling to it. What follows are the resulting attributes:

```
Loc Len  Text/Attributes
--- ---  ---------------
  0  10  "This is a "
            1. NSParagraphStyle: Alignment 4, LineSpacing 0, ParagraphSpacing
16.08, ParagraphSpacingBefore 0, HeadIndent 0, TailIndent 0, FirstLineHeadIndent
0, LineHeight 0/0, LineHeightMultiple 0, LineBreakMode 0, Tabs (
), DefaultTabInterval 36, Blocks (null), Lists (null), BaseWritingDirection 0,
HyphenationFactor 0, TighteningFactor 0, HeaderLevel 1
            2. NSStrokeWidth: 0
            3. NSFont: <UICTFont: 0x8f73470> font-family: "TimesNewRomanPS-BoldMT";
font-weight: bold; font-style: normal; font-size: 24.00pt
            4. NSColor: UIDeviceRGBColorSpace 0.466667 0.466667 0.466667 1
            5. NSStrokeColor: UIDeviceRGBColorSpace 0.466667 0.466667 0.466667 1
            6. NSKern: 0
 10   7  "Heading"
            1. NSParagraphStyle: Alignment 4, LineSpacing 0, ParagraphSpacing
16.08, ParagraphSpacingBefore 0, HeadIndent 0, TailIndent 0, FirstLineHeadIndent
0, LineHeight 0/0, LineHeightMultiple 0, LineBreakMode 0, Tabs (
), DefaultTabInterval 36, Blocks (null), Lists (null), BaseWritingDirection 0,
HyphenationFactor 0, TighteningFactor 0, HeaderLevel 1
            2. NSStrokeWidth: 0
            3. NSFont: <UICTFont: 0x8f67d90> font-family: "TimesNewRomanPS-
BoldItalicMT"; font-weight: bold; font-style: italic; font-size: 24.00pt
            4. NSColor: UIDeviceRGBColorSpace 0.466667 0.466667 0.466667 1
            5. NSStrokeColor: UIDeviceRGBColorSpace 0.466667 0.466667 0.466667 1
            6. NSKern: 0
```

In addition to styles added explicitly, implicit items such as paragraph spacing, stroke width, and kerning appear in this output. They showcase some of the extent of the automated conversion process, which goes well beyond simple style-to-attribute mapping.

Establishing Document Attributes

To this point, this chapter has mostly focused on importing attributes into a form where they can be presented in UIKit views. The reverse process is also important. Your application may have users creating and editing text in views, which you then want to build into a standard document container suitable for saving and sharing, whether on iOS or to other computers.

Document attribute dictionaries express features that go beyond the simple types shown in Listing 4-1. The following code defines a more complex document attribute dictionary. Its entries discuss margins, background color, page size, display size, and more. These attributes are defined as part of the NSStringDrawing extensions for attributed strings and can be found in the NSAttributedString.h header file.

```
NSDictionary *attributes =
    @{
        // Store as RTF
        NSDocumentTypeDocumentAttribute : NSRTFTextDocumentType,

        // Page background color is light gray
        NSBackgroundColorDocumentAttribute :
            [UIColor lightGrayColor],

        // Add 1.5-inch margin to top, 0.75-inch to sides
        // and 1-inch margin on the bottom
        NSPaperMarginDocumentAttribute :
            [NSValue valueWithUIEdgeInsets:
                UIEdgeInsetsMake(1.5 * 72, 0.75 * 72,
                    1.0 * 72, 0.75 * 72)],

        // Pages use a US legal size
        NSPaperSizeDocumentAttribute :
            [NSValue valueWithCGSize:CGSizeMake(612, 1008)],

        // Use a page display sized to a US "half-letter"
        NSViewSizeDocumentAttribute :
            [NSValue valueWithCGSize:CGSizeMake(612, 396)],

        // View the document with page-by-page layout mode
        NSViewModeDocumentAttribute : @(YES),

        // Set the document as read-only
        NSReadOnlyDocumentAttribute : @(YES),
    };
```

You apply document dictionaries when converting an attributed string to document data, as you see in the following snippet:

```
NSData *data = [attributedString
    dataFromRange:NSMakeRange(0, attributedString.length)
    documentAttributes:attributes error:&error];
```

When saved to a file, the data you create in this fashion produces a fully attributed RTF document.

The RTF file shown in Figure 4-6 was created in iOS using this document attribute dictionary. It's been copied to OS X and opened in TextEdit. TextEdit supports the full range of document attributes defined here, so you see the page-by-page layout, the gray background, and the long top margin.

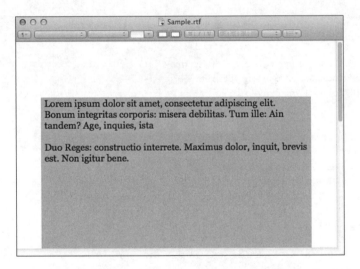

Figure 4-6   Document attributes define how a file will appear when opened using a standards-compliant reader such as TextEdit in OS X.

At this time, iOS does not provide the same standards-compliant support as OS X. So what you see in Figure 4-7 when presenting the RTF data lacks some of the features specified by that document dictionary, such as the gray background and the indentations. The settings are preserved in the attributed string that underlies the text view.

> Carrier 📶   10:11 AM   ▬
>
> Lorem ipsum dolor sit amet, consectetur adipiscing elit. Bonum
> integritas corporis: misera debilitas. Tum ille: Ain tandem? Age,
> inquies, ista
>
> Duo Reges: constructio interrete. Maximus dolor, inquit, brevis est.
> Non igitur bene.

Figure 4-7   iOS's text view does not respect RTF document attributes during presentation the way that OS X does. However, these attributes are maintained internally and will persist in any document files you create.

Enhancing Attributed Strings

With the latest iOS releases focusing ever more on attributed strings, I've found it helpful to create categories to fill gaps that Apple has left open. For example, consider the following two lines of code:

```
NSString *s = [NSString string]; // this works
NSAttributedString *as =
    [NSAttributedString string]; // this won't
```

Although Apple has long since provided a class convenience method for NSString, it fails to provide a parallel version for NSAttributedString.

Listing 4-7 establishes a class category to covers these basics. It enables you to build new attributed string instances with class convenience methods. Each method mirrors the instance method initializer.

Listing 4-7   Extending **NSAttributedString** Instance Creation

```
@implementation NSAttributedString(AttributedStringUtility)
+ (instancetype) stringWithString: (NSString *) string
{
    return [[self alloc] initWithString:string];
}
```

```
+ (instancetype) string
{
    return [self stringWithString:@""];
}


+ (instancetype) stringWithAttributedString:
    (NSAttributedString *) string
{
    return [[self alloc] initWithAttributedString:string];
}
+ (instancetype) stringWithString:(NSString *)string
    attributes: (NSDictionary *) attributes
{
    return [[self alloc] initWithString:string
        attributes:attributes];
}
@end
```

Returning Copies with New Attributes

I can't tell you the number of times I've just wanted to tweak attributed strings without having to create mutable versions from my calling method. The method in Listing 4-8 returns a new copy of the caller by applying an attribute to the entire string. This approach is especially handy, and I use it far more often than I ever anticipated I would.

Listing 4-8   **Adding Attributes**

```
- (NSAttributedString *) stringByAddingAttribute:
        (NSString *) attributeName
    value: (id) value
{
    NSMutableAttributedString *mutable = self.mutableCopy;
    [mutable addAttribute:attributeName value:value
        range:NSMakeRange(0, self.length)];
    return mutable.copy;
}
```

From this starting point, you can easily add any number of attribute customization routines based on Listing 4-8. For example, you might want to return copies of a string by applying a specific font or color, as in the following methods:

```
- (NSAttributedString *) stringWithFont:(UIFont *)font
{
    return [self stringByAddingAttribute:
        NSFontAttributeName value:font];
}
```

```
- (NSAttributedString *) stringWithColor:(UIColor *) color
{
    return [self stringByAddingAttribute:
        NSForegroundColorAttributeName value:color];
}
```

Adjusting Attributes

While Listing 4-8 applies a single attribute across an entire string, some common adjustments require more precise work. The method in Listing 4-9 adjusts font sizes across a string, presumably in response to a user's request to shrink or grow the presentation. This requires an attribute-by-attribute walk across the string, enabling each embedded font to grow or shrink by the requested offset. Figure 4-8 demonstrates the results of growing the fonts in a document-based attributed string.

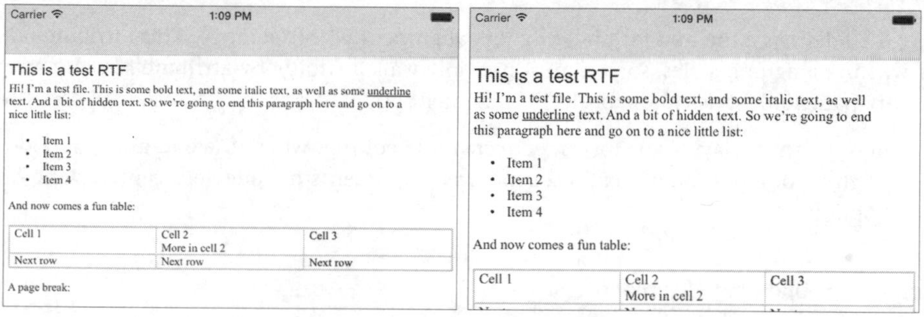

Figure 4-8   After applying Listing 4-9, each font in the text view's attributed string has grown by 25% in point size.

Listing 4-9   **Tweaking Font Sizes**

```
- (NSAttributedString *) stringByAdjustingFontSizesByPercent:
    (CGFloat) percent
{
    NSMutableAttributedString *mutable = self.mutableCopy;
    UIFont *defaultFont = [UIFont systemFontOfSize:12];
    [self enumerateAttributesInRange:NSMakeRange(0, self.length)
        options:0
        usingBlock:^(NSDictionary *attrs, NSRange range, BOOL *stop)
    {
        // Calculate the adjusted font
        UIFont *oldFont = attrs[NSFontAttributeName] ? : defaultFont;
```

```
        UIFont *newFont = [UIFont fontWithName:oldFont.fontName
            size:fabs(oldFont.pointSize * (1.0 + percent))];


        // Apply the update
        [mutable addAttribute:NSFontAttributeName
            value:newFont range:range];
    }];
    return mutable.copy;
}
```

Extending Mutable Attributed Strings

The previous examples focus on creating new versions of existing attributed strings. As Listing 4-10 demonstrates, this approach takes a slightly different form when used with mutable versions. Instead of building new instances, you focus on changing attributes in place.

Listing 4-10 defines a method for updating text alignment within a range. This attribute takes place within paragraph styles, so you must not only walk attribute-by-attribute but also create or modify paragraph styles to establish the alignment you desire.

This kind of method plays a role for user-directed text editing, where the end user can choose how to align all or a portion of text. iOS-supported alignments include, left, center, right, and justified options.

Listing 4-10   **Updating Alignment**

```
- (void) setAlignment: (NSTextAlignment) alignment
    range: (NSRange) requestedRange
{
    [self enumerateAttributesInRange:requestedRange options:0
        usingBlock:^(NSDictionary *attrs, NSRange range, BOOL *stop)
    {
        NSMutableParagraphStyle *style;
        if (attrs[NSParagraphStyleAttributeName])
            style = [attrs[NSParagraphStyleAttributeName] mutableCopy];
        else
            style = [[NSMutableParagraphStyle alloc] init];
        style.alignment = alignment;
        [self addAttribute:NSParagraphStyleAttributeName
            value:style range:range];
    }];
}
```

Text Ranges

When using attributed strings in text views, you encounter two similarly named elements that represent two quite different things. Don't confuse a `UITextView`'s `selectedRange` property, which returns an `NSRange` struct, with `selectedTextRange`, which does not.

These latter user selections are reported as `UITextRange` items. These objects represent a range of characters in a text container. They are distinct from `NSRange`, which is a simple data type.

Text ranges, and their near cousins text positions, are objects not structures, and they are built on the WebKit framework. The `UITextInput` protocol standardizes text input interaction by using text ranges. It uses text position and text range classes to discuss selections and insertion points for material that can be laid out using multiple directions. These semantic elements are designed to represent text layout at a more abstract level than the simple *location-length* tuples used for low-level string manipulation.

Calculating Positions

Every text input–supporting class that includes text views offers access to `beginningOf-Document` and `endOfDocument` properties, in addition to `selectedTextRange`. These document properties each return text position instances. They enable you to calculate the number of positions between the two or between each of them and another text position. This count may or may not correspond to the number of characters of your attributed string's length, as there is not always an exact correspondence between the two, just as there aren't always correspondences between typesetting glyphs and the characters they represent. Attachments and other underlying semantic features may throw off your count. Here's how you calculate all the logical positions in text storage:

```
[self offsetFromPosition:self.beginningOfDocument
    toPosition:self.endOfDocument];
```

When you want to find a character offset rather than a position one, there's a separate `characterOffsetOfPosition:withinRange:` method. Be careful. This method may or may not be implemented by the text input–supporting class. When available, this method accounts for any discrepancies between characters and text positions and offers an index that enables you to look up attributes and content within your associated text storage. Always check to see whether a class has implemented this before calling. If it is not, assume a one-to-one correlation between positions and characters.

Position Geometry

Often you want to recover geometric information about a text position in your view to better interact with touches or hardware key input. Listing 4-11 returns a `CGRect` representing the bounding rectangle at a text position.

Listing 4-11 **Position Bounds**

```
- (NSUInteger) indexAtPosition: (UITextPosition *) position
{
    return [self offsetFromPosition:self.beginningOfDocument
        toPosition:position];
}


- (CGRect) rectAtPosition: (UITextPosition *) position
{
    NSTextContainer *container =
        self.layoutManager.textContainers.firstObject;
    NSInteger index = [self indexAtPosition:position];
    NSInteger glyphIndex = [self.layoutManager
        glyphIndexForCharacterAtIndex:index];
    CGRect rect = [self.layoutManager
        boundingRectForGlyphRange:NSMakeRange(glyphIndex, 1)
        inTextContainer:container];
    return rect;
}
```

To find a position from a point, use the corresponding closestPositionToPoint: method. The following snippet tries to find a character that as closely as possible lies directly above the current selection point. It then moves the selection to that point:

```
// Fetch the rect at the current selection point
CGRect glyphRect =
    [self rectAtPosition:self.selectedTextRange.start];

// Move upwards
CGFloat targetY = MAX(CGRectGetMidY(glyphRect) -
    glyphRect.size.height, 0);
CGPoint targetPoint = CGPointMake(mostRecentXPosition, targetY);

// Find the closest text position to the geometric target
UITextPosition *position = [self closestPositionToPoint:targetPoint];

// Convert the position to a range and select it
UITextRange *range = [self textRangeFromPosition:position
    toPosition:position];
self.selectedTextRange = range;
```

This system uses one more trick, which you indirectly see here. It tracks the most recent deliberate X position (mostRecentXPosition). This enables the cursor to return to an approximate horizontal location even when some lines are blank. Unless you track this value, cursors forced to the left by blank lines (in left-to-right systems like English) may get stuck there.

Updating Selection Points

Using text positions and ranges can be a little frustrating due to the inherent indirection of the underlying classes and the lack of native API expression. Listing 4-12 defines a method to set a selection (a caret in this case, as the start and end of the selection are the same point) at a position offset that you supply.

The helper methods in Listings 4-11 and 4-12 mirror each other. They convert a position to an index and an index to a position, enabling you to enter and withdraw from the text position world on demand.

Listing 4-12   **Setting a Selection Point**

```
- (UITextPosition *) positionAtIndex: (NSUInteger) index
{
    return [self positionFromPosition:self.beginningOfDocument
        offset:index];
}


- (void) setSelectionAtPositionIndex: (NSUInteger) index
{
    UITextPosition *position = [self positionAtIndex:index];
    UITextRange *range =
        [self textRangeFromPosition:position toPosition:position];
    self.selectedTextRange = range;
}
```

Hardware Key Support

Enabling your apps to adapt to hardware key commands provides your users with more consistent experiences across device platforms. First introduced in iOS 7, the UIKeyCommand class enables hardware key combinations and their recognition. With it, your apps recognize keyboard chords that include Control, Option, and Command modifier support.

UIResponder instances can now declare which key combinations they support. When a user enters a chord, iOS walks through the responder chain to find an object that responds to it. Combinations corresponding to system events automatically pass to the appropriate system handler, such as Command-C for copy and Command-X for cut.

You declare key support by implementing a keyCommands method on the view. This method returns an array of commands that a view responds to. Listing 4-13 builds KeySupportTextField, a text field subclass that enables you to iteratively add key commands. When a supported key command is detected, it posts a notification.

This approach creates a reusable system that isn't tied to any specific set of key semantics. With it, you simply instantiate a new text field and then listen for specific key combinations, which are stored to a mutable set. Using a set rather than an array ensures that duplicate key command requests are ignored.

Each time you call `listenForKey:modifiers:`, the custom text field adds a new key command to listen to. You specify an input key and a mask of modifiers, which may include the Shift key, Control key, Alt key, and Command key. Two additional modifiers specify whether the Caps Lock key is engaged (`UIKeyModifierAlphaShift`) and whether the key is located on a numeric keypad (`UIKeyModifierNumericPad`). Here are a few examples of what this might look like:

```
// Listen for Command-Shift-N
[textField listenForKey:@"n"
    modifiers:UIKeyModifierCommand|UIKeyModifierShift];
// Listen for the t key
[textField listenForKey:@"t" modifiers:0];
// Listen for Shift-T
[textField listenForKey:@"t" modifiers:UIKeyModifierShift];
// Listen for Alt-H
[textField listenForKey:@"h" modifiers:UIKeyModifierAlternate];
```

When you listen specifically for the *t* key, as in the preceding example, any occurrence of the letter will be passed to your handler. It will not be entered as a normal keystroke. If you type *Henrietta*, the letters that appear in your text field will be *Hennriea*. This is a problem if your goal is to solicit text entry. If you're writing a game and your first responder wants to listen to vi-like commands such as h, j, k, and l, you don't have to force your users to use modifiers. `UIResponder` supports unmodified keys, as in this example.

Listing 4-13 uses the notification center to broadcast commands. You can easily update it to use any mechanism you like to connect this class with a command consumer. For example, you might implement a delegate (`keySupportTextField:recognizedKeyCommand:`, for example), a target-action, blocks (`keyCommandHandlerBlock`, for example), and so forth.

Listing 4-13   Text Field with Key Support

```
NSString *const KeySupportFieldEvent = @"KeySupportFieldEvent";

@interface KeySupportTextField : UITextField
- (void) resetKeyCommands;
- (void) listenForKey: (NSString *) key modifiers: (UIKeyModifierFlags) flags;
@end

@implementation KeySupportTextField
{
    NSMutableSet *keyCommands;
}
```

```objc
- (instancetype) initWithFrame:(CGRect)frame
{
    if (!(self = [super initWithFrame:frame])) return self;
    keyCommands = [NSMutableSet set];
    self.borderStyle = UITextBorderStyleRoundedRect;
    return self;
}


// Report current set of supported commands
- (NSArray *)keyCommands
{
    return keyCommands.allObjects;
}


- (void) resetKeyCommands
{
    keyCommands = [NSMutableSet set];
}


// Post event
- (void) handleKeyCommand: (UIKeyCommand *) command
{
    [[NSNotificationCenter defaultCenter]
        postNotificationName:KeySupportFieldEvent object:command];
}


// Create a new key command and add it to the supported set
- (void) listenForKey: (NSString *) key modifiers: (UIKeyModifierFlags) flags
{
    UIKeyCommand *command = [UIKeyCommand keyCommandWithInput:key
        modifierFlags:flags action:@selector(handleKeyCommand:)];
    [keyCommands addObject:command];
}
@end
```

Wrap-up

Here are final points to wrap up what you've read in this chapter:

- There's no need to limit yourself to plain-text thinking in your applications. iOS is rich-text ready. Its attributed string classes are profoundly powerful.

- In iOS, text attachments act like any other kind of string attribute. If you're not working with an already-styled RTFD source, add NSAttachmentAttributeName attributes and assign NSTextAttachment values to them. For in-line images, you typically initialize an attachment with image data and a UTI type. If you'd rather lay out your text independently of inline images, use the exclusion zone approach discussed in Chapter 2, "Dynamic Typography."

- When working with documents, keep portability in mind. Although your user may be creating a document in iOS, the resulting RTF or HTML container may end up being used on a Windows or Mac desktop system.

- As a rule, it is far, far easier to use a desktop editor to build documents and import them into your iOS documents than to create complex attributed strings from scratch.

- You can be very, very relaxed when using HTML import. Instead of focusing on standards-based markup, feel free to add just the elements you need to get the job done.

5

Animation

Of the technologies updated in the last couple years, iOS animation is one of the ones that has been most enhanced by recent APIs. Flexible animation styles enable your interfaces to integrate real-world physics for better and more exciting presentations and interactions. If you use animations to add liveliness and interest to your interfaces and want to push them to the next level, this chapter is for you. This chapter offers some fresh approaches to this classic technology.

Keyframe Animation

Although `UIView` animation has long provided ways to smoothly transition from one set of view characteristics to another, until iOS 7, the implementation of `UIView` was always "flat." Beyond tweaking the underlying curve, you couldn't do much to chain sequences without a lot of custom overhead. Your view could go from transparent to opaque, from red to green, from small to large, but view changes were limited to a single bounded sequence.

View animations normally use a known start state and end state. The animation interpolates between these states and produces a smooth transition between the starting and ending visuals. Keyframes add fixed intermediate points to animations. This means you can create animations that not only go from A to B but also to C, then D, then E.

Until iOS 7, I relied on custom classes of my own design to create UIKit-specific keyframe animation sequences. (Keyframes have long been a part of Core Animation.) My older classes are available on GitHub: Search for `AnimationQueue` and Sadun. When iOS 7 debuted, UIKit finally added its own keyframe solution. Although its design was a little counterintuitive, these APIs enabled you to build timed keyframe updates with minimal fuss and overhead.

Keyframe animations tell better stories than do simple flips or fades. They create more realistic interactions than basic interpolation with fixed start and end points. With them, you can repeatedly shake, wiggle, and bounce views. Don't settle for a view that just slides or fades. Realize core animation principles like stretching and squashing, anticipation and exaggeration, follow-through, overlapping action, and so forth. Keyframe animation makes these sequences of change possible using simple progressions.

In the simplest form, UIKit keyframes consist of a custom block that establishes view conditions at specific times. Listing 5-1 builds a shake animation to demonstrate a base implementation. It moves a view repeatedly first up and right, then down and left. It's a perfect way to indicate a negative to the user, such as "operation failed" or "this view is off limits for interaction." The method generates its animation block and passes it to the keyframe animation request.

Here's the tricky bit: Instead of supplying a list of times and updates, the block consists of code that builds keyframes during its execution. This was probably the biggest mental hurdle for me when transitioning from my old way of doing things to the newer approach. The animation block you create to build the keyframe sequence isn't executed until *after* you pass it to the UIView class. You create a block that establishes the keyframes on demand, producing a full and scalable sequence.

Listing 5-1 offers a simple keyframe animation. It creates a shaking effect by toggling repeatedly between two view transformations before ending with a reset to the identity transform. Each change is established in the method's animationBlock, which is passed to the UIView animation request.

The method finishes by calling animateKeyframesWithDuration:delay:options: animations:completion:. Its request parameters consist of a duration in seconds, an optional delay that enables you to start the animation after a fixed time, an options parameter, which describes the way the animation is laid out and paced, and two blocks. The options parameter in the final line is set to 0 in this example. This produces a default linear interpolation between keyframes. The first block establishes keyframes; the second block executes after the animation completes. Once called, this method executes immediately, pausing only for any delay you specify as the second parameter.

> **Note**
>
> The relative start time and relative duration parameters both take floating-point values between 0.0 and 1.0. The animation call multiplies these against the total duration you pass to the view animation request.

Listing 5-1   **Shake Keyframe Animation**

```
- (void) shake: (UIView *) view
{
    // Animation parameters
    NSInteger numberOfShakes = 8; // Repeat 4 times up and down

    // Define the animation block
    void (^animationBlock)() = ^{
        // Create the two transforms: up-right, down-left
```

```
    CGAffineTransform t1 = CGAffineTransformMakeTranslation(2, -2);
    CGAffineTransform t2 = CGAffineTransformMakeTranslation(-2, 2);


    // Iteratively add each keyframe
    for (int i = 0; i < numberOfShakes; i++)
    {
        CGFloat progress = (CGFloat) i / (CGFloat) numberOfShakes;
        [UIView addKeyframeWithRelativeStartTime: progress
            relativeDuration: 1.0 / numberOfShakes
            animations:^{
                view.transform = (i % 2) ? t1 : t2;}];}

    // End by returning to the start position
    [UIView addKeyframeWithRelativeStartTime:
            (numberOfShakes - 1.0) / numberOfShakes
        relativeDuration: 1.0 / numberOfShakes animations:^{
            view.transform = CGAffineTransformIdentity;}];
    };

    // Call the animation
    [UIView animateKeyframesWithDuration:1.0 delay:0.0
        options: 0 animations:animationBlock completion:nil];
}
```

Building Physics with Keyframes

UIKit offers complex physical animations through its dynamic animator class, which you will read about in Chapter 6, "Dynamic Animators." This section isn't about those built-in elements. The keyframe mechanism offers a perfect match for custom animation effects as well, and that's where Listing 5-2 delivers. It uses a damped oscillator to "pop" a view's size. The built-in UIKit effects manipulate a view's position and how it (rigidly) interacts with the views and containers that surround it. Listing 5-2 emulates a stretchable/squashable view that changes in size, not just position.

The `DampedSinusoid()` function (see Figure 5-1) creates a wave whose amplitude approaches zero over time. Each successive cycle decreases, allowing an effect to grow less and less prominent. For Listing 5-2, the damping function controls the size of the view. It allows it to iteratively approach its final size, popping the view out slightly less at each iteration.

Using keyframes powered by a mathematical model enables you to build multistep animations that explore view transformations and properties beyond those offered directly by UIKit. Listing 5-2 explores a scale transformation. By adjusting the two lines in the keyframe block to the following, you could easily adapt this method to rotate instead:

```
CGFloat degree = dampValue * 0.3;
view.transform = CGAffineTransformMakeRotation(M_PI_4 * degree);
```

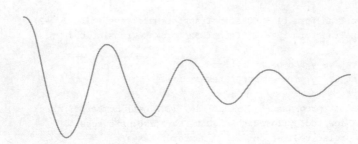

Figure 5-1   A damped sinusoid function decays over time.

So long as there's some kind of underlying function driving an animation, keyframes provide a perfect match between time-based progress and view property updates.

Listing 5-2   **Damped Oscillating Pop Effect**

```
CGFloat DampedSinusoid(CGFloat time,
    CGFloat distance, CGFloat decayAccelerator)
{
    return 1 - cos(distance) * exp(-1.0 * time * decayAccelerator);
}

- (void) pop: (UIView *) view
{
    void (^animationBlock)() = ^{
        // Animation steps in total
        NSInteger numberOfSteps = 30;

        // Amount to oscillate
        CGFloat numberOfOscillations = 2;
        CGFloat oscillationDistance =
            numberOfOscillations * 2 * M_PI;

        // Perform oscillation over n-1 steps
        for (NSInteger step = 1; step < numberOfSteps; step++)
        {
            CGFloat progress = (CGFloat) step / (CGFloat) numberOfSteps;
            CGFloat distance = progress * oscillationDistance;
            CGFloat dampValue = 1 - DampedSinusoid(progress, distance, 2);

            [UIView addKeyframeWithRelativeStartTime: progress
                relativeDuration: 1.0 / numberOfSteps animations:^{
                CGFloat degree = 1.0 + dampValue * 0.3;
                view.transform =
                    CGAffineTransformMakeScale(degree, degree);
            }];
        }
```

```
    // Return to normal
    [UIView addKeyframeWithRelativeStartTime:
            (numberOfSteps - 1.0) / numberOfSteps
        relativeDuration: 1.0 / numberOfSteps animations:^{
        view.transform = CGAffineTransformIdentity;
    }];
};


[UIView animateKeyframesWithDuration:1.5
    delay:0 options:0 animations:animationBlock completion:nil];
}
```

Blocking Animators

Keyframe animations, for all their utility, can require significant overhead for simple do-this-then-that animation sequences. Blocking animators use a run loop to prevent the next call from executing until they have finished their animation. These provide a convenient way to stack calls without building a full keyframe animation or using endless completion-block nesting. Importantly, they don't require relative start times, so you can tweak the durations of your calls without affecting other steps in the process.

Run loops carry risks. The class shown in Listing 5-3 uses old-style UIKit animation, which has been soft deprecated since iOS 4. Apple writes in the class documentation, "[This approach] is discouraged....You should use the block-based animation methods to specify your animations instead." That said, I find the approach used in Listing 5-3 to be highly useful for prototyping keyframe sequences, for creating quick demo apps, and for other primarily in-house uses. I've included the class here because of that level of utility. Being able to sequentially call animateBlockingWithDuration:animations:completion: can be a tremendously effective design first step before formalizing your animations into more modern calls.

Listing 5-3   **Blocking Animations**

```
void (^completion)(BOOL);

// The delegate catches the end of the animation sequence and
// restores the previous run loop
@interface BlockingAnimationDelegate : NSObject
@end

@implementation BlockingAnimationDelegate
- (void) animationDidStop:(CAAnimation *)anim finished:(BOOL)flag
{
    // Execute the completion block at this time
    if (completion) completion(flag);
    CFRunLoopStop(CFRunLoopGetCurrent());
```

```
}
@end

static BlockingAnimationDelegate *delegate;

@implementation UIView (BlockingAnimation)
+ (void) animateBlockingWithDuration:(NSTimeInterval)duration
    animations:(void (^)(void))animations
    completion:(void (^)(BOOL))theCompletion
{
    // Establish the completion delegate
    delegate = [[BlockingAnimationDelegate alloc] init];
    completion = theCompletion;

     // Welcome back to the days of iOS 3
    [UIView beginAnimations:@"BlockingAnimations" context:nil];
    [UIView setAnimationCurve:UIViewAnimationCurveEaseInOut];
    [UIView setAnimationDuration:duration];
    [UIView setAnimationDidStopSelector:@selector(animationDidStop:finished:)];
    [UIView setAnimationDelegate:delegate];
    if (animations) animations();
    [UIView commitAnimations];

    // Block with a new run loop
    CFRunLoopRun();
}
@end
```

UIKit Spring-Based Animations

Although you can always roll your own physics-based animations, UIKit now offers one exceedingly handy built-in solution based on damped harmonics. The following example uses this approach to handle a tap gesture by "closing" a slide-in window:

```
- (void) handleCloseTapGesture: (UITapGestureRecognizer *) tapGestureRecognizer
{
    [handleView removeGestureRecognizer:tapGestureRecognizer];
    [UIView animateWithDuration:0.5
                          delay:0
         usingSpringWithDamping:0.6
          initialSpringVelocity:0
                        options:0
                     animations:^{
                         _constraint.constant = kClosedDrawExtent;
                         [self.superview layoutIfNeeded];
                     }
```

```
          completion:^(BOOL finished) {
              [handleView addGestureRecognizer:
                  panGestureRecognizer];}];
}
```

Instead of just animating the view back to its initial position, it uses UIKit's new spring-based animation to enliven the transition, letting the view bounce a little as it reaches its final position. Based on a damped harmonic oscillator (essentially the same approach used in Listing 5-2), the built-in method enables you to specify the animation's duration, a damping constant, and an initial velocity.

Beyond those extra tweaks, the method works exactly like a standard `animateWithDuration:completion:` call. The animation block updates a constraint and performs a layout. On completion, the method installs a new gesture recognizer to handle the next user drag.

Damping, which ranges from 0 to 1, defaults to 0.5. Lowering this value makes the animation very "springy." Raising it reduces a view's apparent bounciness. The initial velocity parameter enables you to match the view's prior speed before starting the animation. If the view was previously moving at 50 points per second and your animation will traverse 200 points, set an initial velocity of 0.25.

The options parameter uses a mask of standard `UIView` animation options, which are enumerated in the class documentation. This is where you update the animation curve, which normally defaults to the perfectly pleasant ease in-out setting.

I've set up a test bed in the sample code for this chapter (see Figure 5-2) that lets you interactively explore some of these settings and how they affect the view animation. Use this test bed to interactively tweak the view's damping, initial velocity, and overall animation duration.

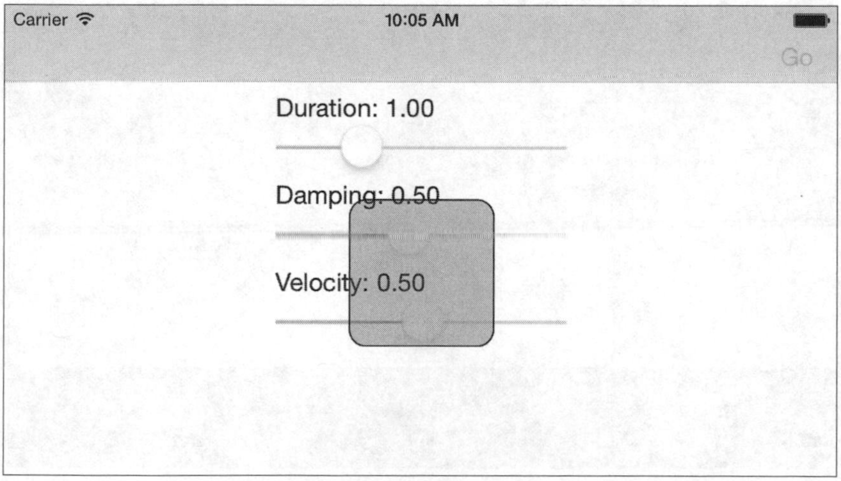

Figure 5-2 This test bed offers sliders to tweak an animation's duration, damping, and initial velocity. This sample is best explored in person as a screenshot cannot do it justice.

Practical Uses for Spring Animations

The spring animation works best when a view is falling back to its natural place or when that natural place updates due to user interaction. The following code represents the opposite approach to the one you saw earlier in this section in the `handleCloseTapGesture:` method. There, a user tapped a view-based drawer to shut it. Here, the user interaction has extended far enough that it passes a trigger point, allowing the drawer to snap into the open position shown in Figure 5-3:

```
if ((amount + kClosedDrawExtent + kHandleInset +
    kHandleExtent / 2) > kTriggerPoint) // moved past the trigger point
{
    [UIView animateWithDuration:0.5
                          delay:0
         usingSpringWithDamping:0.4
          initialSpringVelocity:0
                        options:0
                     animations:^{
                         _constraint.constant = kOpenDrawExtent;
                         [self.superview layoutIfNeeded];
                     }
                     completion:^(BOOL finished) {
                         [handleView addGestureRecognizer:
                             tapGestureRecognizer];
                     }];
    return;
}
```

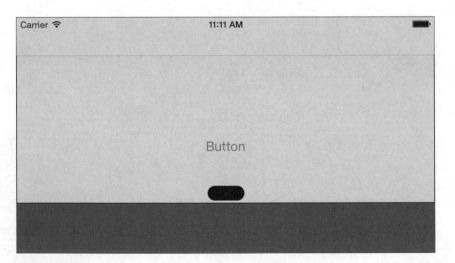

Figure 5-3   This button appears in a virtual drawer that slides in from the top of this interface. Populate your slide-in views with whatever UI content your application demands. You will best experience this UI by running the sample code that accompanies this chapter.

This code is nearly identical to the previous version. The main difference is the damping constant, which provides more bounce at 0.4 than the 0.6 used for normal closing. This extra energy indicates that the user has achieved a new state. If you look at the sample code for the chapter, you'll discover that this class also uses a third animation sequence when the user fails to reach the trigger point. This final sequence uses an even more extreme 0.25 constant, mimicking the physics of an old-fashioned window blind flapping back to its rolled-up position. The degree of energy you use offers hints regarding the success or failure of each action as well as their natural state. These small tweaks to parameters encourage distinct user experiences.

System Animations

iOS now offers a canonical way for you to remove deleted views from your screen. At this time, the UISystemAnimationDelete animation is the only system-supplied animation, although it's likely that Apple will introduce others over time. When you call the following method on an array of views, iOS shrinks and fades those views off the screen on your behalf:

```
[UIView performSystemAnimation:UISystemAnimationDelete
    onViews:@[testView] options:0 animations:nil
    completion:^(BOOL finished)
    {
        // do completion work here
    }];
```

By the end of the animation, the view becomes fully transparent and scales to 25% of its original size:

```
2014-12-08 11:06:08.198 Hello World[75470:60b] <UIView: 0x10976b300; frame =
(147.5 271.5; 25 25); transform = [0.25, 0, 0, 0.25, 0, 0]; alpha = 0; layer =
<CALayer: 0x109761f70>>
```

You can add a parallel animation block by using the animations: parameter. Use this option to update interface positions, taking advantage of the space now vacated by the deleted view or views. Avoid tweaking view properties on the to-be-deleted view, especially those that overlap with the system animation (namely background color and transform). These won't animate smoothly.

Motion Effects

Motion effects lend applications a three-dimensional feel. They enable you to build visual effects tied to device motion. The most common use of motion effects is as virtual planes, shown in Figure 5-4. This affect appears in the iOS home screen, where icons appear to float over the background wallpaper.

With motion effects, views adjust to match the user's angle of perception, creating a sense of depth. Each view's magnitude of change establishes how perceptually far or near that view is with respect to the user. This mimics the natural human stereo-optic effect established by having two eyes. Views with the same magnitude move together. This enables viewers to mentally connect them as being on the same "plane."

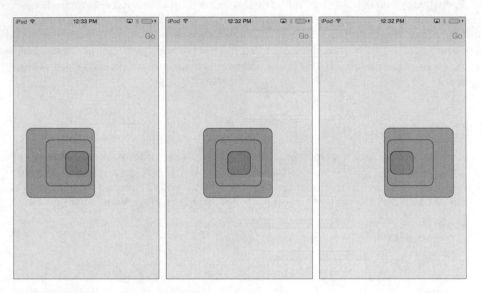

Figure 5-4   Motion effects create visual transformations keyed to the device angle and the user's point of view. Virtual planes enable you to add views to depth-cued "layers."

Users may disable motion effects in Settings > General > Accessibility > Reduce Motion. Unfortunately, you cannot guarantee that this feature is enabled nor officially query this setting from your application. With a quick web search, you'll find a variety of fragile workarounds for this issue, but I cannot recommend the ones I found in production code. As a rule, write your app as if the feature is there, but be aware that users may switch it off on demand.

Building Planes

Listing 5-4 demonstrates how to create a plane effect. This class builds a motion effect group from two UIInterpolatingMotionEffect instances. Each effect is interpolated along one axis, either horizontal or vertical, and updates a specific key path—in this case, for the view's center property. You can supply any key path you like, although there are relatively few choices that make sense and produce a pleasing interface effect.

The UIInterpolatingMotionEffect class used in Listing 5-4 is the most common entry point into motion effects. Although you can work directly with its parent class UIMotionEffect, nearly everything you'll ever want to do is better done with the subclass. As the name suggests, the UIInterpolatingMotionEffect class provides an interpolated effect ranging from –1 to 1. This value is based on the axis you monitor: the left–right horizontal axis or the up–down vertical axis. You set multipliers by adjusting the minimum and maximum relative values. Typically you set these to either [–x through x] or [0 through x].

You can add either single effects or groups to views by using the same `addMotionEffect:` method. Listing 5-4 returns a group instead of individual effects because it's easier to work in both dimensions that way. The following line of code builds a new `CenterMotionEffect` group and adds it to a view:

```
[testView addMotionEffect:[CenterMotionEffect effectWithMagnitude:30]];
```

Increase the magnitude as needed for more pronounced effects. Once added, the motion effects engine takes charge of implementing adjustments. You do no further work. The effect persists until you remove the effect by calling `removeMotionEffect:`.

Listing 5-4   **Adding Motion Effects for View Plane Offsets**

```
@interface CenterMotionEffect : UIMotionEffectGroup
+ (instancetype) effectWithMagnitude: (CGFloat) magnitude;
@end

@implementation CenterMotionEffect
+ (instancetype) effectWithMagnitude: (CGFloat) magnitude
{
    UIInterpolatingMotionEffect *hEffect =
        [[UIInterpolatingMotionEffect alloc] initWithKeyPath:@"center.x"
            type:UIInterpolatingMotionEffectTypeTiltAlongHorizontalAxis];
    hEffect.minimumRelativeValue = @(-1 * fabs(magnitude));
    hEffect.maximumRelativeValue = @(fabs(magnitude));

    UIInterpolatingMotionEffect *vEffect =
        [[UIInterpolatingMotionEffect alloc] initWithKeyPath:@"center.y"
            type:UIInterpolatingMotionEffectTypeTiltAlongVerticalAxis];
    vEffect.minimumRelativeValue = @(-1 * fabs(magnitude));
    vEffect.maximumRelativeValue = @(fabs(magnitude));

    CenterMotionEffect *group =  [[self alloc] init];
    group.motionEffects = @[hEffect, vEffect];
    return group;
}
@end
```

Shadow Effects

Device-controlled view shadows offer another powerful—and easy—way to use motion effects. It takes few changes to Listing 5-4 to create the shadow effects shown in Figure 5-5. Just update the key paths from `center.x` and `center.y` to `layer.shadowOffset.width` and `layer.shadowOffset.height`, and you're good to go.

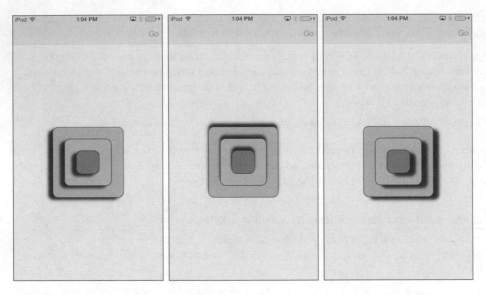

Figure 5-5   These device-driven shadows were implemented via a simple motion effect.

A few final points about motion effects:

- You can easily update Listing 5-4 to apply a motion effect to just one dimension. You are not required to create effects that work across two axes. You can also update the listing to create multiple effects, such as adding the shadows and the view offsets together. As long as the transformations are conceptually tied together, there's no reason to separate them into different effects.

- Motion effects work with any animatable property, not just shadows. This offers you the opportunity to create unique (but probably less generally useful) effects.

- Motion effects are fully compatible with Auto Layout. Unlike with view dynamics, which are discussed in Chapter 6, with motion effects the perceived frame changes do not affect layout rules. You can set up and adjust your interfaces in tandem with running effects. Motion effects do not change actual view placement. Unless you take action to update your views, nothing in the interface actually adjusts as the motion-enabled views appear to move.

- iOS automatically disables motion effects whenever you enable AirPlay mirroring. This makes application demonstrations steadier but less interesting. If you need to re-enable that functionality, workarounds exist, but keep in mind that they are not suitable for App Store.

Custom Transition Animations

The UIViewControllerAnimatedTransitioning protocol enables you to add custom animations between view controllers. In the form discussed in this section, these animations have a fixed timeline and are not interactive. You build custom classes that animate the transition with whatever animation tools you have on hand. This means you can use UIView animation, Core Animation, Core Image filters...whatever. The way you move from one controller to the next is basically unbounded.

The example in Figure 5-6 is built around a navigation controller. The normal sliding transitions are replaced with page curls, which animate either up or down, depending on whether a new controller is being pushed onto the stack or an older controller is being popped off from it.

Figure 5-6   Custom transitions enable you to use standard interaction elements such as navigation controllers, tab controllers, and modal view controllers with animations you specify.

This technology depends on two key elements: a custom transition class that conforms to the animated transitioning protocol and delegation, which allows you to tell controllers which transition class to use.

Delegation

The controller delegates you work with are as follows:

- **UITabBarControllerDelegate**—Supply a transition for moving from one tab to another.

- **UINavigationControllerDelegate**—Create custom transitions for pop and push actions.

For each of these protocols, you create a controller and set its delegate. Here's an example:

```
UINavigationController *nav =
    [[UINavigationController alloc] initWithRootViewController:vc];
nav.delegate = self;
```

The nuances of delegate methods depend on the class you're supporting. Tab bar controller transitions don't have a direction. In contrast, the UINavigationControllerOperation parameter sent to a navigation controller's delegate uses enumeration to differentiate between push operations and pop operations.

The callback signatures are long, as you see in the following example, but the actual implementation is simple. You create a transitioning object instance, set up its parameters, and return it:

```
- (id<UIViewControllerAnimatedTransitioning>)navigationController:
        (UINavigationController *)navigationController
    animationControllerForOperation:
        (UINavigationControllerOperation)operation
    fromViewController:(UIViewController *)fromVC
    toViewController:(UIViewController *)toVC
{
    FlipTransition *transition =
        [[FlipTransition alloc] init];
    BOOL forward = (operation == UINavigationControllerOperationPush);
    transition.forward = forward;
    transition.duration = 0.6;
    return transition;
}
```

Building Transitioning Objects

With custom animations, there is no transitioning class that you subclass. Instead, you build a new class, typically descended from NSObject, and declare the UIViewControllerAnimated-Transitioning protocol. This protocol is uncomplicated. It consists of two required methods, shown in Listing 5-5. The one optional animationEnded: method enables you to perform any post-transition work.

All the elements you need to perform your animation are passed through the UIViewControllerContextTransitioning context. Here you find access to the two controllers you're transitioning between and the container view that parents them. Use object properties to pass any additional state information that goes beyond the information passed by the transitioning context. This example stores the direction of animation and the total animation duration as custom properties. Set these in the delegate method so they're ready to be used when the transition object is called on to execute.

Listing 5-5 uses built-in view-to-view page curls for its animation, but you can replace this animation as you desire. Other built-in view-to-view animations include page flips and cross dissolves. I have also created custom Core Animation transitions, leveraged Core Image filters (avoid them; they're slow, and caching can cause interface delays), and built transitions around the new UIKit keyframing and damped harmonic animations. Whatever approach you end up using, make sure you tie your animation to the duration returned by the transitionDuration: method and call completeTransition: as the final step.

Listing 5-5   **Building an Animated Controller Transition**

```
@interface FlipTransition : NSObject <UIViewControllerAnimatedTransitioning>
@property (nonatomic) BOOL forward;
@property (nonatomic) CGFloat duration;
@end

@implementation FlipTransition
- (instancetype) init
{
    if (!(self = [super init])) return self;
    _duration = 1.0; // default
    _forward = YES;
    return self;
}

- (void)animateTransition:
    (id<UIViewControllerContextTransitioning>)transitionContext
{
    // Retrieve context players
    UIViewController *fromController = [transitionContext
        viewControllerForKey:UITransitionContextFromViewControllerKey];
    UIViewController *toController = [transitionContext
        viewControllerForKey:UITransitionContextToViewControllerKey];
    UIView *containerView = [transitionContext containerView];

    // Set up container
    [containerView addSubview:fromController.view];

    // Animate
    CGFloat duration = [self transitionDuration:transitionContext];
    NSUInteger options = _forward ?
        UIViewAnimationOptionTransitionCurlUp :
```

```
        UIViewAnimationOptionTransitionCurlDown;
    [UIView transitionFromView:fromController.view
        toView:toController.view duration:duration
        options:options completion:^(BOOL finished) {
        [transitionContext completeTransition:YES];
    }];
}

- (NSTimeInterval)transitionDuration:
    (id<UIViewControllerContextTransitioning>)transitionContext
{
    return _duration;
}
@end
```

Implicit Animations

As you've already read in this chapter, iOS offers a wealth of animation routines with both UIKit and Core Animation. iOS 7, in particular, introduced new routines to provide keyframe animations and spring-like physics to extend the way you create fluid interfaces. In addition to these explicit routines, iOS offers several ways, relatively little known, to automatically animate view changes as you update view properties. You add this implicit animation support with simple classes and just a few lines of code. Once this is added, your views automatically animate between their before and after values without any further work on your part.

Imagine updating a `UIView` layer instance's corner radius property, as in Figure 5-7. As the property changes between 32 and 0 and back again, the view corners jump between sharply angled and smoothly rounded. Now imagine that somehow iOS could respond to these property assignments by animating the change between the two values. Instead of jumping, the edges would smoothly interpolate between the two:

```
- (void) go
{
    CGFloat newValue = (customView.layer.cornerRadius < 32) ? 32 : 0;
    customView.layer.cornerRadius = newValue;
}
```

Implicit animations respond to standard property assignments, involving no animation timing, curves, and so forth. The implicit response lies in how the view's layer implementation responds to property changes.

Building an Animation-Ready Layer

You create implicit animations by establishing custom `CALayer` subclasses. In Listing 5-6, updates to the `cornerRadius` property invoke a basic animation. You override the `actionForKey:` method to add dynamic responses to property changes.

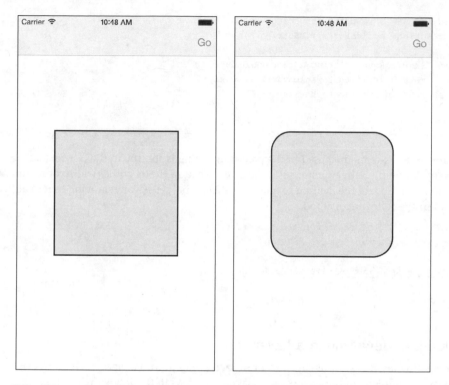

Figure 5-7   iOS can smoothly interpolate between built-in layer properties such as the `cornerRadius` that changes from 0 in the left screen shot to 32 in the right.

Listing 5-6   **Adding Custom Animations to Property Actions**

```
@interface CustomLayer : CALayer
@property (nonatomic, assign) CGFloat animationDuration;
@end

@implementation CustomLayer
// Return a basic animation
- (CABasicAnimation *) customAnimationForKey: (NSString *) key
{
    CABasicAnimation *animation =
        [CABasicAnimation animationWithKeyPath:key];
    animation.fromValue = [self.presentationLayer valueForKey:key];
    // Default to 0.3 second duration
    animation.duration =
        (_animationDuration == 0.0) ? 0.3 : _animationDuration;
    return animation;
}
```

```
// Add a dynamic response for corner radius updates
-(id<CAAction>)actionForKey:(NSString *)key
{
    if ([key isEqualToString:@"cornerRadius"])
        return [self customAnimationForKey:key];
    return [super actionForKey:key];
}
@end
```

The `actionForKey` method used in the preceding listing is specific to the `cornerRadius` property. It doesn't animate changes to the layer's shadow, to its border width, or to any other elements. You update the method to animate all layer properties by removing that qualification, as in the following method:

```
// Add a dynamic response for all properties
-(id<CAAction>)actionForKey:(NSString *)key
{
    return [self customAnimationForKey:key];
}
@end
```

Building a View Around a Layer

After creating a self-animating layer, you can incorporate it into a view. Create a `UIView` subclass and implement the `layerClass` class method, as in the following example:

```
@interface CustomView : UIView
@end

@implementation CustomView
+ (Class) layerClass
{
    return [CustomLayer class];
}
@end
```

Instances of this subclass automatically use the `CustomLayer` layer class and animate its property changes.

Timing

Animations defined in the `CustomLayer` class do not respond to `UIView` animation calls, as you see in the following example:

```
- (void) go
{
    CGFloat newValue = (customView.layer.cornerRadius < 32) ? 32 : 0;
```

```
    NSDate *date = [NSDate date];
    [UIView animateWithDuration:2.0 animations:^{
        customView.layer.cornerRadius = newValue;
    } completion:^(BOOL finished) {
        NSLog(@"Elapsed time: %f",
            [[NSDate date] timeIntervalSinceDate:date]);
    }];
}
```

Consider the updated go method in this example. It embeds its cornerRadius update into a view animation block.

Two things happen—or, more accurately, do not happen—here:

- First, the requested duration (2.0 seconds) is ignored. The animation lasts for the default time defined by the layer (0.3 seconds), not the 2 seconds set by the animation block.

- Second, the completion block runs almost immediately, not after a 2-second delay. As far as the UIView class is concerned, there are no animatable items to update, so the completion block executes at the end of the call.

Here are timing results from testing this a couple times. The elapsed time is close to zero:

```
2014-12-19 09:44:58.968 Hello World[60556:60b] Elapsed time: 0.007392
2014-12-19 09:44:59.529 Hello World[60556:60b] Elapsed time: 0.008787
```

Although there are ways to work around this by catching animation notifications and deriving the implicit animation duration and applying that to the layer, such approaches are brittle and not App Store safe. Instead, consider coordinating your animations.

Coordinating Animations

You coordinate implicit animations by adding them to a standard animation block along with explicit animations, as in the following example:

```
- (void) go
{
    // Retrieve the layer
    CustomLayer *customLayer = (CustomLayer *) customView.layer;

    // Match the animation duration
    customLayer.animationDuration = 2.0;

    CGFloat newValue = (customView.layer.cornerRadius < 32) ? 32 : 0;
    NSDate *date = [NSDate date];
    [UIView animateWithDuration:2.0 animations:^{
        // Coordinate animations
        customLayer.cornerRadius = newValue;
        self.view.backgroundColor = _nextColor;
```

```
    } completion:^(BOOL finished) {
        NSLog(@"Elapsed time: %f", [[NSDate date] timeIntervalSinceDate:date]);
    }];
}
```

Here, the layer's animation duration is manually set to match that of the animation block. By placing both updates in the same block, you cause them to occur simultaneously. The completion block executes after the explicit animation concludes.

The completion block fires properly this time as there is a recognized `UIView` property to animate. The elapsed time moves to the expected 2 seconds:

```
2014-12-19 09:55:10.208 Hello World[60661:60b] Elapsed time: 2.000776
2014-12-19 09:55:13.562 Hello World[60661:60b] Elapsed time: 2.001607
```

Building Implicit Completion Blocks

You needn't rely on `UIView` calls to add completion blocks. You can build a custom completion block for your implicit animations with just a few tweaks. The following interface extends the `CustomLayer` class to add a `completionBlock` property:

```
typedef void (^ImplicitCompletionBlock)(NSString *key, BOOL finished);

@interface CustomLayer : CALayer
@property (nonatomic, assign) CGFloat animationDuration;
@property (nonatomic, strong) ImplicitCompletionBlock completionBlock;
@end
```

The custom `ImplicitCompletionBlock` type takes two arguments: a string corresponding to the animated property key path (for example, `"cornerRadius"`) and a flag that specifies whether the animation completed. The key enables you to distinguish between property updates in your block to better control any wrap-up.

The following methods implement the completion block details:

```
- (void) animationDidStop:(CAAnimation *)anim finished:(BOOL)flag
{
    if (_completionBlock)
    {
        NSString *key = [anim valueForKey:@"Animation Type"];
        _completionBlock(key, flag);
    }
}

- (CABasicAnimation *) customAnimationForKey: (NSString *) key
{
    CABasicAnimation *animation = [CABasicAnimation animationWithKeyPath:key];
    animation.fromValue = [self.presentationLayer valueForKey:key];
    animation.duration = (_animationDuration == 0.0) ? 0.3 : _animationDuration;
```

```
    animation.delegate = self;
    [animation setValue:key forKey:@"Animation Type"];
    return animation;
}
```

The `customAnimationForKey:` method adds an animation delegate and stores the key with the animation. This enables the `CustomLayer` instance to catch the end of the animation and execute the optional block.

Animating Custom Properties

You just read about animating built-in properties. Now it's time to move on to custom ones. If you can connect a visual representation to an inherent instance value and draw that value in some way, you can build an animatable property. This section discusses how. A custom property is as wild or as limited as your imagination. For example, you could fade an associated logo into and out of sight as a view layer's property changes (see Figure 5-8).

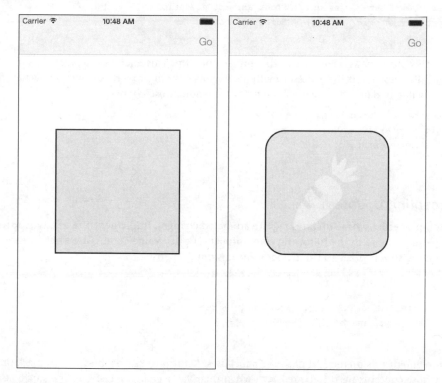

Figure 5-8   In this example, a translucent logo property is implicitly animated as its custom `logoLevel` property updates.

In the example that follows, an NSNumber property called logoLevel triggers the animation. The property ranges from 0.0 (fully transparent) to 1.0 (fully opaque). The layer smoothly adjusts its presentation, no matter what value you set. The following method enables the user to trigger the animations. Every time the user taps the *Go* button, each layer property is assigned a new value:

```
- (void) go
{
    BOOL direction = customView.layer.cornerRadius < 32;
    CustomLayer *layer = (CustomLayer *) customView.layer;
    layer.cornerRadius = direction ? 32 : 0;
    layer.logoLevel = direction ? @(1.0) : @(0.0);
}
```

To build the fading logo, start by creating a custom property. In this example, the logo level property stores an NSNumber instance:

```
@interface CustomLayer : CALayer
@property (nonatomic, assign) CGFloat animationDuration;
@property (nonatomic, strong) NSNumber *logoLevel;
@end
```

Declare this property as @dynamic in the implementation. This enables the layer class to dynamically implement the accessor methods for this custom property at runtime. When the property value updates, the layer will be ready to handle those changes:

```
@implementation CustomLayer
@dynamic logoLevel;
...class implementation...
@end
```

Intercepting Updates

To catch properties whose updates require animated changes, implement the needsDisplay-ForKey: method, as in the following code snippet. The key value coding used here means you compare the supplied key to the name of the custom property:

```
+ (BOOL) needsDisplayForKey:(NSString *) key
{
    if ([key isEqualToString:@"logoLevel"]) return YES;
    return [super needsDisplayForKey:key];
}
```

You implement this method in CALayer subclasses. Returning YES enables you to mark properties whose contents need to be redrawn when their value changes. Defer to the superclass's implementation for any property you don't handle.

Drawing Properties

The magic behind custom property animation lies in implementing drawInContext:. This method is superficially similar to the drawRect: method used in UIView subclasses. As with drawRect:, you implement a custom presentation by drawing your changes into a context. Here's an example that shows the relationship between the custom logoLevel property and the drawing it produces. Dividing the logoLevel value by 2.0 ensures the logo is drawn at a maximum alpha level of 0.5:

```
- (void) drawInContext:(CGContextRef) context
{
    UIGraphicsPushContext(context);

    UIBezierPath *path = [self path]; // any path will do
    CGFloat alpha = self.logoLevel.floatValue / 2.0;
    [[[UIColor whiteColor] colorWithAlphaComponent:alpha ] set];
    [path fill];

    UIGraphicsPopContext();
}
```

This method is called repeatedly as the layer interpolates between its old and new values. Each time it's called, the new alpha level creates a different fill result.

You aren't, of course, limited to a single animatable property. In the following method, both the logoLevel and imageLevel properties control the drawing produced by the layer subclass. The imageLevel property allows the image to fade in and out, just as the logo drawing does, but without having to do so in tandem:

```
- (void) drawInContext:(CGContextRef) context
{
    UIGraphicsPushContext(context);

    // Draw the path
    UIBezierPath *path = [self path]; // supply a path
    CGFloat alpha = self.logoLevel.floatValue / 2.0;
    [[[UIColor whiteColor] colorWithAlphaComponent:alpha ] set];
    [path fill];

    // Draw an image
    static UIImage *image = nil;
    if (!image) image = [UIImage imageNamed:IMAGE_NAME];
    [image drawInRect:CGRectMake(20, 20, 64, 64) blendMode:kCGBlendModeCopy
        alpha:self.imageLevel.floatValue];

    UIGraphicsPopContext();
}
```

As a rule of thumb, keep your drawing simple and local, using resources set as instance variables within the layer rather than adjusted by outside properties. When in doubt, slow down your animation. Properly behaving items update gradually. A good candidate for custom intrinsic animation is any view that updates to reflect state. For example, you might indicate items selected by the user by applying check marks, thickening frames, or changing the opacity of an overlay. The best applications, though, are ones with nuance. Instead of switching a display feature on or off, adjust it continuously within a range of values. The implicit animations ensure that your visual properties update and display smoothly.

Wrap-up

Here are final points to wrap up what you've read in this chapter:

- UIKit animations have really stepped up over the past few years. There's little you can imagine that cannot be implemented using today's toolset. Standout additions include keyframe animation and motion effects.

- Although blocking animations may not be suitable for production work, they are darn handy to have around for prototyping.

- Custom transitions enable your applications to change state in new ways, using familiar controllers. Make sure you budget your time to allow extra room for tuning these classes. Getting them just right can be maddening.

- Implicit animations provide an exciting way to create smooth transitions between view properties, enabling you to grab a viewer's eye with a minimum of programming. Use these features to draw and resign user focus in your interfaces.

Dynamic Animators

Dynamic animators are some of the most exciting elements of iOS, even if they are among the least practical. Their physics-based view behaviors create lively and curious interfaces. At the same time, they can be fussy to work with. They don't happily coexist with Auto Layout because they directly update frame values and can rotate views. That said, dynamic animators are tremendously fun. They help make your UIs pop and are well worth exploring to discover what features they can provide your users.

Physics-Based Behaviors

The UIDynamicAnimator class emulates interface "physics." It coalesces this functionality into distinct behaviors like snapping, pushing, attachment, and collision. Here's a quick overview of the primitive UIKit dynamic behaviors:

- **Attachments**—UIAttachmentBehavior instances tie a view either to a position or to another view. It's basically a virtual string with a set length, although you can make it act more like a spring by updating damping and frequency properties.

- **Collisions**—UICollisionBehavior instances allow views to collide with each other or with path-based boundaries. In a collision, energy can be passed from one item to another, and a view's trajectory can be changed.

- **Gravity**—UIGravityBehavior instances apply acceleration to views. You set where "down" is and allow the gravity vector to act on velocities over time.

- **Pushes**—UIPushBehavior instances add an impulse force to views, adding new energy to the system.

- **Snaps**—UISnapBehavior instances act as magnets, drawing views to attachment points.

- **Dynamic items**—UIDynamicItemBehavior is the odd man out in this list. Instead of acting as a force, dynamic items are objects affected by forces. These behaviors enable your views to participate in the other behaviors listed here. You can attach, collide, push, snap, and weigh down views by treating them as having physical properties. The dynamic item behavior defines density, elasticity, friction, and resistance and manages linear and angular item velocities.

You can best explore how these items work by running Apple's UIKit Dynamic Catalog sample code (https://developer.apple.com/library/ios/samplecode/DynamicsCatalog). This sample code illustrates available dynamic behaviors, presenting a wide range of effects you can create in your own apps. Most importantly, it lets you see, interact with, and explore each behavior on its own.

Building Dynamics

Once you've finished exploring Apple's dynamics catalog, start building your own examples. To begin, you need to create a dynamic animator, like this:

```
self.animator = [[UIDynamicAnimator alloc]
    initWithReferenceView:self.view];
```

This top-level class acts as an intermediary between your views and any dynamic behaviors you add to the system. The animator provides context for the animations, establishing either a reference view to create a coordinate system or a reference layout when working with collection views.

Typically, you use a view controller's primary view as a reference, although you are not limited to this. Use any view backdrop that's large enough to contain the actors in your drama. And, as you'll see, you can extend animated views beyond the parent view, if needed.

Dynamics Delegation

Delegation enables you to know when an animator pauses, an important tool for tracking the end of an animation sequence. An animator delegate declares the `UIDynamicAnimatorDelegate` protocol and conforms to that protocol by implementing the optional `dynamicAnimatorDidPause:` and `dynamicAnimatorWillResume:` methods. Assign a delegate like this:

```
self.animator.delegate = self;
```

When you implement a delegate, you know when animation sequences coalesce, which enables you to clean up your simulation after the physics have come to a static resting point. Be aware that some animations may never "stop," especially those that do not employ energy-lowering strategies like friction and resistance.

Creating and Adding Behaviors

Each dynamic animator can coordinate many behaviors at once. For example, you might want to create a dynamic system where views "fall" in the direction of gravity but bounce off each other and remain within the boundaries of the view controller's view. Or you might create a snapping behavior that involves collision detection, bumping some views out of the way.

Add each behavior to the animator with the `addBehavior:` method. This method applies the behavior to the current state. If the animator is active, the behavior will immediately start. The following snippet creates a new snapping behavior and adds it to an animator:

```
UISnapBehavior *snapBehavior = [[UISnapBehavior alloc]
    initWithItem:testView snapToPoint:point];
[self.animator addBehavior:snapBehavior];
```

The standard behavior-creation pattern is to allocate an instance and initialize it with one or more items. This example uses a single item (`testView`) and sets a single parameter, a snap-to point. When this is added to the animator, the view moves until its center co-aligns with the snap point.

Each dynamic behavior is distinct in terms of the details associated with the class's API. Gravity behavior initializers accept an array of child items, although you can add and remove items at later times. Attachment behaviors include a suite of initializers that supply anchor points, dynamic items, and offsets away from the anchors. Each behavior class is a new adventure, and it's well worth your time to read through their APIs as they are all quite different from each other.

Detecting Pauses

Behavior lifetimes vary. After adding a behavior to an animator, you leave it in place for varying degrees of time: until some application state has changed, until the animation has come to a stopping point (or has reasonably coalesced to the point where the user perceives it as having stopped), or until the application ends. The lifetime you select depends on the kind of behavior you define. For example, a collision behavior that keeps views inside a parent view controller may persist indefinitely. You might remove a snap behavior as soon as the view has moved to the newly requested position or a push behavior as soon as the impulse has finished.

The problem is, however, that the built-in dynamic animator can take a long time to detect that the views it manages have stopped moving. Consider the following list of times and frames for a snapped view:

```
[0.03] NSRect: {{121.55639, 217.55638}, {66.88723, 66.88723}}
[0.07] NSRect: {{91.418655, 206.41866}, {81.162689, 81.162689}}
[0.10] NSRect: {{60.333874, 201.33388}, {83.332253, 83.332253}}
[0.13] NSRect: {{44.293236, 204.29323}, {79.413528, 79.413528}}
[0.17] NSRect: {{42.394054, 213.39406}, {68.211891, 68.211891}}
[0.20] NSRect: {{44.46402, 221.46402}, {60.071957, 60.071957}}
[0.23] NSRect: {{44.94722, 222.94722}, {61.105556, 61.105556}}
[0.27] NSRect: {{47.207447, 223.70744}, {60.58511, 60.58511}}
[0.30] NSRect: {{49.458027, 223.45802}, {60.083942, 60.083942}}
[0.33] NSRect: {{50.481998, 222.48199}, {60.035999, 60.035999}}
```

```
[0.37] NSRect: {{50.987999, 221.98801}, {60.023998, 60.023998}}
[0.40] NSRect: {{51, 221.5}, {60, 60}}
[0.43] NSRect: {{50.5, 221.5}, {60, 60}}
[0.47] NSRect: {{50, 221.5}, {60, 60}}
[0.50] NSRect: {{50, 222}, {60, 60}}
[0.53] NSRect: {{50, 222}, {60, 60}}
[0.57] NSRect: {{50, 222}, {60, 60}}
...[snipped 0.60 to 1.10]...
[1.13] NSRect: {{50, 222}, {60, 60}}
[1.17] NSRect: {{50, 222}, {60, 60}}
Elapsed time: 1.167326
```

This view reaches its final position after half a second has passed. The dynamic animator does not pause until 1.17 seconds—more than double the required time. In user experience terms, those extra 0.67 seconds can feel like forever.

The reason for the delay becomes clear when you sneak down into the animator and look up the view's linear and angular velocity:

```
[0.60] NSRect: {{50, 222}, {60, 60}}
    Linear Velocity: NSPoint: {1.8314272, 1.0867469}
    Angular Velocity: 0.000001
```

Those values do not drop to 0 until that extra time has passed:

```
[1.17] NSRect: {{50, 222}, {60, 60}}
    Linear Velocity: NSPoint: {0, 0}
    Angular Velocity: 0.000000
```

In a practical sense, the velocities are meaningless once the view frame stops changing. When you know in advance that no outside forces will impel a view to start moving again after it's reached a resting point, leverage this information. Trim down your waiting time by tracking a view's frame.

Listing 6-1 defines a watcher class that monitors views until they stop changing. After a view has remained fixed for a certain period of time (here for at least 0.1 seconds), this class contacts a delegate and lets it know that the view has stopped moving. That callback enables you to update your dynamic animator and remove the behavior so the animator can more quickly come to a pause.

When run with the same snap animation as the previous example, the new watcher detects the final frame at 0.50. By 0.60, the delegate knows to stop the animation, and the entire sequence stops nearly 0.55 seconds earlier:

```
[0.47] NSRect: {{50, 221.5}, {60, 60}}
[0.50] NSRect: {{50, 222}, {60, 60}}
[0.53] NSRect: {{50, 222}, {60, 60}}
[0.57] NSRect: {{50, 222}, {60, 60}}
[0.60] NSRect: {{50, 222}, {60, 60}}
Elapsed time: 0.617352
```

Use this kind of short-cutting approach to re-enable GUI items that might otherwise be inaccessible to users once you know that the animation has come to a usable end point. While this example implements a pixel-level test, you might vary this approach to detect low angular velocities and other "close enough" tests to help end the animation effects within a reasonable amount of time.

Listing 6-1   **Watching Views**

```objc
// Info stores the most recent frame, count, delegate
@interface WatchedViewInfo : NSObject
@property (nonatomic) CGRect frame;
@property (nonatomic) NSUInteger count;
@property (nonatomic) CGFloat pointLaxity;
@property (nonatomic) id <ViewWatcherDelegate> delegate;
@end

@implementation WatchedViewInfo
@end

// Watcher class
@implementation ViewWatcher
{
    NSMutableDictionary *dict;
}

- (instancetype) init
{
    if (!(self = [super init])) return self;
    dict = [NSMutableDictionary dictionary];
    _pointLaxity = 10;
    return self;
}

// Determine whether two frames are "close enough"
BOOL CompareFrames(CGRect frame1, CGRect frame2, CGFloat laxity)
{
    if (CGRectEqualToRect(frame1, frame2)) return YES;
    CGRect intersection = CGRectIntersection(frame1, frame2);
    CGFloat testArea =
        intersection.size.width * intersection.size.height;
    CGFloat area1 = frame1.size.width * frame1.size.height;
    CGFloat area2 = frame2.size.width * frame2.size.height;
    return ((fabs(testArea - area1) < laxity) &&
            (fabs(testArea - area2) < laxity));
}
```

```objc
// See whether the view has stopped moving
- (void) checkInOnView: (NSTimer *) timer
{
    int kThreshold = 3; // must remain for 0.3 secs

    // Fetch the view and the info
    UIView *view = (UIView *) timer.userInfo;
    NSNumber *key = @((int)view);
    WatchedViewInfo *watchedViewInfo = dict[key];

    // Matching frame? If so update count
    BOOL steadyFrame = CompareFrames(watchedViewInfo.frame,
        view.frame, _pointLaxity);
    if (steadyFrame) watchedViewInfo.count++;

    // Threshold met
    if (steadyFrame && (watchedViewInfo.count > kThreshold))
    {
        [timer invalidate];
        [dict removeObjectForKey:key];
        [watchedViewInfo.delegate viewDidPause:view];
        return;
    }

    if (steadyFrame) return;

    // Replace frame with new frame
    watchedViewInfo.frame = view.frame;
    watchedViewInfo.count = 0;
}

- (void) startWatchingView: (UIView *) view
    withDelegate: (id <ViewWatcherDelegate>) delegate
{
    NSNumber *key = @((int)view);
    WatchedViewInfo *watchedViewInfo = [[WatchedViewInfo alloc] init];
    watchedViewInfo.frame = view.frame;
    watchedViewInfo.count = 1;
    watchedViewInfo.delegate = delegate;
    dict[key] = watchedViewInfo;

    [NSTimer scheduledTimerWithTimeInterval:0.03 target:self
        selector:@selector(checkInOnView:) userInfo:view repeats:YES];
}
@end
```

Creating a Frame-Watching Dynamic Behavior

While the solution in Listing 6-1 provides general view oversight, you can implement the frame checker in a much more intriguing form: as the custom dynamic behavior you see in Listing 6-2. This approach that adapts Listing 6-1 to a new form requires just a couple adjustments to work as a behavior:

- The behavior from the `checkInOnView:` method is now implemented in the behavior's `action` property. This block is called directly by the animator, using its own timing system, so the threshold is slightly higher in this implementation than in Listing 6-1.

- Instead of calling back to a delegate, this approach unloads both the watcher and the client behavior directly in the `action` block. This may be problematic if the behavior controls additional items, but for snap behaviors and their single items, it is a pretty safe approach.

To enable the watcher, you must add it to the animator as a separate behavior. Here's how you allocate it and initialize it with a client view and an affected behavior:

```
UISnapBehavior *snapBehavior = [[UISnapBehavior alloc]
    initWithItem:testView snapToPoint:p];
[self.animator addBehavior:snapBehavior];
WatcherBehavior *watcher = [[WatcherBehavior alloc]
    initWithView:testView behavior:snapBehavior];
[self.animator addBehavior:watcher];
```

Once it is added, it works just like Listing 6-1, iteratively checking the view's frame to wait for a steady state.

Listing 6-2   Watching Views with a Dynamic Behavior

```
// Create custom frame watcher
@interface WatcherBehavior : UIDynamicBehavior
- (instancetype) initWithView: (UIView *) view
    behavior: (UIDynamicBehavior *) behavior;
@property (nonatomic) CGFloat pointLaxity; // defaults to 10
@end

// Store the view, its most recent frame, and a count
@interface WatcherBehavior ()
@property (nonatomic) UIView *view;
@property (nonatomic) CGRect mostRecentFrame;
@property (nonatomic) NSInteger count;
@property (nonatomic) UIDynamicBehavior *customBehavior;
@end
```

```objc
@implementation WatcherBehavior
- (instancetype) initWithView: (UIView *) view
    behavior: (UIDynamicBehavior *) behavior
{
    if (!(self = [super init])) return self;

    // Initialize instance
    _view = view;
    _mostRecentFrame = _view.frame;
    _count = 0;
    _pointLaxity = 10;
    _customBehavior = behavior;

    // Create custom action for the behavior
    __weak typeof(self) weakSelf = self;
    self.action = ^{
        __strong typeof(self) strongSelf = weakSelf;
        UIView *view = strongSelf.view;

        CGRect currentFrame = view.frame;
        CGRect recentFrame = strongSelf.mostRecentFrame;
        BOOL steadyFrame = CompareFrames(currentFrame,
            recentFrame, strongSelf.pointLaxity);
        if (steadyFrame) strongSelf.count++;

        NSInteger kThreshold = 5;
        if (steadyFrame && (strongSelf.count > kThreshold))
        {
            [strongSelf.dynamicAnimator
                removeBehavior:strongSelf.customBehavior];
            [strongSelf.dynamicAnimator removeBehavior:strongSelf];
            return;
        }

        if (!steadyFrame)
        {
            strongSelf.mostRecentFrame = currentFrame;
            strongSelf.count = 0;
        }
    };

    return self;
}
@end
```

Implementing Snap Zones

One of my favorite dynamic animator tricks involves creating snap zones—areas of your interface that pull in dragged items once they overlap a particular region. This approach allows you to collect items into well-managed zones and offer a pleasing "snap-into-place" animation. In the general form shown in Listing 6-3, there's no further test beyond whether a dragged view has strayed into a zone. However, you might want to expand the approach to limit blue items to blue zones or red items to red zones, and so forth.

Listing 6-3 assumes that users will have access to multiple zones and even that a view might move from one zone directly to another. It uses a tagging scheme to keep track of this potential reparenting. A free view has no current parent and can move freely about. When a free view overlaps a snap zone, however, it suspends dragging by disabling the view's gesture recognizer and adds a snap-to-parent behavior. The view slides into place into its new parent. Once it arrives, as the dynamic animator pauses, the recognizer is re-enabled.

Allowing a view to escape from its new parent's bounds is the tricky bit—and the motivating reason for the view tagging. You do not want a view to recapture its child unless the dragging gesture has ended, which is why this method keeps track of the gesture state. With new parents, however, the snap behavior is added (and the gesture is suspended) as soon as a view strays over the line. Balancing the escapes and the captures ensures that the user experience is snappy and responsive and does not thwart the user's desires to remove a view from a parent.

Listing 6-3   **Handling Multiple Snap Zones**

```
- (void) draggableViewDidMove: (NSNotification *) note
{
    // Check for view participation
    UIView *draggedView = note.object;
    UIView *nca = [draggedView nearestCommonAncestorWithView:
        _animator.referenceView];
    if (!nca) return;

    // Retrieve state
    UIGestureRecognizer *recognizer = (UIGestureRecognizer *)
        draggedView.gestureRecognizers.lastObject;
    UIGestureRecognizerState state = [recognizer state];

    // View frame and current attachment
    CGRect draggedFrame = draggedView.frame;
    BOOL free = draggedView.tag == 0;

    for (UIView *dropZone in _dropZones)
    {
        // Make sure all drop zones are views
```

```
if (![dropZone isKindOfClass:[UIView class]])
    continue;

// Overlap?
CGRect dropFrame = dropZone.frame;
BOOL overlap = CGRectIntersectsRect(draggedFrame, dropFrame);

// Free moving
if (!overlap && free)
{
    continue;
}

// Newly captured
if (overlap && free)
{
    if (suspendedRecognizer)
    {
        NSLog(@"Error: attempting to suspend second recognizer");
        break;
    }

    // New parent.
    // CAPTURED is an integer offset for tagging
    suspendedRecognizer = recognizer;
    suspendedRecognizer.enabled = NO; // stop!
    draggedView.tag = CAPTURED + dropZone.tag; // mark as captured
    UISnapBehavior *behavior = [[UISnapBehavior alloc]
        initWithItem:draggedView
        snapToPoint:RectGetCenter(dropFrame)];
    [_animator addBehavior:behavior];
    break;
}

// Is this the current parent drop zone?
BOOL isParent = (dropZone.tag + CAPTURED == draggedView.tag);

// Current parent
if (overlap && isParent)
{
    switch (state)
    {
        case UIGestureRecognizerStateEnded:
        {
            // Recapture
            UISnapBehavior *behavior = [[UISnapBehavior alloc]
                initWithItem:draggedView
```

```
                    snapToPoint:RectGetCenter(dropFrame)];
                [_animator addBehavior:behavior];
                break;
            }
            default:
            {
                // Still captured but no op
                break;
            }
        }
        break;
    }

    // New parent
    if (overlap)
    {
        suspendedRecognizer = recognizer;
        suspendedRecognizer.enabled = NO; // stop!
        draggedView.tag - CAPTURED + dropZone.tag;
        UISnapBehavior *behavior = [[UISnapBehavior alloc]
            initWithItem:draggedView
            snapToPoint:RectGetCenter(dropFrame)];
        [_animator addBehavior:behavior];
        break;
    }
}
}
```

Leveraging Real-World Physics

The built-in gravity dynamic animator consists of a downward force. You can adjust the force's vector to point gravity in other directions, but it's a static system. You can, however, integrate the gravity behavior with Core Motion to produce a much more satisfying effect. Apple's Core Motion framework enables your apps to receive motion-based data from device hardware, including the onboard accelerometer and gyroscope. The framework converts motion data into a form of input that your device can use to coordinate application changes with the way your user's device is held and moved over time.

Listing 6-4 builds a motion manager singleton. It uses Core Motion to listen for accelerometer updates, and when it receives them, it calculates a working vector and posts notifications with that information. You may be curious about that extra 0.5 added to the y component; it produces a more natural vector for holding a device in your hand.

Listing 6-4   **Broadcasting Motion Updates**

```
#define VALUE(struct) ({ __typeof__(struct) __struct = struct; \
    [NSValue valueWithBytes:&__struct \
    objCType:@encode(__typeof__(__struct))]; })


NSString *const MotionManagerUpdate = @"MotionManagerUpdate";
NSString *const MotionVectorKey = @"MotionVectorKey";

static MotionManager *sharedInstance = nil;

@interface MotionManager ()
@property (nonatomic, strong) CMMotionManager *motionManager;
@end

@implementation MotionManager
+ (instancetype) sharedInstance
{
    if (!sharedInstance)
        sharedInstance = [[self alloc] init];

    return sharedInstance;
}

- (void) shutDownMotionManager
{
    NSLog(@"Shutting down motion manager");
    [_motionManager stopAccelerometerUpdates];
    _motionManager = nil;
}

- (void) establishMotionManager
{
    if (_motionManager)
        [self shutDownMotionManager];

    // Establish the motion manager
    NSLog(@"Establishing motion manager");
    _motionManager = [[CMMotionManager alloc] init];
}

- (void) startMotionUpdates
{
    if (!_motionManager)
        [self establishMotionManager];
```

```
if (_motionManager.accelerometerAvailable)
    [_motionManager
    startAccelerometerUpdatesToQueue:[[NSOperationQueue alloc] init]
    withHandler:^(CMAccelerometerData *data, NSError *error)
    {
        CGVector vector = CGVectorMake(data.acceleration.x, -
            (data.acceleration.y + 0.5));
        NSDictionary *dict = @{MotionVectorKey:VALUE(vector)};
        [[NSNotificationCenter defaultCenter]
            postNotificationName:MotionManagerUpdate
            object:self userInfo:dict];
    }];

}
@end
```

Connecting a Gravity Behavior to Device Acceleration

On the other end of things, create an observer for motion updates. The following snippet builds a gravity behavior and updates its `gravityDirection` property whenever the physical device moves:

```
// Build device gravity behavior
_deviceGravityBehavior = [[UIGravityBehavior alloc] initWithItems:@[]];

// Add observer
__weak typeof(self) weakSelf = self;
id observer = [[NSNotificationCenter defaultCenter]
    addObserverForName:MotionManagerUpdate object:nil
    queue:[NSOperationQueue mainQueue]
    usingBlock:^(NSNotification *note) {
        __strong typeof(self) strongSelf = weakSelf;

        // Retrieve vector
        NSDictionary *dict = note.userInfo;
        NSValue *value = dict[MotionVectorKey];
        CGVector vector;
        [value getValue:&vector];

        // Set gravity direction to that vector
        strongSelf.deviceGravityBehavior.gravityDirection = vector;
}];
[_observers addObject:observer];
```

As the `gravityDirection` property updates, any child items (none are yet added in this code) respond to the new force, moving in the appropriate direction.

Creating Boundaries

One of the biggest annoyances about gravity is that it never stops. When you apply a gravity behavior to a view, it will accelerate off the screen and keep going on essentially forever. Bye-bye, view. To avoid this, add a boundary. The UICollisionBehavior has a built-in solution for enclosures. Enable its translatesReferenceBoundsIntoBoundary property, and it sets the animator's reference view as a default boundary for its items:

```
_boundaryBehavior = [[UICollisionBehavior alloc] initWithItems:@[]];
_boundaryBehavior.translatesReferenceBoundsIntoBoundary = YES;
```

When building behaviors like this, it's important to spot-check your key steps. Remember that animators own behaviors, and behaviors own items, which are typically views. Don't forget to add items to each behavior that affects them. For this example of device-based gravity, add views to both the gravity behavior *and* the boundary behavior. Also, make sure to add the behaviors to the animator. Always make sure your views fall fully within the collision boundaries *before* adding a behavior to the animator. Views that cross the boundary or lie outside the boundary will not respond properly to the "keep items within the reference bounds" rule.

Collision behaviors also enable views to bounce off each other. By default, any view added to a collision behavior will participate not only in view-to-boundary collisions but also in view-to-view collisions. If for any reason you don't want this to happen, you can update the behavior's collisionMode property to exclude item-to-item collisions:

```
_boundaryBehavior = [[UICollisionBehavior alloc] initWithItems:@[]];
_boundaryBehavior.translatesReferenceBoundsIntoBoundary = YES;
_boundaryBehavior.collisionMode = UICollisionBehaviorModeBoundaries;
```

Enhancing View Dynamics

Dynamic item behaviors customize view traits—making them springier or duller, heavier or lighter, smoother or stickier, and so forth. Unlike the other built-in behaviors, dynamic item behaviors focus less on external forces and more on individual view properties. For example, say you have views that you want to add bounce to. Create a dynamic item behavior and adjust its elasticity property:

```
_elasticityBehavior = [[UIDynamicItemBehavior alloc] initWithItems:items];
_elasticityBehavior.elasticity = 0.8; // Higher values are more elastic
[_animator addBehavior:_elasticityBehavior];
```

Dynamic item properties include the following:

- **Rotation (allowsRotation)**—This property allows or disallows view rotation as the view participates in the dynamic system. When it is enabled (the default), views may rotate as they collide with other items.

- **Angular resistance (angularResistance)**—Angular resistance creates a damping effect on rotation. As the value of this property rises from 0 to 1, views stop tumbling more quickly.

- **Resistance (`resistance`)**—Also ranging from 0 to 1, the linear resistance property is analogous to angular resistance. Instead of damping rotation, it limits linear velocity. You can think of this as a natural viscosity in the view's "atmosphere," where 0 is close to operating in a vacuum, and 1 is like moving through thick syrup.

- **Density (`density`)**—An item's `density` property controls its virtual mass. Any dynamic behavior that uses mass as a factor (such as collisions and friction) responds to the current value of this property, which defaults to 1. Because items have density, a view that's twice the size of another along each dimension will contribute four times the effective mass when set to the same density or equal mass when set to a quarter of the density.

- **Elasticity (`elasticity`)**—Ranging from 0 to 1, this property establishes how elastic a view's collisions will be. At 0, collisions are lifeless, with no bounce at all. A setting of 1 creates completely elastic collisions with wildly bouncy items.

- **Friction (`friction`)**—The `friction` property creates linear resistance, producing a kind of "stickiness" for when items slide across each other. As the `friction` setting rises from 0 (friction-free) to 1 (the strongest possible friction), views tend to disperse energy on contact and connect more strongly to each other and to boundaries.

Custom Behaviors

Apple provides a library of default behaviors that includes forces (attachments, collisions, gravity, pushes, and snaps) and "dynamic items" that describe how a physics body reacts to forces. You can also create your own behaviors that operate with dynamic animators. This section discusses how you might do this in your own projects.

You choose from two approaches when creating custom dynamic behaviors. First, you can hook your changes onto an existing behavior and transform its updates to some new style. That's the approach Apple uses in the Dynamic Catalog example that converts an attachment point animator to a boundary animation. It transforms an elastic attachment to view morphing. Second, you can create a new behavior and establish your own rules for coalescing its results over time. This approach enables you create any kind of behavior you can imagine, as long as you express it with regard to the animator's timeline. Both have advantages and drawbacks.

Creating Custom Dynamic Items

Before jumping into custom behaviors, you need to understand dynamic items more fully. Dynamic items are the focal point of the dynamic animation process. Until this point, I have used views as dynamic items—after all, they provide the `bounds`, `center`, and `transform` properties required to act in this role—but dynamic items are not necessarily views. They are merely objects that conform to the `UIDynamicItem` protocol. This protocol ensures that these properties are available from conforming objects. Because of this abstraction, you can dynamically animate custom objects as easily as you animate views.

Consider the following class. It consists of nothing more than three properties, ensuring that it conforms to the UIDynamicItem protocol:

```
@interface CustomDynamicItem : NSObject <UIDynamicItem>
@property (nonatomic) CGRect bounds;
@property (nonatomic) CGPoint center;
@property (nonatomic) CGAffineTransform transform;
@end
@implementation CustomDynamicItem
@end
```

After adding this class to your project, you can instantiate and set properties however you like. For example, you might use the following lines of code to create a new custom item:

```
item = [[CustomDynamicItem alloc] init];
item.bounds = CGRectMake(0, 0, 100, 100);
item.center = CGPointMake(50, 50);
item.transform = CGAffineTransformIdentity;
```

Once you have established a dynamic item, you may pass it to a behavior and add that behavior to an animator, just as you would with a view:

```
animator = [[UIDynamicAnimator alloc] init];
UIPushBehavior *push = [[UIPushBehavior alloc]
    initWithItems:@[item] mode:UIPushBehaviorModeContinuous];
push.angle = M_PI_4;
push.magnitude = 1.0;
[animator addBehavior:push];
push.active = YES;
```

What happens next, however, may surprise you. If you monitor the item, you'll find that its center property updates, but its bounds and transform remain untouched:

```
2014-12-01 13:33:08.177 Hello World[55151:60b] Bounds: [0, 0, 100, 100], Center:
(86 86), Transform: Theta: {0.000000 radians, 0.000000°} Scale: {1.000000,
1.000000} Translation: {0.000000, 0.000000}
2014-12-01 13:33:09.176 Hello World[55151:60b] Bounds: [0, 0, 100, 100], Center:
(188 188), Transform: Theta: {0.000000 radians, 0.000000°} Scale: {1.000000,
1.000000} Translation: {0.000000, 0.000000}
2014-12-01 13:33:10.175 Hello World[55151:60b] Bounds: [0, 0, 100, 100], Center:
(351 351), Transform: Theta: {0.000000 radians, 0.000000°} Scale: {1.000000,
1.000000} Translation: {0.000000, 0.000000}
2014-12-01 13:33:11.176 Hello World[55151:60b] Bounds: [0, 0, 100, 100], Center:
(568 568), Transform: Theta: {0.000000 radians, 0.000000°} Scale: {1.000000,
1.000000} Translation: {0.000000, 0.000000}
```

This curious state of affair happens because the dynamic animator remains completely agnostic as to the kind of underlying object it serves. This abstract CustomDynamicItem class provides no links between its center property and its bounds property the way a view would. If you want these items to update synchronously, you must add corresponding methods. For example, you might implement a solution like this:

```
- (void) setCenter:(CGPoint)center
{
    _center = center;
    _bounds = RectAroundCenter(_center, _bounds.size);
}


- (void) setBounds:(CGRect)bounds
{
    _bounds = bounds;
    _center = RectGetCenter(bounds);
}
```

I'm not going to present a full implementation that allows the item to respond to transform changes—for two reasons. First, in real life, you almost never want to create custom items in this fashion. Second, when you actually do need this, you'll be far better off using an actual view as an underlying model. Allowing a UIView instance to do the math for you will save you a lot of grief, especially since you're trying to emulate a view in the first place.

> **Note**
>
> I am unaware of any workaround that will allow you to create non-rectangular dynamic items at this time.

Subverting Dynamic Behaviors

As mentioned earlier, Apple created a Dynamic Catalog example that redirects the results of an attachment behavior to create a bounds animation. It accomplishes this by building an abstract dynamic item class. This class redirects all changes applied to the item's center to a client view's width and height. This means that while the physics engine thinks it's bouncing around a view in space, the actual expressions of those dynamics are producing bounds shifts. The following code performs this mapping:

```
// Map bounds to center
- (CGPoint)center
{
    return CGPointMake(_item.bounds.size.width, _item.bounds.size.height);
}

// Map center to bounds
- (void)setCenter:(CGPoint)center
{
    _item.bounds = CGRectMake(0, 0, center.x, center.y);
}
```

I dislike this approach for the following reasons:

- The animator isn't animating the view's center at the point you think it is. You must establish an anchor point within the view's own coordinate system so the center values make any sense to use.

- All you're getting back from this exercise is a damped sinusoid, as in Listing 5-2. Just use a damped sinusoid to begin with, and you'll avoid any unintentional side effects.

- How often are you just sitting around in your development job, thinking, "Hey, I'll just take the output of a physics emulation system and map its results into another dimension so I can create an overly complex sample application that has no general reuse value?" Right, me either.

Better Custom Dynamic Behaviors

As you read this section, remember that *better* is a relative term. The biggest problem when it comes to custom dynamic behaviors is that Apple has not released a public API that keeps a completely custom item animating until it reaches a coalesced state. This means that while Listing 6-5 offers a more satisfying solution than Apple's solution, it's still a hack.

The main reason for this is that while built-in dynamic behaviors can tell the animator "Hey, I'm done now" by using private APIs that allow the animator to stop, you and I cannot tickle the animator to make sure it keeps on ticking. Enter this class's "clock mandate." It's a gravity behavior added to the `ResizableDynamicBehavior` as a child.

The gravity behavior works on an invisible view, which is itself added to the animated view so that it belongs to the right hierarchy. (This is an important step so you don't generate exceptions.) Once it is added, the gravity behavior works forever. When you're ready for the dynamic behavior to end, simply remove it from its parent. Without this extra trick, the animation ends on its own about a half second after you start it.

I developed the damped equation used in the `action` block after playing with graphing. As Figure 6-1 shows, I was looking for a curve that ended after about one and a half cycles. You cannot depend on the animator's elapsed time, which doesn't reset between behaviors. To power my curve, I made sure to create a clock for each behavior and use that in the action block.

Figure 6-1   A fast-decaying sin curve provides a nice match to the view animation.

A few final notes on this one:

- You need to attach some sort of built-in animator like gravity, or your `action` property will not be called. Gravity offers the simple advantage of never ending.

- You must establish the `bounds` as is done here, or your view immediately collapses to a 0 size.

- The `identity` transform in the last step isn't strictly necessary, but I wanted to ensure that I cleaned up after myself as carefully as possible.

- To slow down the effect, reduce the number of degrees traveled per second. In this case, it goes 2 * pi every second.

- To increase or decrease the animation magnitude, adjust the multiplier. Here it is 1 + 0.5 * *the scale*. The 1 is the identity scale, and you should keep it as is. Tweak the 0.5 value up to expand the scaling or down to diminish it.

- You can bring the animation to coalescence faster or slower by adjusting the final multiplier in the exponentiation. Here it is set to 2.0, which produces fairly rapid damping. Higher values produce stronger damping; lower values allow the animation to continue longer.

Listing 6-5 **Extending a Custom Behavior's Lifetime**

```
@interface ResizableDynamicBehavior ()
@property (nonatomic, strong) UIView *view;
@property (nonatomic) NSDate *startingTime;
@property (nonatomic) CGRect frame;
@property (nonatomic) UIGravityBehavior *clockMandate;
@property (nonatomic) UIView *fakeView;
@end

@implementation ResizableDynamicBehavior
- (instancetype) initWithView: (UIView *) view
{
    if (!view) return nil;
    if (!(self = [super init])) return  self;
    _view = view;
    _frame = view.frame;

    // Establish a falling view to keep the timer going
    _fakeView = [[UIView alloc] initWithFrame:CGRectMake(0, 0, 10, 10)];
    [view addSubview:_fakeView];
    _clockMandate = [[UIGravityBehavior alloc] initWithItems:@[_fakeView]];
    [self addChildBehavior:_clockMandate];

    // The action block is called at every animation cycle
    __weak typeof(self) weakSelf = self;
```

```
    self.action = ^{
        __strong typeof(self) strongSelf = weakSelf;

        // Start or update the clock
        if (!strongSelf.startingTime)
            strongSelf.startingTime = [NSDate date];
        CGFloat time = [[NSDate date]
            timeIntervalSinceDate:strongSelf.startingTime];

        // Calculate the current change
        CGFloat scale = 1 + 0.5 * sin(time * M_PI * 2) *
            exp(-1.0 * time * 2.0);

        // Apply the bounds and transform
        CGAffineTransform transform =
            CGAffineTransformMakeScale(scale, scale);
        strongSelf.view.bounds = (CGRect){.size = strongSelf.frame.size};
        strongSelf.view.transform = transform;
        [strongSelf.dynamicAnimator
            updateItemUsingCurrentState:strongSelf.view];

        // Stop after 3 * Pi
        if (time > 1.5)
        {
            [strongSelf removeChildBehavior:strongSelf.clockMandate];
            [strongSelf.fakeView removeFromSuperview];
            strongSelf.view.transform = CGAffineTransformIdentity;
        }
    };

    return self;
}
@end
```

Custom Secondary Behaviors

You do far less work when your custom behavior acts side-by-side with a known system-supplied one. You don't have to establish an overall animation end point, the way Listing 6-5 does. Consider Listing 6-6, which creates a behavior that modifies a view transformation over time. This class is duration agnostic. Its only customizable feature is an acceleration property, which establishes how fast the changes accelerate to an end point.

With custom behaviors, it's really important that you not tie yourself to a set timeline. While a system-supplied snap behavior might end after 80 updates or so, you should never rely on knowing that information in advance. In contrast, with keyframes, you are free to interpolate a function over time. With dynamics, you establish a system that *coalesces*, reaching a natural stopping point on its own.

For example, Listing 6-6 uses velocity and acceleration to drive its changes from 0% to 100%, applying an easing function to that transit to produce a smooth animated result. At no point does the behavior reference elapsed time. Instead, all updates are driven by the dynamic animation's heartbeat and applied whenever the `action` method is called.

Figure 6-2 shows the animation in action, with the two behaviors acting in parallel. As the views draw near to their snap points, they apply the requested transforms to finish with a coordinated pile of views.

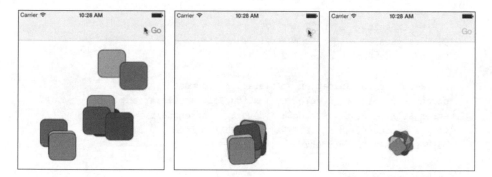

Figure 6-2   In this animation, a snap behavior draws the views together, and a transformation behavior angles each item to form a tight nest.

Listing 6-6   **Building a Transform-Updating Behavior**

```
- (instancetype) initWithItem: (id <UIDynamicItem>) item
      transform: (CGAffineTransform) transform;
{

    if (!(self = [super init])) return self;

    // Store the passed information
    _item = item;
    _originalTransform = item.transform;
    _targetTransform = transform;

    // Initialize velocity and acceleration
    _velocity = 0;
    _acceleration = 0.0025;

    // The weak and strong workarounds used here avoid retain cycles
    // when using blocks.
    ESTABLISH_WEAK_SELF;
    self.action = ^(){
        ESTABLISH_STRONG_SELF;
```

```
        // Pull out the original and destination transforms
        CGAffineTransform t1 = strongSelf.originalTransform;
        CGAffineTransform t2 = strongSelf.targetTransform;

        // Original
        CGFloat xScale1 = sqrt(t1.a * t1.a + t1.c * t1.c);
        CGFloat yScale1 = sqrt(t1.b * t1.b + t1.d * t1.d);
        CGFloat rotation1 = atan2f(t1.b, t1.a);

        // Target
        CGFloat xScale2 = sqrt(t2.a * t2.a + t2.c * t2.c);
        CGFloat yScale2 = sqrt(t2.b * t2.b + t2.d * t2.d);
        CGFloat rotation2 = atan2f(t2.b, t2.a);

        // Calculate the animation acceleration progress
        strongSelf.velocity = velocity + strongSelf.acceleration;
        strongSelf.percent = strongSelf.percent + strongSelf.velocity;
        CGFloat percent = MIN(1.0, MAX(strongSelf.percent, 0.0));
        percent = EaseOut(percent, 3);

        // Calculated items
        CGFloat targetTx = Tween(t1.tx, t2.tx, percent);
        CGFloat targetTy = Tween(t1.ty, t2.ty, percent);
        CGFloat targetXScale = Tween(xScale1, xScale2, percent);
        CGFloat targetYScale = Tween(yScale1, yScale2, percent);
        CGFloat targetRotation = Tween(rotation1, rotation2, percent);

        // Create transforms
        CGAffineTransform scaleTransform =
            CGAffineTransformMakeScale(targetXScale, targetYScale);
        CGAffineTransform rotateTransform =
            CGAffineTransformMakeRotation(targetRotation);
        CGAffineTransform translateTransform =
            CGAffineTransformMakeTranslation(targetTx, targetTy);

        // Combine and apply transforms
        CGAffineTransform t = CGAffineTransformIdentity;
        t = CGAffineTransformConcat(t, rotateTransform);
        t = CGAffineTransformConcat(t, scaleTransform);
        t = CGAffineTransformConcat(t, translateTransform);
        strongSelf.item.transform = t;
    };

    return self;
}
```

Collection Views and Dynamic Animators

Leveraging the power of dynamic animators in collection views is possible courtesy of a few UIKit extensions. Dynamic animators add liveliness to your presentations during scrolling and when views enter and leave the system. The dynamic behavior set is identical to that used for normal view animation, but the collection view approach requires a bit more overhead and bookkeeping as views may keep appearing and disappearing during scrolls.

The core of the dynamic animator system is the UIDynamicItem protocol. The UICollectionViewLayoutAttributes class, which represents items in the collection view, conforms to this protocol. Each instance provides the required bounds, center, and transform properties you need to work with dynamic animators. So although you don't work directly with views, you're still well set to introduce dynamics.

Custom Flow Layouts

The key to using dynamic animation classes with collection views is to build your own custom UICollectionViewFlowLayout subclass. Flow layouts create organized presentations in your application. Their properties and instance methods specify how the flow sets itself up to place items onscreen. In the most basic form, the layout properties provide you with a geometric vocabulary, where you talk about row spacing, indentation, and item-to-item margins. With custom subclasses, you can extend the class to produce eye-catching and nuanced results.

To support dynamic animation, your custom class must coordinate with an animator instance. You typically set it up in your flow layout initializer by using the UIDynamicAnimator collection view-specific initializer. This prepares the animator for use with your collection view and enables it to take control of reporting item attributes on your behalf. As you'll see, the dynamic animator takes charge of many methods you normally would have to implement by hand.

The following init method allocates an animator and adds a custom "spinner" behavior. The UIDynamicItemBehavior class enables you to add angular velocity to views, creating a spinning effect, which you see in action in Figure 6-3:

```
- (instancetype) initWithItemSize: (CGSize) size
{
    if (!(self = [super init])) return self;
    _animator = [[UIDynamicAnimator alloc]
        initWithCollectionViewLayout:self];
    _spinner = [[UIDynamicItemBehavior alloc] init];
    _spinner.allowsRotation = YES;
    [_animator addBehavior:_spinner];
    self.scrollDirection = UICollectionViewScrollDirectionHorizontal;
    self.itemSize = size;
    return self;
}
```

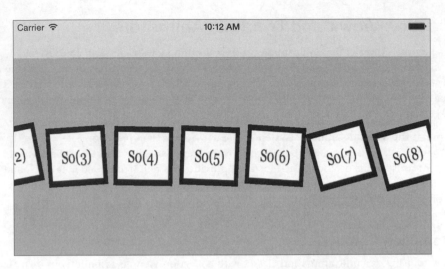

Figure 6-3 Allowing dynamic items to rotate enables you to add angular velocities, causing views to tilt and spin.

Returning Layout Attributes

As mentioned earlier, a dynamic animator can take charge of reporting layout attributes. The following methods do all the work, redirecting the normal geometry through the animator:

```
- (NSArray *)layoutAttributesForElementsInRect:(CGRect)rect
{
    return [_animator itemsInRect:rect];
}


- (UICollectionViewLayoutAttributes *)layoutAttributesForItemAtIndexPath:
    (NSIndexPath *)indexPath
{
    UICollectionViewLayoutAttributes *dynamicLayoutAttributes =
        [_animator layoutAttributesForCellAtIndexPath:indexPath];

    // Check whether the attributes were properly generated
    return dynamicLayoutAttributes ?
        [_animator layoutAttributesForCellAtIndexPath:indexPath] :
        [super layoutAttributesForItemAtIndexPath:indexPath];
}


- (BOOL)shouldInvalidateLayoutForBoundsChange:(CGRect)newBounds
{
    return YES;
}
```

For safety, the second method checks that the animator properly reports attributes. If it fails, the method falls back to the default implementation.

Updating Behaviors

With collection views, the hardest work involves coordinating items with behaviors. Although you can allow behaviors to control items that are no longer onscreen, as a general rule, you probably want to weed out any items that have left the display and add any items that have moved into place. Listing 6-7 demonstrates this approach.

You start by calculating the onscreen rectangle and request the array of items that appear in that space. Use each item's index path to compare it to items owned by a behavior. If a behavior item does not appear in the onscreen list, remove it. If an onscreen item isn't yet owned by the behavior, add it.

Although you mostly just add physics behaviors and let them run, I decided to tie Listing 6-7 to user interaction. The speed and direction of the backing scroll view add "impulses" to each view, nudging their angular velocity in one direction or the other.

Listing 6-7   **Adding Physics-Based Animation to Collection Views**

```
// Scroll view delegate method establishes the current speed
- (void)scrollViewDidScroll:(UIScrollView *)scrollView
{
    scrollSpeed = scrollView.contentOffset.x - previousScrollViewXOffset;
    previousScrollViewXOffset = scrollView.contentOffset.x;
}


// Prepare the flow layout
- (void) prepareLayout
{
    [super prepareLayout];

    // The collection view isn't established in init, catch it here.
    if (!setupDelegate)
    {
        setupDelegate = YES;
        self.collectionView.delegate = self;
    }

    // Retrieve onscreen items
    CGRect currentRect = self.collectionView.bounds;
    currentRect.size = self.collectionView.frame.size;
    NSArray *items = [super layoutAttributesForElementsInRect:currentRect];

    // Clean up any item that's now offscreen
    NSArray *itemPaths = [items valueForKey:@"indexPath"];
```

```
    for (UICollectionViewLayoutAttributes *item in _spinner.items)
    {
        if (![itemPaths containsObject:item.indexPath])
            [_spinner removeItem:item];
    }


    // Add all onscreen items
    NSArray *spinnerPaths = [_spinner.items valueForKey:@"indexPath"];
    for (UICollectionViewLayoutAttributes *item in items)
    {
        if (![spinnerPaths containsObject:item.indexPath])
            [_spinner addItem:item];
    }


    // Add impulses
    CGFloat impulse = (scrollSpeed /
        self.collectionView.frame.size.width) * M_PI_4 / 4;
    for (UICollectionViewLayoutAttributes *item in _spinner.items)
    {
        CGAffineTransform t = item.transform;
        CGFloat rotation = atan2f(t.b, t.a);
        if (fabs(rotation) > M_PI / 32) impulse = - rotation * 0.01;
        [_spinner addAngularVelocity:impulse forItem:item];
    }
}
```

Building a Dynamic Alert View

I stumbled across developer Victor Baro's dynamic iOS "jelly view" (http://victorbaro.com/
2014/07/vbfjellyview-tutorial/), which instantly caught my eye. This clever hack uses dynamic
attachment behaviors that wiggle in harmony, enabling you to create views that emulate Jell-O.
Although its utility is limited in practical deployment, it provides a superb example of how
traditional iOS elements like alerts can be re-imagined using modern APIs. Figure 6-4 shows a
jelly view alert in motion, squashing and stretching as it bounces off an invisible center ledge
within the main UI.

Connecting Up the Jelly

The secret to the jelly effect lies in an underlying 3×3 grid of tiny views, all attached to each
other and to the main view's center using UIAttachmentBehavior instances (see Figure 6-5).
These views and their attachments create a semi-rigid backbone that provides the view physics.
Listing 6-8 details how these views and attachments are made and installed. The elasticity
of the connections allows the views to move toward and away from each other, creating a
deformed skeleton for the view presentation.

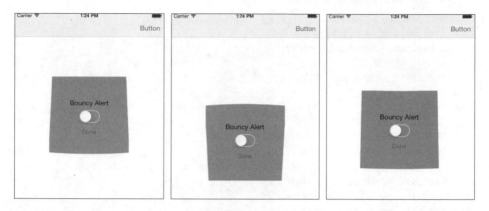

Figure 6-4   This "jelly view" distorts its shape as it uses UIKit dynamics to emulate a view built onto a blob of Jell-O.

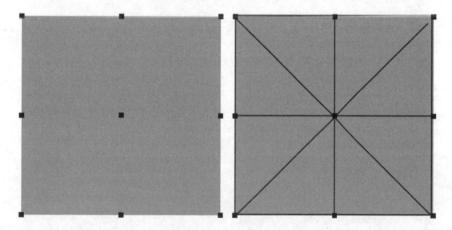

Figure 6-5   The nine connected points form a spring-based skeleton for the Jell-O animation.

Listing 6-8   **Establishing Jelly Dynamics**

```
- (void) establishDynamics : (UIDynamicAnimator *) animator
{
    if (animator) _animator = animator;

    // Create baseline dynamics for primary view
    UIDynamicItemBehavior *dynamic =
        [[UIDynamicItemBehavior alloc] initWithItems:@[self]];
    dynamic.allowsRotation = NO;
    dynamic.elasticity = _elasticity / 2;
```

```
dynamic.density = _density;
dynamic.resistance = 0.9;
[_animator addBehavior:dynamic];

// Establish jelly grid
for (int i = 0; i < 9; i++)
{
    // Add dynamics
    UIView *view = [self viewWithTag:(i + 1)];
    UIDynamicItemBehavior *behavior =
        [[UIDynamicItemBehavior alloc] initWithItems:@[view]];
    behavior.elasticity = _elasticity * 2;
    behavior.density = _density;
    behavior.resistance = 0.2;
    [_animator addBehavior:behavior];

    // Attach each grid view to main jelly view center
    UIAttachmentBehavior *attachment =
        [[UIAttachmentBehavior alloc] initWithItem:view attachedToItem:self];
    attachment.damping = _damping;
    attachment.frequency = _frequency;
    [_animator addBehavior:attachment];

    // Attach views to each other
    if ((i + 1) != 5) // skip center
    {
        NSInteger xTag = [@[@(1), @(2), @(5), @(0), @(4), @(8),
            @(3), @(6), @(7)][i] integerValue] + 1;
        UIView *nextView = [self viewWithTag:xTag];
        attachment = [[UIAttachmentBehavior alloc]
            initWithItem:view attachedToItem:nextView];
        attachment.damping = _damping;
        attachment.frequency = _frequency;
        [_animator addBehavior:attachment];
    }
}
}
```

Drawing the View

UIView instances are rectangular, not gelatinous. To create a view that *looks* as if it deforms, even if the underlying view remains rectangular, you must hide each of the underlying views from Figure 6-5 and draw a unified shape that represents the adjusted skeleton. You do this by observing changes on each of the component views. When they move, which you detect by observing the center property, the jelly view needs a redraw. Listing 6-9 shows the redrawing code.

This code works by building a Bezier path from corner point to corner point to corner point. It uses the center views along each edge as control points to produce its inflected curves. Once the curved path is calculated, a standard drawRect: method fills in the curve to present the view.

Listing 6-9 **Drawing the Jelly View**

```
- (void) observeValueForKeyPath:(NSString *)keyPath
                       ofObject:(id)object
                         change:(NSDictionary *)change
                        context:(void *)context
{
    // Update whenever a child view center changes
    [self setNeedsDisplay];
}

- (UIBezierPath *) cornerCurve
{
    // Build a series of quad curve elements from point to point to point
    UIBezierPath *path = [UIBezierPath bezierPath];
    UIView *v0 = [self viewWithTag:1];
    [path moveToPoint:v0.center];

    // The corner points are view destinations.
    // The centers act as control points.
    NSArray *destinations = @[@(2), @(8), @(6), @(0)];
    NSArray *controlPoints = @[@(1), @(5), @(7), @(3)];

    for (int i = 0; i < 4; i++)
    {
        NSInteger dTag = [destinations[i] integerValue] + 1;
        NSInteger cTag = [controlPoints[i] integerValue] + 1;
        UIView *vd = [self viewWithTag:dTag];
        UIView *vc = [self viewWithTag:cTag];
        [path addQuadCurveToPoint:vd.center controlPoint:vc.center];
    }
    return path;
}

- (void) drawRect:(CGRect)rect
{
    // Build the curves and draw the shape
    [_color set];
    [[self cornerCurve] fill];
}
```

Deploying Jelly

While the jelly view is fun to create, deploy with care. Most users have a fixed limit of patience. Any dynamic elements will tend to run longer in presentation and dismissal than standard system-supplied UI elements. They have more complicated visual stories to tell. Because of this, you might need to trade off the cool visual flourishes that excite a developer if you want to put the user experience first. A jelly-based alert may be exciting to develop, but an overly long alert that takes precious seconds to settle may add one-star reviews to your product.

A user will not be able to tell if your app was developed using UIKit, OpenGL, Cocos2D, or SpriteKit. Just because you can now do exciting dynamics in UIKit is not sufficient reason to include those solutions. Your apps must defer to and serve the needs of your users rather than pad your resume and augment your portfolio. Keep this in mind and use dynamic animators sparingly.

Wrap-up

Here are final points to wrap up what you've read in this chapter:

- Dynamic animators and behaviors are like a UI building toy set. They are enormously fun to work with and produce a really great range of results. I best like interactions that direct the user to natural results like the snap zones shown in Listing 6-3 and ones that provide a user-based experience like the device gravity that coordinates with a motion manager in Listing 6-4.

- Although it's easy to get super-flashy with all the built-in physics, some of the best effects are the subtlest. It's the little flourishes—such as bounces when views enter and leave a screen, or collisions when collection items interact with each other—that produce the best results.

- Layering and coordinating behaviors can stylize and customize the otherwise default animations. The scaling, stacking, and rotation I added for Figure 6-2 help send the message that these items have been "put away."

- Some things you might not initially think of as behaviors can turn out to be super-handy. You saw this with the "watcher" behavior in Listing 6-2. Although this custom behavior doesn't introduce any view changes, it helps tune the dynamic system to produce greater responsiveness.

- Always consider behavior lifetimes. You should clean up after your behaviors if they're short lived and retain them if they persist.

- Sometimes it's simpler to create basic and keyframe animations like the ones you saw in Chapter 5, "Animation," than to implement dynamic behaviors with the associated overhead.

7

Presentations

iOS's adaptive redesign brings presentation elements into a new generation. User alerts are re-imagined, and popovers are now universally available, not just on tablets. Special effects highlight presentations to provide the greatest visual impact when you overlay content for modal interaction. This chapter introduces several of the presentation changes you'll work with. You'll read about the new alert controller class and about the mask and view effects that support presentation styling. You'll also learn how to create phone-style popovers.

Alerts

Alerts benefited from a full redesign in iOS 8. The UIAlertController class provides one-stop shopping for your user messaging needs, deprecating older UIAlertView and UIActionSheet calls. This redesign moves toward Apple's class origins—the alert view and action sheet were once a single class—and picks up the essential modern extras of completion blocks.

In addition, the new API provides simpler implementation details. In keeping with adaptive themes, it is suitable for use on both tablets and phones. You no longer need to worry about how and where items are presented. Instead, you focus on alert contents and responses to user interactions. Yes, there are still a few platform-specific implementation details to take into account, as discussed in this chapter, but you'll discover that the move toward universal deployment continues forward for presentation items.

Class Deprecations

Both UIAlertView and UIActionSheet class header files urge you to update your implementation, as you see in the following excerpts pulled from UIKit framework headers:

```
// UIAlertView is deprecated. Use UIAlertController with a preferredStyle of
UIAlertControllerStyleAlert instead
// UIActionSheet is deprecated. Use UIAlertController with a preferredStyle
of UIAlertControllerStyleActionSheet instead
```

> **Note**
>
> While discussing deprecations, it's worth noting that Swift prevents you from using APIs depre-cated as of iOS 7 and earlier in your apps.

Building Alerts

The `UIAlertController` class builds universal user cross-platform alerts for iOS 8-and-later targets. Using this new class involves the following steps:

1. **Use class constructors to create a new controller instance.** Supply a primary title and message and indicate the kind of alert to build. Choose from `UIAlertControllerStyle-Alert` for pop-up alerts or `UIAlertControllerStyleActionSheet` to prompt users to select from a set of choices:

   ```
   UIAlertController *controller = [UIAlertController
       alertControllerWithTitle:@"Title" message:@"Message"
       preferredStyle:UIAlertControllerStyleAlert];
   if (!controller) {
       NSLog(@"Unable to create controller");
       return;
   }
   ```

   Once they are instantiated, both styles use identical customization steps.

2. **Establish a weak reference to the controller.** This reference enables you to dismiss the controller in completion blocks and refer to its properties for text field access:

   ```
   __weak typeof(controller) weakController = controller;
   ```

   Each handler block accepts one parameter, the `UIAlertAction` object itself. The strong/weak approach used in this example eliminates reference cycles. You do not want to use `self` within blocks because the instance may be holding onto the block at the same time that the block is holding on to `self`. This creates a memory release nightmare. Instead, use a weak reference workaround. This enables you to access `self`'s properties while avoiding reference cycles.

   Assigning a weak reference to a strong one, as you see here, holds on to that reference. If that `self` view controller reference still exists and is still valid when the handler block begins execution, assigning it immediately to a strong variable reference, as you see in the next step, retains it throughout the block's lifetime.

3. **Build actions.** Each action describes a button and its handler block. The action controller uses these actions to construct its presentation and respond to touches. As all actions belong to a single `UIAlertAction` class, their associated style tells the action controller how to present and handle each item. Actions use default (`UIAlertActionStyleDefault`), cancel (`UIAlertActionStyleCancel`), and destructive (`UIAlertActionStyleDestructive`) styles:

```
UIAlertAction *defaultAction = [UIAlertAction
    actionWithTitle:@"Default"
    style:UIAlertActionStyleDefault
    handler:^(UIAlertAction *action) {
        __strong typeof(controller) strongController = weakController;
        // Perform action here
        [strongController dismissViewControllerAnimated:YES completion:nil];
    }];
```

A cancel item should dismiss the controller without taking further action. Destructive items may change or delete data. Default items present plain actions without additional meaning. Make sure each handler dismisses the controller as its final step.

4. **Add the actions to the controller.** For the most part, the order in which you add the actions specifies the order used to present items. If you add a cancel action and then a default action to an action style controller (see Figure 7-1), the cancel appears to the left:

```
[controller addAction:cancelAction];
[controller addAction:defaultAction];
```

Reverse this order, and the cancel appears to the right. This changes when you add a third action. Alerts with three actions display vertically with stacked buttons. In that case, the cancel button follows its siblings and automatically appears at the bottom.

Figure 7-1   Alert button order depends on the `addAction:` sequence used to populate an action controller. These alerts present identically on tablets and phones.

With action sheets in their default phone presentation, the cancel button always appears at the bottom and is physically spaced away from other items (see Figure 7-2, left). In popover presentations, the cancel button is omitted. Users tap on the background to dismiss the sheet without selecting an item (see Figure 7-2, right).

You can now add destructive items to pop-up alerts as well as action sheets. They appear in red, as they did traditionally in action sheets; in the screen shown in Figure 7-3, the Destructive Action button text displays in red on a real device.

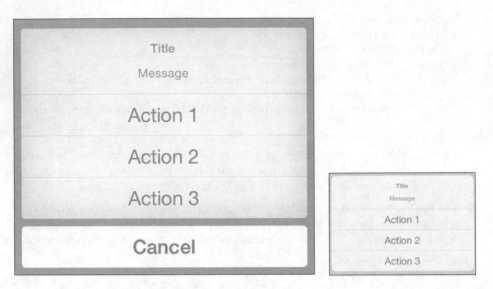

Figure 7-2   When using action sheets on phone destinations, the cancel button is always set apart from actions. Cancel buttons do not appear on tablets. You can use at most one cancel action per sheet or alert.

Figure 7-3   Red button text indicates a destructive action. The red text helps users identify which actions might change or delete data. The "Destructive Action" choice in this screenshot normally appears in red, which you won't see in the printed book.

You may add any number of default or destructive items to your action controllers, but you add no more than one cancel item at a time. Multiple cancel buttons raise a runtime exception ('UIAlertController can only have one action with a style of UIAlertActionStyleCancel').

5. **When working with action sheets on the iPad, set a view or bar button item and an arrow direction.** Without arrow direction, the popover presents randomly on the screen. You can set these properties on phone targets without cost, so it's always a good choice to add these directives to your code:

```
controller.popoverPresentationController.barButtonItem =
    self.navigationItem.rightBarButtonItem;
controller.popoverPresentationController.permittedArrowDirections =
    UIPopoverArrowDirectionAny;
```

Popover presentation controllers and their features are explored in more depth later in this chapter.

6. **Present the controller.** When the user taps a button, the action item's associated completion block fires, taking responsibility for handling that tap and dismissing the controller:

```
[self presentViewController:controller animated:YES completion:nil];
```

Listing 7-1 builds and presents a trivial action sheet that showcases all the steps used to build these elements in a single method.

Listing 7-1   **Building and Presenting Action Controllers**

```
- (void) presentActionSheet
{
    // Build the controller
    UIAlertController *controller =
        [UIAlertController alertControllerWithTitle:@"Title"
            message:@"Message"
            preferredStyle:UIAlertControllerStyleActionSheet];
    if (!controller) {
        NSLog(@"Unable to create controller");
        return;
    }

    // Establish weak reference
    __weak typeof(controller) weakController = controller;

    // Build actions
    UIAlertAction *action1 = [UIAlertAction actionWithTitle:@"Action 1"
```

```objc
    style:UIAlertActionStyleDefault handler:^(UIAlertAction *action) {
    __strong typeof(controller) strongController = weakController;
    NSLog(@"Action1: %@", action);
    [strongController dismissViewControllerAnimated:YES completion:nil];
}];

UIAlertAction *action2 = [UIAlertAction actionWithTitle:@"Action 2"
    style:UIAlertActionStyleDefault handler:^(UIAlertAction *action) {
    __strong typeof(controller) strongController = weakController;
    NSLog(@"Action2: %@", action);
    [strongController dismissViewControllerAnimated:YES completion:nil];
}];

UIAlertAction *destructive1 = [UIAlertAction
    actionWithTitle:@"Destructive Action"
    style:UIAlertActionStyleDestructive handler:^(UIAlertAction *action) {
    __strong typeof(controller) strongController = weakController;
    NSLog(@"Destruct1: %@", action);
    [strongController dismissViewControllerAnimated:YES completion:nil];
}];

UIAlertAction *destructive2 = [UIAlertAction
    actionWithTitle:@"Destructive Action2"
    style:UIAlertActionStyleDestructive handler:^(UIAlertAction *action) {
    __strong typeof(controller) strongController = weakController;
    NSLog(@"Destruct2: %@", action);
    [strongController dismissViewControllerAnimated:YES completion:nil];
}];

UIAlertAction *cancelAction = [UIAlertAction
    actionWithTitle:@"Cancel" style:UIAlertActionStyleCancel
    handler:^(UIAlertAction *action) {
    __strong typeof(controller) strongController = weakController;
    NSLog(@"Cancel Action: %@", action);
    [strongController dismissViewControllerAnimated:YES completion:nil];
}];

// Add actions in order (Cancel will pop to end)
[controller addAction:action1];
[controller addAction:action2];
[controller addAction:destructive1];
[controller addAction:destructive2];
[controller addAction:cancelAction];

// Customize popover presentations
controller.popoverPresentationController.barButtonItem =
    self.navigationItem.rightBarButtonItem;
```

```
controller.popoverPresentationController.permittedArrowDirections =
    UIPopoverArrowDirectionAny;

// Present controller
[self presentViewController:controller animated:YES completion:nil];
}
```

Enabling and Disabling Alert Buttons

The new generation of alerts introduces an `enabled` property for actions. Figure 7-4 demonstrates the strength and weakness of this new feature. When used with default action items, it provides a consistent button context. You present an alert whose grayed-out items indicate choices that might otherwise be available. This creates a predictable interface with buttons always appearing in the same positions, regardless of whether they're enabled.

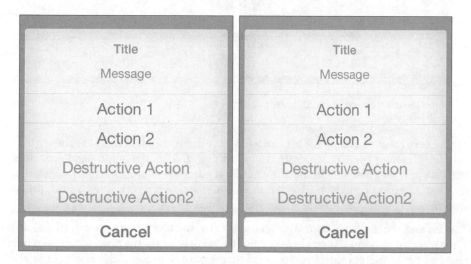

Figure 7-4   In the right-hand version, both Action 1 and the first Destructive Action have been disabled. Disabled destructive items are visually indistinguishable from their enabled counterparts, which may baffle users.

The action item marked Destructive Action in Figure 7-4 showcases this property's weakness. Although this action is disabled in the right screen shot, the destructive item presents no visual indication that user touches will be ignored. Users may confuse this deliberately disabled item with a broken application, which is never a good thing for overall app ratings.

Because of this, limit your disabled buttons to `UIAlertActionStyleDefault` items only. If you *must* disable a destructive action, consider modifying its text to indicate that the option is not available or simply leave it out. This breaks the "same everywhere, all the time" pattern but may diminish end-user confusion.

Adding Text Fields

Text fields extend alerts to enable users to enter prompted information such as user credentials or other application-specific text. Figure 7-5 shows an example of alert controller text entry. As with iOS 7 and earlier, you're limited to the alert style presentation for this feature. However, as Listing 7-2 demonstrates, the process of creating and accessing text fields is far cleaner and more intuitive than in earlier systems.

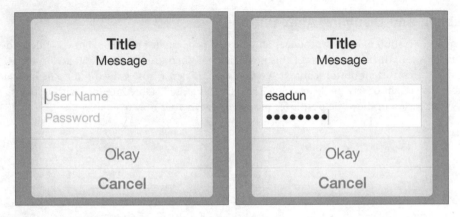

Figure 7-5   Text fields are stacked in alert controllers.

You build text fields by adding them to an action controller using addTextFieldWith-ConfigurationHandler:, as demonstrated in Listing 7-2. A configuration handler enables you to initialize and set up each field. Here is where you establish secure text entry, add placeholder text, adjust fonts and correction styles, and so forth. If you're pre-populating a field, the configuration handler creates the context where you set those values.

You access and process fields from your action handler, the block that responds to user actions with meaningful responses. It's a mystery why the handler passes the (useless) action parameter instead of a (very useful) controller. You need that controller to access the textFields array property to retrieve each text field. The fields appear in the array in the order in which you added them. In this example, the name field is item 0, and the password field is item 1.

Listing 7-2   **Building Alert Text Fields**

```
- (void) go
{
    // Text fields work only with alerts, not action sheets
    // "You can add a text field only if the preferredStyle
    // property is set to UIAlertControllerStyleAlert."
    UIAlertController *controller = [UIAlertController
        alertControllerWithTitle:@"Title" message:@"Message"
        preferredStyle:UIAlertControllerStyleAlert];
```

```objc
    if (!controller) {
        NSLog(@"Unable to create controller");
        return;
    }

    __weak typeof(controller) weakController = controller;

    // Handle successful entry
    UIAlertAction *okAction = [UIAlertAction actionWithTitle:@"Okay"
        style:UIAlertActionStyleDefault handler:^(UIAlertAction *action) {
        __strong typeof(controller) strongController = weakController;
        UITextField *nameField = strongController.textFields[0];
        UITextField *passField = strongController.textFields[1];
        NSLog(@"Name %@", nameField.text);
        NSLog(@"Pass %@", passField.text);
        [strongController dismissViewControllerAnimated:YES completion:nil];
    }];

    // Handle cancel
    UIAlertAction *cancelAction = [UIAlertAction actionWithTitle:@"Cancel"
        style:UIAlertActionStyleCancel handler:^(UIAlertAction *action) {
        __strong typeof(controller) strongController = weakController;
        [strongController dismissViewControllerAnimated:YES completion:nil];
    }];

    // Add user name field
    [controller addTextFieldWithConfigurationHandler:^(UITextField *textField) {
        textField.placeholder = @"User Name";
        textField.autocapitalizationType = UITextAutocapitalizationTypeNone;
        textField.autocorrectionType = UITextAutocorrectionTypeNo;
    }];

    // Add password field
    [controller addTextFieldWithConfigurationHandler:^(UITextField *textField) {
        textField.placeholder = @"Password";
        textField.autocapitalizationType = UITextAutocapitalizationTypeNone;
        textField.autocorrectionType = UITextAutocorrectionTypeNo;
        textField.secureTextEntry = YES;
    }];

    // Install both actions
    [controller addAction:okAction];
    [controller addAction:cancelAction];

    // Present
    [self presentViewController:controller animated:YES completion:nil];
}
```

Mask Views

You've now read about creating and presenting alerts, which overlay content with modal, inter-active dialogs. Presentations that integrate with the material behind them aren't limited to OK/Cancel interactions. Mask views are an important part of the presentation story, creating ways to display content while retaining a fundamental tie to the most recently shown views that lie beneath them.

iOS 8 introduced `UIView maskView` properties. These properties enable you to create shaped views, commonly used in presentations to adapt overlays with visual material that lies beneath. Both edge adjustments and integrated holes provide views that better merge with material that lies below the view itself, allowing another feature of adaptive display.

Mask functionality is not new. If you've used shape layers, you've already encountered more or less the same feature under new APIs. The updated calls are, however, fragile enough that the `maskView` property probably shouldn't have made the cut for iOS 8. Because of this, this section reviews both the time-tested and new methods for masking.

Shape Layer Masking

Listing 7-3 shows a shape layer approach to creating round image views. This class masks a view by using an oval `CAShapeLayer`. Despite some fiddly bits—namely the key-value observing used to detect bounds changes—this implementation is robust and time tested.

This approach works by assigning a shape layer mask to a view's primary layer. An underlying Bezier path establishes the mask boundaries. When used with well-chosen paths (built around curves rather than pixels), this approach produces smooth masking, regardless of the size of the parent or the shape of the mask; you could easily extend the class in Listing 7-3 to mask with any Bezier path, not just round ones.

Masks do not naturally scale with the parent. Key-Value Observing catches bounds changes. This lets you respond with a dynamically sized mask that consistently matches the view frame.

Listing 7-3 **Shape Layer Masking**

```
@implementation RoundedImageView
// Fit the shape to the new bounds
- (void) updateLayer
{
    if (CGSizeEqualToSize(self.bounds.size, CGSizeZero))
        return;
    CGFloat minimum = fminf(self.bounds.size.width, self.bounds.size.height);
    UIBezierPath *path = [UIBezierPath
        bezierPathWithOvalInRect:CGRectMake(
            CGRectGetMidX(self.bounds) - minimum / 2.0,
            CGRectGetMidY(self.bounds) - minimum / 2.0, minimum, minimum)];
```

```objc
    CAShapeLayer *maskLayer = [CAShapeLayer layer];
    maskLayer.path = path.CGPath;
    self.layer.mask = maskLayer;
}


// Update on bounds changes
- (void) observeValueForKeyPath:(NSString *)keyPath
                       ofObject:(id)object
                         change:(NSDictionary *)change
                        context:(void *)context
{
    if ([keyPath isEqualToString:@"bounds"])
        [self updateLayer];
}


- (void) setup
{
    // Listen for bounds changes
    [self addObserver:self forKeyPath:@"bounds"
        options:NSKeyValueObservingOptionNew context:NULL];
}


// Handle all likely inits

- (instancetype) initWithImage:(UIImage *)image
   highlightedImage:(UIImage *)highlightedImage
{
    if (!(self = [super initWithImage:image
        highlightedImage:highlightedImage])) return self;
    [self setup];
    return self;
}

- (instancetype) initWithImage:(UIImage *)image
{
    if (!(self = [super initWithImage:image])) return self;
    [self setup];
    return self;
}

- (instancetype) initWithFrame:(CGRect)frame
{
    return [self initWithImage:nil];
}
```

```
// Clean up on dealloc
- (void) dealloc
{
    [self removeObserver:self forKeyPath:@"bounds"];
}
@end
```

Building Mask Views

UIView introduced the maskView property in iOS 8. This is essentially a subview whose alpha levels established which pixels to show on the parent. View pixels corresponding to transparent mask pixels get clipped, while nontransparent ones show through. This creates a masked result equivalent to Listing 7-3, using UIView assignment. Masks enable you to create clipping that goes beyond simple shapes and can include embedded holes.

As you can tell from Listing 7-4, view masking relies just as heavily on key-value bounds observing as the shape layer. Without this step, masking uses the default size of the mask view—however big or small—often with unexpected, unpleasant, and incorrect results. You cannot use Auto Layout to tie the two together or just connect the mask view property to a child view.

What you're left with is Listing 7-4, which bears a strong resemblance to Listing 7-3, with its KVO approach. As the parent view updates its size, its mask view dynamically adjusts to match. Because of this mask management, the MaskedImageView class proactively hides its maskView property. It offers a custom maskImage property instead. Assignments to this property create and update the internal mask view, enabling it to grow and shrink with the parent's display.

What you're left with is a solution that's neither as robust nor as simple as the shape layer approach. That's because:

- Mask views are more vulnerable to content mode changes both for the view that masks and the view being masked. As content size scales, coordinating those changes with a second view is far more difficult than adjusting a Bezier path. Use particular care here.

- Even when working with a one-to-one correlation between mask pixels and parent pixels, this may not persist during device orientation changes.

- Any content that does not stretch edge-to-edge in the mask may cause extra, unintended clipping on the parent.

- Mask images at low resolution may produce pixilated clipping effects in the parent, unlike resolution-independent vector clipping used by shape layers.

The bottom line: I prefer vectors for clipping. Using bitmap clipping isn't as clean, isn't as reliable, and isn't as predictable as the vector solution.

Listing 7-4   **Masking with Views**

```objc
@interface MaskedImageView ()
@property (nonatomic, readonly) UIImageView *internalMaskView;
@end

@implementation MaskedImageView

#pragma mark - Bounds observing
- (void) updateMask
{
    self.internalMaskView.frame = self.bounds;
}

- (void) observeValueForKeyPath:(NSString *)keyPath
                       ofObject:(id)object
                         change:(NSDictionary *)change
                        context:(void *)context
{
    if ([keyPath isEqualToString:@"bounds"])
        [self updateMask];
}


- (void) dealloc
{
    [self removeObserver:self forKeyPath:@"bounds"];
}

#pragma mark - Hide mask view from external consumption

- (void) setMaskView:(UIView *)maskView
{
    // no op.
    NSLog(@"Mask view is not externally settable");
}

- (UIView *) maskView
{
    // no op.
    NSLog(@"Mask view is not externally settable");
    return nil;
}

// Provide internal access only
- (UIImageView *) internalMaskView
{
```

```objc
        return (UIImageView *) super.maskView;
}

- (void) setMaskImage:(UIImage *)maskImage
{
    if (!maskImage)
    {
        super.maskView = nil;
        return;
    }

    if (!self.internalMaskView)
    {
        UIImageView *imageView = [UIImageView new];
        imageView.contentMode = UIViewContentModeScaleAspectFit;
        super.maskView = imageView;
    }
    self.internalMaskView.image = maskImage;
    [self updateMask];
}

- (UIImage *) maskImage
{
    return self.internalMaskView.image;
}

#pragma mark - Initializers

- (void) setup
{
    // Default content mode is aspect fit
    self.contentMode = UIViewContentModeScaleAspectFit;

    // Listen for bounds changes
    [self addObserver:self forKeyPath:@"bounds"
        options:NSKeyValueObservingOptionNew context:NULL];
}

- (instancetype) initWithImage:(UIImage *)image
    highlightedImage:(UIImage *)highlightedImage
{
    if (!(self = [super initWithImage:image
        highlightedImage:highlightedImage])) return self;
    [self setup];
    return self;
}
```

```
- (instancetype) initWithImage:(UIImage *)image
{
    if (!(self = [super initWithImage:image])) return self;
    [self setup];
    return self;
}

- (instancetype) initWithFrame:(CGRect)frame
{
    return [self initWithImage:nil];
}
@end
```

Building Effect Views

The `UIVisualEffectView` class introduced in iOS 8 provides a simple view abstraction for visual effects. These effects pick up hints from the views they overlay. As with masks, this technology brings presented material more closely into the world of its parent screens, the backgrounds they're shown over. Figure 7-6 showcases two distinct visual effects combined into an effect view overlay.

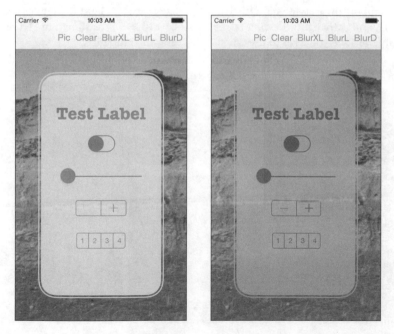

Figure 7-6   Blurring (left) and vibrancy (right) are now built into the iOS API. A blur softens background pixels. Vibrancy picks up and enhances the colors behind a blur.

Background image courtesy of the National Park Service.

The primary effect is a blur. A blur obscures details behind a view to offer barely distinct color traces that bleed through to provide visual context. In these examples, the blur picks up elements of the pixels from the picture of the Agate Fossil Beds used as a backdrop. Although it is hard to see this in a black-and-white book, the prevailing color of the background image and the strongest visual elements are preserved and can be perceived by the user.

A vibrancy effect amplifies and adjusts the presentation color. In Figure 7-6, it applies that color to a set of sample controls, including a label, a switch, and a slider. If you're reading this book on paper rather than in an e-book, you can best see that effect by testing the sample code that accompanies this chapter. That hue derives from the vibrancy effect's parent blur effect. You always configure your vibrancy effect with respect to a blur effect.

Building a Blur Effect

You create a blur by instantiating an effect, installing it to a custom view, and adding the view to your presentation. The steps go like this:

1. **Create a blur instance.** Blurs belong to the `UIBlurEffect` class. This is a concrete subclass of the abstract `UIVisualEffect` class. An effect transforms content placed behind a view. You build a new effect like this:

   ```
   blur = [UIBlurEffect effectWithStyle:UIBlurEffectStyleDark];
   ```

   Blurs support three styles: dark (`UIBlurEffectStyleDark`), light (`UIBlurEffectStyle-Light`), and extra light (`UIBlurEffectStyleExtraLight`), as shown in Figure 7-7. Supply the style you wish to use when initializing the blur effect.

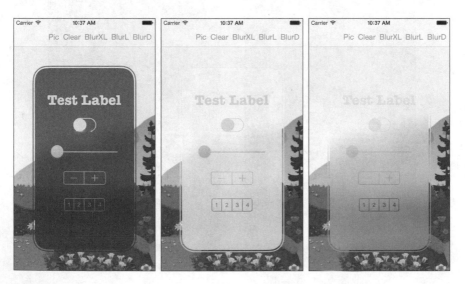

Figure 7-7   These screen shots show dark, light, and extra light blur effects.

Background image courtesy of Glitch the Game (http://glitchthegame.com) public domain assets.

2. **Install the blur effect to an effect view.** Build a new effect view instance and initialize it with the blur you just created:

```
blurView = [[UIVisualEffectView alloc] initWithEffect:blur];
```

3. **Add the blur view to your interface**.

Use blur views sparingly and meaningfully. If using mask views, as in this example, follow the KVO practices from the preceding section to ensure that the mask properly adjusts during resize and layout.

Adding Vibrancy Effects

The vibrancy effect you've seen enables you to embed controls into a blurred overlay to create a seamless blend of functionality with background color cues. Although Apple doesn't provide specific guidance about integrating controls with vibrancy, limit this use to monochrome controls. Figure 7-8 demonstrates why. When enabled (set to ON), a switch oval can no longer be casually distinguished. Compare Figure 7-8 with Figure 7-7. The switch loses its visual role and usage hints.

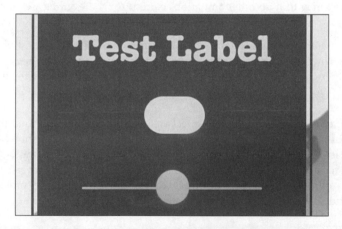

Figure 7-8   Non-monochrome controls lose distinguishing information when used with vibrancy effects.

Build vibrancy effects with respect to blurs. In the following example, the vibrancy effect picks up and adjusts its hues based on the parent blur:

```
UIVibrancyEffect *vibrancy = [UIVibrancyEffect effectForBlurEffect:blur];
vibrancyView = [[UIVisualEffectView alloc] initWithEffect:vibrancy];
[blurView.contentView addSubview:vibrancyView];
```

After creating the vibrancy view, you add it to the blur view's `contentView`. Make sure you lay out the blur view, whether with Auto Layout (recommended) or by manually setting its frame.

To participate in the vibrancy effect, add subviews to the vibrancy view's `contentView`, as in the following example:

```
for (UIView *view in @[testLabel, theSwitch, slider, stepper, segment])
{
    [vibrancyView.contentView addSubview:view];
}
```

When a view is owned this way, the vibrancy view controls its presentation. You can opt out of the vibrancy effect on a view-by-view basis. Add your views to the parent blur view's content view instead of the vibrancy view's content view.

Using Auto Layout remains the best way to lay out subviews within either effect's content view.

Animating Effect Views

Effect views are somewhat brittle. You may encounter animation errors when attempting to animate these views directly. For example, effect views cannot animate their opacity. A quick search on the web may turn up other limitations current to whatever release you're working with.

Normally you work around such issues by taking a screen shot of a view and then animating the screen shot. With effect views, workarounds like screen shots may also present problems, as in Figure 7-9. The right-hand screen shot was created using the following standard API:

```
UIView *newView = [blurView snapshotViewAfterScreenUpdates:YES];
```

It's not practical to avoid animations with effect views. Animation creates fluid transitions for users, helping them mentally move from one state to another. Listing 7-5 showcases both the broken effect (case 3) and a workaround (case 0). This workaround screen shows the main interface and uses it to hide the new effect view. Fading the screen shot away reveals the effect view as if it had been animated into view. The other two examples in Listing 7-5 provide examples that translate and scale an effect view into place.

Figure 7-9 Effect views can be difficult to animate in some cases. Screen shot workarounds may return artifacts when captured, such as the label edges shown in the right screen shot or other improperly blended elements.

Background image courtesy of Glitch the Game (http://glitchthegame.com) public domain assets.

Listing 7-5   Animating Effect Views

```
- (void) go: (UIBarButtonItem *) bbi
{
    [self buildBlurView];
    NSInteger choice = [self.navigationItem.rightBarButtonItems
        indexOfObject:bbi];
    switch (choice) {
        case 0:
        {
            // Screen shot main view with the blur view hidden
            blurView.hidden = YES;
            UIView *newView = [self.view snapshotViewAfterScreenUpdates:YES];
            blurView.hidden = NO;
            [self.view addSubview:newView];
```

```
        [UIView animateWithDuration:1 animations:^{
            newView.alpha = 0.0;
        } completion:^(BOOL finished) {
            [newView removeFromSuperview];
        }];
        break;
    }
    case 1:
    {
        // Scale
        blurView.transform = CGAffineTransformMakeScale(0.001, 0.001);
        [UIView animateWithDuration:1 animations:^{
            blurView.transform = CGAffineTransformIdentity;
        }];
        break;
    }
    case 2:
    {
        // Translate
        [NSLayoutConstraint deactivateConstraints:
            blurView.externalConstraintReferences];
        PlaceViewInSuperview(blurView, @"tc", 0, -500, 1000);
        [self.view layoutIfNeeded];
        [NSLayoutConstraint deactivateConstraints:
            blurView.externalConstraintReferences];

        [UIView animateWithDuration:1 animations:^{
            PlaceViewInSuperview(blurView, @"cc", 0, 0, 1000);
            [self.view layoutIfNeeded];
        }];
        break;
    }
    case 3:
    {
        // broken
        blurView.alpha = 0.0;
        [UIView animateWithDuration:1.0 animations:^{
            blurView.alpha = 1.0;
        }];
    }
    default:
        break;
    }
}
```

Building Popovers

iOS 8 soft-deprecated the standard popover classes, replacing them with its new presentation controller system. Popovers are now universal and can be used on both phone and tablet targets, as shown in Figure 7-10. While this approach provides a lot more power, it also changes the process of building and presenting simple popovers.

Figure 7-10   Popovers now work on both phone (left) and tablet (right) targets.

A view controller's popover identity is now set as a modal presentation style, as you see in Listing 7-6. When you set the style to popover, the view controller knows to create an internal popover presentation controller. You customize this the same way you used to customize single-purpose popover controllers: Set the source view or bar button item, arrow directions, layout margins, background color, and so forth.

Listing 7-6   **Building an iPhone-Ready Popover**

```
- (UIViewController *) buildPopoverController
{
    // Build a view controller
    UIViewController *vc = [UIViewController new];
```

```
    // ... set up the contents here ...

    // Set its presentation style to popover
    vc.modalPresentationStyle = UIModalPresentationPopover;

    // Establish presentation details
    vc.preferredContentSize = CGSizeMake(200, 200);
    vc.popoverPresentationController.barButtonItem =
        self.navigationItem.rightBarButtonItem;
    vc.popoverPresentationController.permittedArrowDirections =
        UIPopoverArrowDirectionAny;
    vc.presentationController.delegate = self; // 1

    return vc;
}

- (UIModalPresentationStyle)adaptivePresentationStyleForPresentationController:
    (UIPresentationController *)controller // 2
{
    return UIModalPresentationNone;
}
```

At this writing, the popover content size is still a little wonky, which is why Listing 7-6 sets the old-style `preferredContentSize` property as well.

Supporting Bubbles

The default phone popover implementation does not look like Figure 7-10. It is a standard slide-up modal presentation that covers the parent. While a well-written adaptive app should involve code that you write once and that behaves properly on whatever device it's deployed to, I'm not entirely convinced that the default phone "popover" presentation is either aesthetically pleasing or expected. If you want to get the content-in-a-bubble you see in Figure 7-10, you must take care to follow these steps.

1. Set the popover view controller's delegate, as shown in Listing 7-6 on the line marked with the number 1. The delegate must conform to the `UIAdaptivePresentationControllerDelegate` protocol.

2. Implement the adaptive style callback (numbered 2) in the delegate. By returning `UIModalPresentationNone`, you override the normal presentation style that covers the parent controller.

Every view controller contains two presentation controllers: a vanilla `presentation-Controller` and a specialized `popoverPresentationController`. The popover version is created once you set a view controller's presentation style to `UIModalPresentationPopover`. You then access and customize its features.

The default controller lingers until you tell it to step back via the delegation. You cannot set the presentationController's presentation style directly. It's a read-only property, so you must use the delegation implementation instead.

Although the unified presentation system represents a big step forward on the overall iOS design front, using separate internal controllers for normal and popover presentations fails to impress. This feature may have been a rush job that lacked time for refinement and refactoring before iOS 8 shipped to developers.

Presenting Popovers

Starting in iOS 8, popover creation details moved to the child view controller. This means presentation code is simplified to the bare minimum, as you see in the following snippet. You simply create your popover-ready view controller, as in Listing 7-6, and then present as shown here:

```
UIViewController *presentationVC = [self buildPopoverController];
[self presentViewController:presentationVC animated:YES completion:nil];
```

Wrap-up

Here are a few final points to wrap up what you've read in this chapter:

- Despite some wobbly implementation details, the presentations first introduced in iOS 8 are incredibly promising. They represent a long-overdue rethinking of how to present critical elements to users. Providing blocks-based action buttons is one of my favorite presentation features.

- While you can customize a popover action sheet by setting its arrow direction and anchor view or bar button, you cannot at this time present popover action sheets on phone targets. Attempting to do so by overriding the delegate raises exceptions.

- Use effect views and mask views with care. Although they are visually luscious, I'm told by reliable sources that the internal implementation is held together by spit and bandages.

8

Shape Magic

Shaping views goes beyond the simple cropping and mask layers you've read about so far. Nonrectangular views enable your apps to expand possibilities with fun and clever effects. For example, you might draw attention to a view by animating a halo behind it. Or you might use shapes to better stack buttons together for visual seamlessness. This chapter covers many advanced shape techniques you can use to add this pizzazz to your user interfaces.

How to Shape a View

A round view clips its presentation into a circular shape. Contrast the two screen shots in Figure 8-1. View clipping differentiates these otherwise identical layouts. Removing corners changes the way the onscreen elements pack together, enhancing whitespace while retaining the key visual story of the material they present.

You can create round views using one of the following approaches:

- A `CAShapeLayer` masks a view's underlying layer. You assign it to `view.layer.mask`. This is a time-tested robust solution.

- A view's `maskView` property stores an image view. The alpha levels in the associated image establish the view's mask. This solution is quite new and still slightly less robust than you might like.

- You can round the corners of a view's layer (`view.layer.cornerRadius`) to half the view's extent, producing a nicely circled output. While this solution has been around forever, it's really only useful for circles and rounded rectangles. It cannot be generalized to most other shapes.

All three approaches are vulnerable to frame changes. Regardless of your choice, adding a key-value observer to monitor a view's `bounds` enables you to update a view as needed when it resizes.

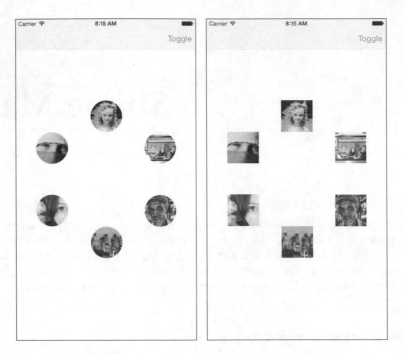

Figure 8-1   Two identical layouts using round (left) and square (right) presentation elements. Round image views help visually de-clutter your interface.

Sample pictures courtesy of Lorem Pixel (http://lorempixel.com) under Creative Commons attribution share alike license (http://creativecommons.org/licenses/by-sa/3.0/). Images by Neils Photography (http://www.flickr.com/photos/neilspicys/), Rolands Lakis (http://www.flickr.com/photos/rolandslakis/), Rodrigo Basure (http://www.flickr.com/photos/rodrigobasaure/), LuzA (http://www.flickr.com/photos/luchilu/), Pink Sherbet (http://www.flickr.com/photos/pinksherbet/), Visual Panic (http://www.flickr.com/photos/visualpanic/).

Expanding Beyond Circles

Chapter 7, "Presentations," introduced RoundImageView. This class, which was used to create the items in Figure 8-1, rounds its content into a circular presentation. As Figure 8-2 suggests, there are many more shapes under the sun than just circles. By preserving the class's bounds observations but expanding the utility to work with any shape, not just circles, you create a far more flexible tool.

Resizing Bezier Paths

One of the big advantages to working with circles is simplicity. The UIBezierPath class includes a built-in constructor called bezierPathWithOvalInRect:. You pass a view's bounds to it, and it returns an oval that fits exactly within that rectangle. Limit your frames to squares, and you produce circles that fit your views as they resize. As you're about to see, arbitrary Bezier paths are not nearly as easy to work with. This is because the coordinate system for the path almost never matches up with the view. To scale a path, you translate its center to the origin of an absolute coordinate system, apply a scale transform, and then translate it into the view's coordinate system. What's more, you often want to scale the path so it does not squash or stretch in either axis. This means calculating a fitting rectangle centered within the view.

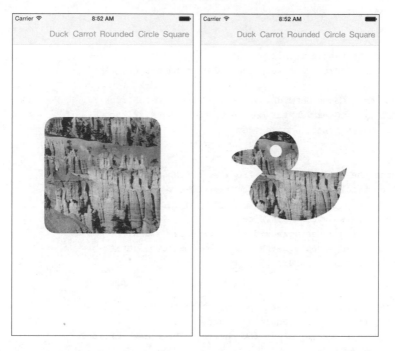

Figure 8-2   A more general view shaping class can mask views to an arbitrary Bezier path.
Background image courtesy of the National Park Service.

Listing 8-1 demonstrates the math involved in all this. I'm not going to pretend this material is exciting to look at or immediately obvious to follow. This Bezier mini pack offers just enough math to get you through the task of mapping a path to a view, enabling you to expand the `RoundImageView` example to a more general solution.

Listing 8-1   **Bezier Mini Pack**

```
// Return a rectangle's center point
CGPoint RectGetCenter(CGRect rect)
{
    return CGPointMake(CGRectGetMidX(rect), CGRectGetMidY(rect));
}

// Construct a rectangle around a center point to a given size
CGRect RectAroundCenter(CGPoint center, CGSize size)
{
```

```
    CGFloat halfWidth = size.width / 2.0;
    CGFloat halfHeight = size.height / 2.0;

    return CGRectMake(center.x - halfWidth, center.y - halfHeight,
        size.width, size.height);
}

// Center one rectangle within another
CGRect RectCenteredInRect(CGRect rect, CGRect mainRect)
{
    CGFloat dx = CGRectGetMidX(mainRect)-CGRectGetMidX(rect);
    CGFloat dy = CGRectGetMidY(mainRect)-CGRectGetMidY(rect);
    return CGRectOffset(rect, dx, dy);
}

// Determine the scale factor to fit a size within a rectangle
CGFloat AspectScaleFit(CGSize sourceSize, CGRect destRect)
{
    CGSize destSize = destRect.size;
    CGFloat scaleW = destSize.width / sourceSize.width;
    CGFloat scaleH = destSize.height / sourceSize.height;
    return fmin(scaleW, scaleH);
}

// Fit a rect into another rect, centering it in the second rect
// and using the first rectangle's aspect
CGRect RectByFittingRect(CGRect sourceRect, CGRect destinationRect)
{
    CGFloat aspect = AspectScaleFit(sourceRect.size, destinationRect);
    CGSize targetSize = CGSizeMake(sourceRect.size.width * aspect,
        sourceRect.size.height * aspect);
    return RectAroundCenter(RectGetCenter(destinationRect), targetSize);
}

// Apply a transform with respect to a path's center point
void ApplyCenteredPathTransform(UIBezierPath *path,
    CGAffineTransform transform)
{
    CGPoint center = RectGetCenter(path.bounds);
    CGAffineTransform t = CGAffineTransformIdentity;

    // Establish center as origin
    t = CGAffineTransformTranslate(t, center.x, center.y);

    // Apply transform
    t = CGAffineTransformConcat(transform, t);
```

```
    // Restore original origin
    t = CGAffineTransformTranslate(t, -center.x, -center.y);

    [path applyTransform:t];
}


// Offset a path
void OffsetPath(UIBezierPath *path, CGSize offset)
{
    CGAffineTransform t = CGAffineTransformMakeTranslation(
        offset.width, offset.height);
    ApplyCenteredPathTransform(path, t);
}


// Scale a path
void ScalePath(UIBezierPath *path, CGFloat sx, CGFloat sy)
{
    CGAffineTransform t = CGAffineTransformMakeScale(sx, sy);
    ApplyCenteredPathTransform(path, t);
}


// Move a path's center to a given point
void MovePathCenterToPoint(UIBezierPath *path, CGPoint destPoint)
{
    CGRect bounds = path.bounds;
    CGPoint p1 = bounds.origin;
    CGPoint p2 = destPoint;
    CGSize vector = CGSizeMake(p2.x - p1.x, p2.y - p1.y);
    vector.width -= bounds.size.width / 2.0;
    vector.height -= bounds.size.height / 2.0;
    OffsetPath(path, vector);
}


// Fit and center a path within a rectangle
void FitPathToRect(UIBezierPath *path, CGRect destRect)
{
    CGRect bounds = path.bounds;
    CGRect fitRect = RectByFittingRect(bounds, destRect);
    CGFloat scale = AspectScaleFit(bounds.size, destRect);

    CGPoint newCenter = RectGetCenter(fitRect);
    MovePathCenterToPoint(path, newCenter);
    ScalePath(path, scale, scale);
}
```

Building a Bezier-Based Shape Image View

Listing 8-2 leverages the path resizing from Listing 8-1 to re-imagine Chapter 7's
RoundImageView class. It introduces a UIBezierPath property called shape. Whenever this
property updates or the view bounds change, the instance recalculates its mask so it always
presents a perfect match between the latest shape and the view's size.

Beyond that change, there's not much difference between this implementation and the one
originally created for Chapter 7. These small changes enable the flexible presentations shown
in Figure 8-2.

Listing 8-2 **Shape Image View**

```
@implementation ShapeImageView

// Respond to bounds changes by updating the view mask
- (void) updateLayer
{
    if ((CGSizeEqualToSize(self.bounds.size, CGSizeZero)) || !self.shape)
    {
        self.layer.mask = nil;
        return;
    }

    // Always use a copy to minimize math errors to the original shape
    UIBezierPath *path = [_shape copy];
    FitPathToRect(path, self.bounds);

    // Create a mask
    CAShapeLayer *maskLayer = [CAShapeLayer layer];
    maskLayer.path = path.CGPath;
    self.layer.mask = maskLayer;
}

- (void) setShape:(UIBezierPath *)shape
{
    if (_shape != shape)
    {
        _shape = shape;
        [self updateLayer];
    }
}

// Use KVO to watch for bounds changes
- (void) observeValueForKeyPath:(NSString *)keyPath
                       ofObject:(id)object
                         change:(NSDictionary *)change
                        context:(void *)context
```

```
{
    if ([keyPath isEqualToString:@"bounds"])
        [self updateLayer];
}

- (void) setup
{
    // Listen for bounds changes
    [self addObserver:self forKeyPath:@"bounds"
        options:NSKeyValueObservingOptionNew context:NULL];
}

// All the init functions (initWithFrame:, initWithCoder:,
// initWithImage:, initWithImage:highlightedImage:) redirect
// to the common setup method
- (instancetype) initWithFrame:(CGRect)frame
{
    if (!(self = [super initWithFrame:frame])) return self;
    [self setup];
    return self;
}

// ... other inits ...

- (void) cleanup
{
    [self removeObserver:self forKeyPath:@"bounds"];
}

- (void) removeFromSuperview
{
    // dealloc isn't always called in time
    [self cleanup];
    [super removeFromSuperview];
}

- (void) dealloc
{
    [self cleanup];
}
@end
```

Working with Unclosed Shapes

As Figure 8-2 shows, shape layers support holes by employing what's called the "even/odd" fill rule. This algorithm tests containment by projecting a ray (a line with one fixed end that points in a given direction) from points within the path to a distant point outside it. The algorithm counts the number of times that ray crosses any line. If the ray passes through an even number of intersections, the point is outside the shape; if odd, inside. Rays starting within the duck's eye cross two borders, which means the eye is considered a hole. Other points within the duck pass through one border (if pointed away from the eye) or three (if passing through the eye), so they are filled in when applying the view mask.

With shape layers, unclosed paths are a little dangerous, as you see in the following example:

```
UIBezierPath *path = [UIBezierPath bezierPath];
[path moveToPoint:CGPointZero];
[path addLineToPoint:CGPointMake(0, 1)];
[path addLineToPoint:CGPointMake(1, 1)];
shapedImageView.shape = path;
```

What is the mask supposed to do? In theory, this shape consists of two infinitely thin lines going down from the origin and then to the right. If you run this example, you get the results shown in Figure 8-3. iOS closes the shape on your behalf and applies a triangle mask.

Figure 8-3   iOS generally closes paths on your behalf if it can do so.

Background image courtesy of the National Park Service.

But what if you remove the path segment that goes to the right, leaving only a single vertical line? You end up with an invisible view. Even closed, there's no two-dimensional content available to view.

On a similar note, imagine moving to point (1, 1) after adding the first line segment and then adding a new segment back from (1, 1) to (0, 1):

```
UIBezierPath *path = [UIBezierPath bezierPath];
[path moveToPoint:CGPointZero];
[path addLineToPoint:CGPointMake(0, 1)];
```

```
[path moveToPoint:CGPointMake(1, 1)];
[path addLineToPoint:CGPointMake(0, 1)];
```

Once again, you end up with an invisible view. Although this shape is "equivalent" from a human perspective, to iOS it represents two distinct subpaths, and neither subpath creates a fill region.

Adding Borders to Shaped Views

The built-in layer border style is fixed to rectangular views, as you see in Figure 8-4. You cannot update a shaped view's `borderWidth` and `borderColor` properties and expect them to work with custom presentations like this. Fortunately, it's fairly easy to build a solution that adapts to the shapes and sizes of a parent view.

Figure 8-4   Standard layer borders (left) support only rectangular views and path-based sublayers to create custom borders that fit shaped views (right).

Background image courtesy of the National Park Service.

The solution starts by adding two new properties to the view that mimic the look and feel of the layer properties. I took the liberty of using a `UIColor` property instead of a `CGColor` one to better match the UIKit view class:

```
@interface ShapeImageView : UIImageView
@property (nonatomic) UIBezierPath *shape;
@property (nonatomic) UIColor *borderColor;
@property (nonatomic) CGFloat borderWidth;
@end
```

These properties force the view's layer to update when their values change. This ensures that the view always reflects the current border color and width settings:

```
- (void) setBorderColor: (UIColor *)borderColor
{
    if (![borderColor isEqual:_borderColor])
    {
        _borderColor = borderColor;
        [self updateLayer];
    }
}

- (void) setBorderWidth:(CGFloat)borderWidth
{
    if (borderWidth != _borderWidth)
    {
        _borderWidth = borderWidth;
        [self updateLayer];
    }
}
```

Listing 8-3 tells the rest of the story. Its updateLayer method now creates borders based on the view's shape layer. Setting the border layer's stroke color and line width enables the border to be drawn on top of the view. Since the drawing is centered on the shape mask path, and the mask clips half the border (any material from the center of the path and outward), a doubled line width ensures that the border is drawn exactly to the requested extent. For this reason, the border always extends from the clipped edge of the view inward, overlaying any material in the view that falls under its width. If needed, use a partially transparent alpha value to enable that material to bleed through the border. Borders can become a significant issue when they grow large enough to obscure view details.

A reference to the border is stored using key/value pairs in the primary view layer. Make sure you remove this reference before attempting to release the view. If this approach, with its mandatory clean-up step, bothers you, consider naming the layer instead. Use the layer name property to store a key and then search the views to find a sublayer with a matching name.

Listing 8-3 Generating Border Layers

```
// Return the view's shape layer
- (CAShapeLayer *) shapeLayer
{
    CAShapeLayer *shapeLayer = (CAShapeLayer *) self.layer.mask;
```

```
        return shapeLayer;
}


// Remove any border layer
- (void) removeBorderLayer
{
    CAShapeLayer *borderLayer = [self.layer valueForKey:BorderLayerKey];
    if (borderLayer)
    {
        [borderLayer removeFromSuperlayer];
        [self.layer setValue:nil forKey:BorderLayerKey];
    }
}


// Update the view layer and border
- (void) updateLayer
{
    // No masks or borders for zero-sized views
    if (CGSizeEqualToSize(self.bounds.size, CGSizeZero))
    {
        self.layer.mask = nil;
        return;
    }

    // Generate a shape if none has been assigned
    if (!_shape)
    {
        _shape = [UIBezierPath bezierPathWithRect:self.bounds];
    }

    // Always use a copy to minimize math errors to the original shape
    UIBezierPath *path = [_shape copy];
    FitPathToRect(path, self.bounds);

    // Create a mask
    CAShapeLayer *maskLayer = [CAShapeLayer layer];
    maskLayer.path = path.CGPath;
    self.layer.mask = maskLayer;

    // Create / Update border layer
    [self removeBorderLayer];
    CAShapeLayer *borderLayer = [CAShapeLayer new];
    borderLayer.frame = self.bounds;
    borderLayer.path = [self shapeLayer].path;
    borderLayer.anchorPoint = CGPointMake(0.5, 0.5);
    borderLayer.lineWidth = _borderWidth * 2.0;
    borderLayer.strokeColor = _borderColor.CGColor;
```

```
    borderLayer.fillColor = [UIColor clearColor].CGColor;
    [self.layer addSublayer:borderLayer];
    [self.layer setValue:borderLayer forKey:BorderLayerKey];
}
```

Building Shaped Buttons

Shaped elements aren't limited to image views. Layer masking works with any view class. Buttons provide an excellent match, especially in the iOS 7-and-later days of sparse minimalism. While standard system buttons are now primarily borderless, shaped buttons can still work with iOS aesthetics, enabling you to create visual groups that unify multiple views into a single cohesive presentation.

Figure 8-5 shows a stacked set of buttons. The top and bottom buttons curve their corners to emphasize the grouping. Although there are three separate button instances, their presentation shows how these views primarily relate to each other.

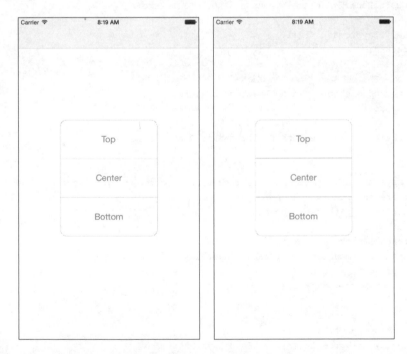

Figure 8-5   Grouped buttons work best when their borders complement each other. The top and center buttons in the left screen shot have their bottom edges removed. This avoids the visual excess shown in the right screen shot between each button pair.

The left and right screen shots illustrate a common problem encountered when building grouped views. In the right screen shot, the bottom border of the first button and top border of the second have doubled. This creates a too-thick section line between each pair as the abutting borders reinforce each other and draw too much attention to the separators. The more streamlined look in the left screen shot omits the bottom edge from each button except the lowest one.

To create this effect, Listing 8-4 modifies the approach from Listing 8-3 to differentiate the mask path used to clip the view from the border layer path that outlines the view. It builds an open path (except for the case of bottom buttons, which provide their own bottom edge) and creates a closed copy for layer masking. Each path created by `pathInRect:role:` is applied to the border layer, enabling the buttons to stack without doubling.

Listing 8-4 **Stackable Paths**

```
- (UIBezierPath *) pathInRect: (CGRect) rect role: (NSInteger) role
{
    // Establish a new path
    UIBezierPath *path = [UIBezierPath bezierPath];

    // Reference Points
    CGPoint topLeft = CGPointZero;
    CGPoint topRight = CGPointMake(rect.size.width, 0);
    CGPoint bottomLeft = CGPointMake(0, rect.size.height);
    CGPoint bottomRight = CGPointMake(rect.size.width, rect.size.height);

    switch (role)
    {
        case 0: // top
        {
            path = [UIBezierPath bezierPath];
            [path moveToPoint:bottomLeft];
            [path addLineToPoint:
                    CGPointMake(topLeft.x, topLeft.y + _cornerRadius)];
            [path addQuadCurveToPoint:
                    CGPointMake(topLeft.x + _cornerRadius, topLeft.y)
                controlPoint:topLeft];
            [path addLineToPoint:
                    CGPointMake(topRight.x - _cornerRadius, topRight.y)];
            [path addQuadCurveToPoint:
                    CGPointMake(topRight.x, topRight.y + _cornerRadius)
                controlPoint:topRight];
            [path addLineToPoint:bottomRight];
            break;
        }
```

```
        case 1: // center
        {
            path = [UIBezierPath bezierPath];
            [path moveToPoint:bottomLeft];
            [path addLineToPoint:topLeft];
            [path addLineToPoint:topRight];
            [path addLineToPoint:bottomRight];
            break;
        }
        case 2: // bottom
        {
            path = [UIBezierPath bezierPath];
            [path moveToPoint:topLeft];
            [path addLineToPoint:
                    CGPointMake(bottomLeft.x, bottomLeft.y - _cornerRadius)];
            [path addQuadCurveToPoint:
                    CGPointMake(bottomLeft.x + _cornerRadius, bottomLeft.y)
                controlPoint:bottomLeft];
            [path addLineToPoint:
                    CGPointMake(bottomRight.x - _cornerRadius, bottomRight.y)];
            [path addQuadCurveToPoint:
                    CGPointMake(bottomRight.x, bottomRight.y - _cornerRadius)
                controlPoint:bottomRight];
            [path addLineToPoint:topRight];
            [path closePath]; // bottom paths are closed
            break;
        }
        default: break;
    }
    return path;
}

- (void) updateLayer
{
    if (CGSizeEqualToSize(self.bounds.size, CGSizeZero)) return;

    // Create a role-specific path
    UIBezierPath *path = [self pathInRect:self.frame role:_role.integerValue];

    // Close the path for masking
    UIBezierPath *closedPath = [path copy];
    [closedPath closePath];

    // Mask the layer
    CAShapeLayer *maskLayer = [CAShapeLayer layer];
```

```
    maskLayer.path = closedPath.CGPath;
    self.layer.mask = maskLayer;

    // Establish a border layer if needed
    if (!borderLayer)
    {
        borderLayer = [[CAShapeLayer alloc] init];
        [self.layer addSublayer:borderLayer];
        borderLayer.fillColor = [UIColor clearColor].CGColor;
    }

    // Set the path for the border
    borderLayer.strokeColor =
        _borderColor ? _borderColor.CGColor : APP_TINT_COLOR.CGColor;
    borderLayer.lineWidth = _borderWidth * 2;
    borderLayer.path = path.CGPath;
}
```

Adding Attention-Grabbing Animations to Shaped Views

Shaped views and their layers naturally lend themselves to any number of animation effects. Figure 8-6 shows two effects in action. On the left, a view's outline repeatedly expands and fades over time. This effect lends itself well to a state of "requires attention" or, if you combine the view with your user's contacts, perhaps "is requesting access to you." On the right are marching dots, showing a selected or highlighted view. (It's far easier to see in action than in a simple screen shot.) A series of dashed lines moves around the view's shape outline.

Listing 8-5 subclasses the ShapedImageView developed in Listing 8-2 to add support for these effects. It offers the setAnimation: method as a primary entry point. Pass it a key to start either effect or pass it nil to stop any ongoing animation.

Because the animations extend beyond the scope of the masked shaped view, animation layers are installed to the view's superview. This enables users to view the effects unclipped by the view. It's important then to associate the animations with a particular view, to prevent one view from overriding another's presentation. The animationKey method associates a class-based key with a view's hexadecimal address to provide a unique correspondence between the animations and the view in question.

The two effects used here are very simple. The first builds an animation group that fades a layer's alpha level to 0.0 and scales it to 1.5x its original size. It does this twice, offsetting each part of the two-second effect by second second. This creates the ring-in-ring look you see in Figure 8-6, to add visual interest. The second builds a border shape, establishes a line dash pattern, and then animates the offset of that pattern (its *phase*) so the dashes appear to move around the view.

Figure 8-6   Shaped views naturally lend themselves to animation effects. In the left images, the view's shape repeatedly expands and fades. In the right images, a line of "marching ants" travels the shape's border.

As with the parent class, the `AnimatingShapeImageView` must respond to shape changes. It does this by watching the `shape` property established in its superclass. When updated, the class must reestablish both its mask, as provided by the superclass implementation, and any animation, as these are tied to the view's shape.

You can easily expand Listing 8-5 for additional animations. Just add a new constant key, build a method to implement the new animation, and update `setAnimation:` to redirect by associating the key with the instance method.

Listing 8-5   **Animated Shapes**

```
// All animations are marked with this key and the view's address, enabling
// you to remove animations currently associated with a particular view
NSString *const AnimatingShapeKey = @"AnimatingShapeKey";

// The two animations defined for this class
NSString *const ScaleAndFadeKey = @"ScaleAndFadeKey";
NSString *const MarchingAntsKey = @"MarchingAntsKey";
```

```objc
// Return all animation layers associated with a key
NSArray *FetchAnimationLayersWithKey(UIView *view, NSString *key)
{
    NSMutableArray *layers = [NSMutableArray array];
    for (CALayer *layer in view.superview.layer.sublayers)
    {
        if ([layer.name isEqualToString:key])
            [layers addObject:layer];
    }
    return layers.copy;
}

@implementation AnimatingShapeImageView
- (NSString *) animationKey
{
    // Append the animation key with the view's address
    return [NSString stringWithFormat:@"%@%X",
        AnimatingShapeKey, (unsigned int) self];
}

- (void) removeAnimations
{
    // Remove all shape animations associated with this view
    NSArray *layers = FetchAnimationLayersWithKey(self, self.animationKey);
    if (layers.count > 0)
    {
        for (CALayer *layer in layers)
            [layer removeFromSuperlayer];

        // Alternatively:
        // [layers makeObjectsPerformSelector:@selector(removeFromSuperlayer)]

        return;
    }
}

// Animation where the shape expands and fades
- (void) establishScaleAndFadeAnimation
{
    // Clean up existing animations
    [self removeAnimations];

    CAShapeLayer *shapeLayer = self.shapeLayer;
    UIColor *color = _primaryColor ? :
        [[UIColor grayColor] colorWithAlphaComponent:0.5];
```

```
// Build two visible rings
for (NSInteger ring = 0; ring < 2; ring++)
{
    CAShapeLayer *borderShapeLayer = [CAShapeLayer layer];
    borderShapeLayer.frame = self.frame;
    borderShapeLayer.opacity = 0.5;
    borderShapeLayer.lineWidth = 2.0;
    borderShapeLayer.strokeColor = color.CGColor;
    borderShapeLayer.fillColor = color.CGColor;
    borderShapeLayer.path = shapeLayer.path;
    borderShapeLayer.name = self.animationKey;

    // Mask the animating layer
    CAShapeLayer *maskLayer = [CAShapeLayer layer];
    maskLayer.path = shapeLayer.path;
    borderShapeLayer.mask = maskLayer;

    // Gently fade to 0
    CABasicAnimation *opacityAnimation =
        [CABasicAnimation animationWithKeyPath:@"opacity"];
    opacityAnimation.toValue =  @0;

    // Scale to 1.5x the original view size
    CABasicAnimation *scaleAnimation =
        [CABasicAnimation animationWithKeyPath:@"transform"];
    scaleAnimation.toValue = [NSValue valueWithCATransform3D:
        CATransform3DMakeScale(1.5, 1.5, 1.5)];

    // Create a group from the animations, and offset the
    // start time for each ring
    CAAnimationGroup *animationGroup = [CAAnimationGroup new];
    animationGroup.repeatCount = HUGE_VALF;
    animationGroup.duration = 2.0;
    animationGroup.beginTime = [borderShapeLayer
        convertTime:CACurrentMediaTime() fromLayer:nil] + ring;
    animationGroup.timingFunction = [CAMediaTimingFunction
        functionWithControlPoints:0.3:0:1:1];
    animationGroup.animations = @[scaleAnimation, opacityAnimation];

    // Add the animation as a layer in the view's superview, so it can expand
    // beyond the view's intrinsic limits
    [borderShapeLayer addAnimation:animationGroup forKey:ScaleAndFadeKey];
    [self.superview.layer sendSublayerToBack:borderShapeLayer];
}
}
```

```objc
- (void) establishMarchingAntsAnimation: (CGFloat) width
{
    // Clean up existing animations
    [self removeAnimations];

    CAShapeLayer *shapeLayer = self.shapeLayer
    UIColor *color = _primaryColor ? : [[UIColor grayColor]
        colorWithAlphaComponent:0.5];

    // Create a base border layer
    CAShapeLayer *borderShapeLayer = [CAShapeLayer layer];
    borderShapeLayer.frame = self.frame;
    borderShapeLayer.opacity = 0.5;
    borderShapeLayer.lineWidth = width;
    borderShapeLayer.strokeColor = color.CGColor;
    borderShapeLayer.fillColor = [UIColor clearColor].CGColor;
    borderShapeLayer.lineDashPattern = @[@8, @8];
    borderShapeLayer.path = shapeLayer.path;
    borderShapeLayer.name = self.animationKey;

    // Mask the border layer
    CAShapeLayer *maskLayer = [CAShapeLayer layer];
    UIBezierPath *path = [UIBezierPath bezierPathWithCGPath:shapeLayer.path];
    ScalePath(path, 1.1, 1.1); // Expand slightly - YMMV
    maskLayer.path = path.CGPath;
    borderShapeLayer.mask = maskLayer;

    // Build an animation around the line dash phase, that is the
    // offset at which the dashes are drawn
    CABasicAnimation *animation = [CABasicAnimation
        animationWithKeyPath:@"lineDashPhase"];
    animation.fromValue = @(0.0);
    animation.toValue = @(-32.0);
    animation.repeatCount = HUGE_VALF;
    animation.duration = 1.0;

    // Install the animation to the view's superview.
    [borderShapeLayer addAnimation:animation forKey:MarchingAntsKey];
    [self.superview.layer sendSublayerToBack:borderShapeLayer];
}

// Start an animation. Pass nil to end a current animation
- (void) setAnimation: (NSString *) animationNameKey
{
    _currentAnimation = animationNameKey;
```

```objc
    if (!animationNameKey)
    {
        _animating = NO;
        [self removeAnimations];
        return;
    }

    if ([animationNameKey isEqualToString:ScaleAndFadeKey])
    {
        [self establishScaleAndFadeAnimation];
        _animating = YES;
    }
    else if ([animationNameKey isEqualToString:MarchingAntsKey])
    {
        [self establishMarchingAntsAnimation:8.0];
        _animating = YES;
    }
    else
    {
        NSLog(@"This is a no-op");
    }
}

- (void) observeValueForKeyPath:(NSString *)keyPath
                       ofObject:(id)object
                         change:(NSDictionary *)change
                        context:(void *)context
{
    [super observeValueForKeyPath:keyPath ofObject:object
        change:change context:context];

    // In addition to the superclass's bounds observer,
    // observe a view's shape to detect border changes.
    if ([keyPath isEqualToString:@"shape"])
    {
        [self setAnimation:_currentAnimation];
    }
}

- (void) setup
{
    [super setup];

    // Observe Shape Changes
    [self addObserver:self forKeyPath:@"shape"
        options:NSKeyValueObservingOptionNew context:NULL];
}
```

```objc
- (instancetype) initWithFrame:(CGRect)frame
{
    if (!(self = [super initWithFrame:frame])) return self;
    [self setup];
    return self;
}

// ... other init methods ...

- (void) cleanup
{
    [self removeAnimations];

    [[NSNotificationCenter defaultCenter] removeObserver:self];
    [self removeObserver:self forKeyPath:@"shape"];
}

- (void) removeFromSuperview
{
    [self cleanup];
    [super removeFromSuperview];
}

- (void) dealloc
{
    [self cleanup];
}
@end
```

Wrap-up

Here are a few final points to wrap up what you've read in this chapter:

- Shaped views are easy to implement and flexible to use. With restraint and good style choices, you can use them to build creative and intriguing interfaces that set your apps apart.

- Indulge yourself with borders. While the major UI redesign that started in iOS 7 emphasizes simplicity and sparseness, borders can work well with shaped views. They reinforce the distinction between unusual visual shapes and the UI that lies behind them.

- Use animations judiciously. The ones discussed in this chapter are meant to grab a user's attention and show interface state. A little, however, goes a very long way. Just because you can make your shaped views pop doesn't mean your users will appreciate having every part of your screen demand attention at once. With these kinds of effects, less is usually more.

9

Adaptive Deployment

As the iOS family continues to grow, apps should automatically support all new displays, orientations, and screens. Although iOS targets are not nearly as splintered as Android's multitude, interfaces face numerous configurations for universal deployment. Until recently, routines specific to iPads or iPhones, to landscape or portrait orientation, and to Retina or non-Retina screens have transformed many iOS apps into a tangle of special-purpose code.

Auto Layout, a descriptive system for interface design, enabled developers to use rule-based view placement that automatically adjusts to screen dimensions and orientation. It was a first step on the road to true universal apps. Now new classes and protocols enable apps to retrieve specifics of the current runtime environment. Apps adjust not only to hardware limitations but also to whatever screen space has been allocated to their presentations.

A truly adaptive app gracefully responds with a well-designed and engaging interface, ready for the user at any size. This chapter explores the basics of these new technologies and the APIs you need to learn for moving your apps forward.

Traits

A trait collection describes a single point in deployment space, a vector of user interface attributes. This space represents the range of possible conditions an interface might encounter in the real world, including height allowances, width allowances, screen resolution, and platform. By making these traits concrete via the UITraitCollection class, Apple enters into a somewhat implicit (but limited) contract with you, the developer, specifying the types and ranges of flexibility you must design for.

Under the current system, your apps handle "compact" and "regular" interface sizes, corresponding to the overall available space on the device screen. In theory, you shouldn't have to worry that Apple will suddenly add some "ultra compact" or "large" game-changer where you have to worry about designing forms for 100-pixel or 10,000-pixel destinations. I'm not saying this won't ever happen in the long term, but iOS's current limited deployment design space gives a sense of where iOS devices will be in the near term.

No matter what kind of apps you design, a tension always exists between pixel-perfect control and adaptability. An interface that looks stunning on a 4-inch iPhone may look cramped on a 3.5-inch screen and sparse on a tablet or 6 Plus. This has led some developers to build what is essentially multiple code bases under a single app umbrella.

With trait collections and standardized callbacks, iOS 8 and later attempt to bring sanity back to those apps. As long as the presentation specifics don't get too ridiculous, Auto Layout and trait-driven assets should be able to handle adaptive presentation at runtime. Whether Apple introduces a new display resolution or a new geometry or adds side-by-side multi-application display, iOS is ready to offer developers the support they need to create adaptive interfaces that work even as the range of target types grows.

Trait Properties

Each trait collection consists of four axes, each set by a distinct property:

- **userInterfaceIdiom**—User interface idioms describe the target platform family, specifically tablet (UIUserInterfaceIdiomPad) or phone (UIUserInterfaceIdiomPhone).

- **horizontalSizeClass and verticalSizeClass**—A size class specifies the amount of space available to the interface. Values include regular (UIUserInterfaceSizeClassRegular) and compact (UIUserInterfaceSizeClassCompact) classes.

- **displayScale**—The iOS family currently includes regular (1.0), Retina (2.0), and Retina HD (3.0) display scales. These scales are represented as floating-point values rather than specific enumerations.

A single trait collection instance may define values for each of these axes or may leave some elements undefined. An unspecified idiom is UIUserInterfaceIdiomUnspecified, an unspecified size class is UIUserInterfaceSizeClassUnspecified, and a 0.0 value indicates a display scale that is yet unset.

Defining Traits

The UITraitCollection constructor methods build a single axis at a time. Here are examples across each axis:

```
// Scale
UITraitCollection *scale1Collection =
    [UITraitCollection traitCollectionWithDisplayScale:1.0];
UITraitCollection *scale2Collection =
    [UITraitCollection traitCollectionWithDisplayScale:2.0];
```

```
UITraitCollection *scale3Collection =
    [UITraitCollection traitCollectionWithDisplayScale:3.0];

// Idiom
UITraitCollection *padCollection = [UITraitCollection
    traitCollectionWithUserInterfaceIdiom:UIUserInterfaceIdiomPad];
UITraitCollection *phoneCollection = [UITraitCollection
    traitCollectionWithUserInterfaceIdiom:UIUserInterfaceIdiomPhone];

// Horizontal size class
UITraitCollection *hRegSizeCollection = [UITraitCollection
    traitCollectionWithHorizontalSizeClass:UIUserInterfaceSizeClassRegular];
UITraitCollection *hCompactSizeCollection = [UITraitCollection
    traitCollectionWithHorizontalSizeClass:UIUserInterfaceSizeClassCompact];

// Vertical size class
UITraitCollection *vRegSizeCollection = [UITraitCollection
    traitCollectionWithVerticalSizeClass:UIUserInterfaceSizeClassRegular];
UITraitCollection *vCompactSizeCollection = [UITraitCollection
    traitCollectionWithVerticalSizeClass:UIUserInterfaceSizeClassCompact];
```

Combining Trait Collections

Traits easily combine to create more complicated collections. You merge single-axis collections using the `traitCollectionWithTraitsFromCollections:` method. The following example passes an array containing the individual collections to build from:

```
UITraitCollection *coll1 = [UITraitCollection
    traitCollectionWithTraitsFromCollections: @[padCollection,
        hCompactSizeCollection, vRegSizeCollection, scale1Collection]];
```

This call returns a unified collection whose traits match the array's components. Here are the traits built from this particular collection:

```
User Interface Idiom: Tablet
Display Scale: 1x
Size class: [H.Compact, V.Regular]
```

Later items in the passed array always override earlier ones. They are added in the sequence you supply them. Say, for example, that you add contradictory items, as in the following example:

```
UITraitCollection *coll2 = [UITraitCollection
    traitCollectionWithTraitsFromCollections:@[padCollection,
    hCompactSizeCollection, vRegSizeCollection, scale1Collection,
    scale2Collection, phoneCollection]];
```

You still end up with a consistent collection that represents the most recently added elements. Here are the resulting traits:

```
User Interface Idiom: Phone
Display Scale: 2x
Size class: [H:Compact, V:Regular]
```

This consistency is important. It provides predictable results when you add new traits to an existing collection, such as when you inherit a trait collection environment from a parent view controller but wish to adapt those traits for a child.

Designing for Traits

With traits, your goal isn't to create a magical adaptive declarative system like Auto Layout. Size classes enable you to architect your app at the most fundamental level. Apple recognized that the process of designing for a *compact* layout is similar for both full-screen phone targets and tablet child controllers that take up a fraction of the available screen space.

Size classes guide structural layout decisions. They offer a base categorization on which you hang your code for universal deployment. Instead of asking "Does this interface run on the iPhone or the iPad?" size classes enable you to ask "Does this interface run in compact or regular space?" This one change re-imagines universal design.

Is this system perfect or even fully baked at this time? No, it is not. As Table 9-1 shows, the regular/compact language is limited. Trait space definitions break down interfaces into the crudest of categories.

It's notable that the current paradigm cannot distinguish between portrait and landscape iPad orientations. This creates an architectural mismatch as a preponderance of iPad apps adapt their UIs in some way to adjust between orientations. As things stand, iPad view layout code cannot use trait environments to distinguish between these orientations.

Other trait design choices may also seem baffling. For example, how is it that a 480-point height is "regular" and a 586-point width is "compact"? A WWDC 2014 presentation stated the cutoffs were set at 480 points for regular height and 768 points for regular width. These evolved with the introduction of the iPhone 6 and 6 Plus, where both the 667-point and 736-point heights are reported as "regular" in newer iOS releases. Table 9-1 shows the default size classes for each device family.

In summary, Apple gets an A for effort on the trait space front. It's a great idea and an excellent direction for this technology, but there's still a lot of room to grow. Apple wants developers to move away from designing customized UIs based on orientation, has deprecated rotation callbacks, and encourages developers to drive their layouts based on traits but ignores how many real-world tablet apps critically rely on orientation-specific layout.

Table 9-1   **Default Device Traits**

Size Classes	Regular Width	Compact Width
Regular Height	Portrait Tablet, Landscape Tablet	Portrait Phone
Compact Height	Landscape 6 Plus	Landscape Phone

UIScreen Properties

Size classes provide high-level design traits for architecting your layout. Despite this, you want to customize presentations based on details like available screen points. The most obvious application for this is the portrait and landscape tablet scenario, where your application might use distinct interface layouts for each orientation.

To support finer-grained queries, iOS offers a number of screen properties consisting of both old and new elements. The following section reviews these properties and discusses the values they return.

Coordinate Spaces

Coordinate space properties report the primary interface bounds and hardware bounds. Use these to distinguish device characteristics at the highest level. Spaces tell you how big the target screen is, enabling you to deduce both device type and primary orientation. (These derived values can also be queried through the UIDevice class.)

To access bounds, retrieve either space property and then query the returned space for its bounds, as shown here:

```
[UIScreen mainScreen].coordinateSpace.bounds
[UIScreen mainScreen].fixedCoordinateSpace.bounds
```

The coordinateSpace property is tied to an application's primary interface orientation. For example, the first-generation iPad Air reports (0, 0, 768, 1024) when being held in portrait orientation and (0, 0, 1024, 768) in landscape. As the orientation changes, the coordinate space updates synchronously. The values for the bounds are in points.

The fixedCoordinateSpace property, also reported in points, is tied to device hardware. Specifically, it's linked to the top-left corner of the hardware in portrait mode. For a first-generation iPad Air, this property reports (0, 0, 768, 1024), regardless of orientation. Again, these values are in points.

Although the 6 Plus screen offers 1920×1080 pixels, its coordinate space is rendered to 414×736 addressable points, which use scaling and down-sampling to render to physical pixels. A rasterization process converts from point-based app-based drawing to pixel rendering on the device screen. Find an excellent description of the current state of the art from the PaintCode team in the *Ultimate Guide to iPhone Resolutions* (www.paintcodeapp.com/news/ultimate-guide-to-iphone-resolutions).

Several key features define themselves in terms of this orientation-specific coordinate space. Starting in iOS 8, the screen bounds, app frame, status bar frame, and key bounds are tied to the new coordinate space. In iOS 7 and earlier, those items were fixed to the top left of the device hardware in portrait position—to what is now called the fixed coordinate space.

For times when you may need to move between hardware space values and orientation space values, `UIView` offers the following conversion methods for transforming points and rectangles between coordinate spaces:

- `(CGPoint)convertPoint:(CGPoint)point toCoordinateSpace:`
    `(id <UICoordinateSpace>)coordinateSpace`
- `(CGPoint)convertPoint:(CGPoint)point fromCoordinateSpace:`
    `(id <UICoordinateSpace>)coordinateSpace`
- `(CGRect)convertRect:(CGRect)rect toCoordinateSpace:`
    `(id <UICoordinateSpace>)coordinateSpace`
- `(CGRect)convertRect:(CGRect)rect fromCoordinateSpace:`
    `(id <UICoordinateSpace>)coordinateSpace`

Application Frame

A screen's application frame returns a rectangle that represents the frame of the application screen area minus the status bar (if visible). On a first-generation iPad Air, the default application frame with a visible status bar is (0, 0, 768, 1004) in portrait and (0, 0, 1024, 748) in landscape. Each size is "missing" 20 points in the vertical dimension due to the status bar. All values refer to points:

```
[UIScreen mainScreen].applicationFrame
```

Screen Bounds

The two bounds properties report the screen's bounds in points (`bounds`) and pixels (`nativeBounds`):

```
[UIScreen mainScreen].bounds
[UIScreen mainScreen].nativeBounds
```

The `bounds` property is orientation aware; it corresponds to the `coordinateSpace.bounds`. The native bounds property is not; it represents a pixel-specific version of the `fixedCoordinateSpace.bounds`. So if the fixed space bounds are (0, 0, 768, 1024) for a first-generation iPad Air, the native bounds are (0, 0, 1536, 2048). The fixed and native bounds do not change as the device is handled.

Scale

The `scale` property reports the device screen scale. This corresponds to 1.0 for non-Retina devices like the first-generation iPad mini, 2.0 for Retina screens, and 3.0 for Retina HD screens. The `nativeScale` property reports the "native scale factor of the physical screen," which is exactly the same value as the `scale` property for devices that do not use down-sampling. On the Retina HD iPhone 6 Plus, which does, it is 2.9. The difference between the 6 Plus display's logical pixel count (1242×2208) and its hardware pixel count (1080×1920) creates a mismatch between the two scale properties:

```
[UIScreen mainScreen].scale
[UIScreen mainScreen].nativeScale
```

> **Note**
>
> At this writing, non-universal phone-specific apps run on tablets using a 3.5-inch form factor. While the 3.5-inch iPhone 4s appears to be on its last legs, the 3.5-inch form may continue to live on through tablet deployment.

Rotation

iOS 8 does away with rotation. It deprecates nearly all the previous rotation callbacks, such as `willRotateToInterfaceOrientation:duration:` and `didRotateFromInterface-Orientation`. You no longer consider a view controller's interface orientation. You don't forward rotation methods to child view controllers. As part of its move to adaptive interfaces, iOS 8 takes the position that all device rotation should be treated as animated bounds changes.

In this one step forward, iOS views and windows become far more like those found on desktop systems. While the likely geometries are better defined than the full window-sizing on the desktop, iOS now treats views and their controllers as flexible presentation units whose sizes can vary programmatically outside device orientation. This is a huge philosophical change.

Use `viewWillTransitionToSize:withTransitionCoordinator:` to apply interface adjustments. Fortunately, using this new approach is easy. Your implementation will look something like the following. Add any changes that need to occur to the first of the two blocks. The second block handles any updates that take place once the transition finishes:

```
- (void) viewWillTransitionToSize:(CGSize)size
    withTransitionCoordinator:
        (id<UIViewControllerTransitionCoordinator>)coordinator
{
    [coordinator animateAlongsideTransition:
        ^(id<UIViewControllerTransitionCoordinatorContext> context) {
        // add coordinated changes here
```

```
    } completion:^(id<UIViewControllerTransitionCoordinatorContext> context) {
        // add completion tasks here
    }];
}
```

Don't limit yourself to orientation-only thoughts when implementing this method. It's fair to assume that you may need to apply these changes in the near future not only to device orientation but also to side-by-side presentation on tablets or user-adjustable split view controllers. A well-designed app and good iOS citizen should be ready for all orientations and trait environments in its layout.

Size Classes and Assets

Prior to iOS 8, you could specialize an image for Retina and non-Retina display and supply device-specific art using image-naming schemes and asset catalogs. For example, the @2x infix distinguishes art meant for standard (non-HD) Retina deployment. The ~ipad and ~iphone keys specify art specific to the tablet and phone. With asset catalogs, you slide art into slots (see Figure 9-1), and Xcode names and stores those items on your behalf.

Figure 9-1   Asset catalogs enable you to install deployment-specific art.

With size categories, iOS 8 expands the way you define deployment-sensitive assets. Figure 9-2 shows a simple asset with slots available for wildcard (*) and compact (-) sizes. These variations on a theme do not include regular sizes, which would be shown with a + indicator. As a rule, you either select Any & Compact or Any & Regular assets. As you can see in this figure, a single asset can be expressed in a multitude of ways.

While iOS would be better served with full vector art support, UIImage does not offer this option yet. iOS 8 introduced limited PDF asset support where UIImage rasterizes the vector art. This limitation derives from UIImage's internal representation, which is backed by the bitmap-based CGImage. Despite what you see in Figure 9-2, iOS 8 offers a much better way for handling adaptive images than adding 32 variations at a time.

Basic Deployment

In reality, most applications do not need dozens of images for each possible deployment and size category variation. Most can get by with either two images (a simple Retina pair) or four (two Retina pairs—one for normal presentations and one for compact presentations).

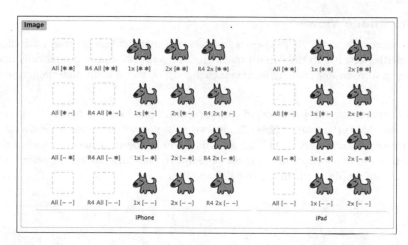

Figure 9-2   Size categories establish new ways to create deployment-specific art. Assets added apart from the wildcard Any indicator (*) are substituted when the presentation environment switches to regular (+) or compact (-) traits. The art used depends on the target geometry (such as R4) and screen density. Retina screens use 2x assets, Retina HD use 3x, and non-Retina screens use 1x assets.

Figure 9-3 shows a simpler and more typical deployment set. It contains Retina pairs for regular (top row) and compact-height (bottom row) presentations. With this configuration, the smaller assets will be used only when the height size class is compact, such as with a landscape iPhone. Labels on each dog indicate the use pattern for the art: + means regular, - means compact, and @2x means Retina. Labels like these enable you to visually inspect assets and ensure that the size class scenarios are being properly deployed as you explore the new trait-driven system. They are not meant for actual production work.

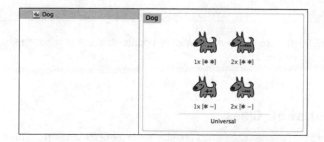

Figure 9-3   Two Retina pairs are generally sufficient to handle compact scenarios. The sizes for these images are 128×128 (@1x regular), 256×256 (@2x regular), 64×64 (@1x, vertically compact), and 128×128 (@2x, vertically compact). I added the * and + and @2x overlay marks to visually distinguish the assets that otherwise all appeared with exactly the same height and width in the Xcode asset editor.

UIKit and Image Views

When you request an image via UIImage's imageNamed: method, iOS chooses a bundle asset whose properties best match the current traits. The UIImageView class automatically updates contents as its surrounding trait environment changes. There's no additional programming required.

Figure 9-4 demonstrates this behavior. In landscape, the iPhone vertical height class is compact. The image view loads the smaller 128×128 pixel asset. In portrait, the regular height class allows the larger 256×256 version to load. Each time you re-orient the device, the image view's embedded trait-aware implementation checks and updates its image to best represent the current situation, thanks to the magic of iOS 8 and later.

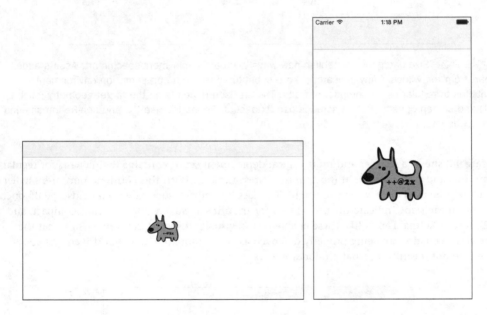

Figure 9-4   In iOS 8, UIImageView automatically updates assets in response to changes in the surrounding trait environment.

The UIImageAsset Class

For finer control, the UIImageAsset class enables you to override relationships between assets and trait collections. When you register an asset for a trait collection, you create a relationship between a specific asset and the traits that determine when to load it.

Listing 9-1 demonstrates an admittedly prosaic implementation that mirrors the default behavior. As you query the asset at runtime, the image asset instance uses its internal rules to produce a matching image.

Normally, you do not approach image loading in this manner. In typical deployment, image views own UIImageAsset instances—not the other way around. The direct access shown in Listing 9-1 offers a way of bypassing the default behavior to install your own rules, whatever they might be.

Use this approach to select items for classes not based on UIImageView. For example, you might use Quartz drawing to composite your images, selecting image sources via the current trait environment. Or you could create custom UIControl elements that adjust their drawn contents on trait collection updates to provide miniaturized versions in compact presentations and standard versions in regular ones. There are a lot of great real-world reasons you might want to build your own image asset instances that smartly adapt to trait environments.

Listing 9-1 Traits-Based Art

```
- (void) traitCollectionDidChange:
    (UITraitCollection *)previousTraitCollection
{
    NSLog(@"Trait collection did change");
    imageView.image =
        [imageAsset imageWithTraitCollection:self.traitCollection];
}

- (void) viewDidLoad
{
    [super viewDidLoad];

    UITraitCollection *compactHeight = [UITraitCollection
        traitCollectionWithVerticalSizeClass:UIUserInterfaceSizeClassCompact];
    UITraitCollection *regularHeight = [UITraitCollection
        traitCollectionWithVerticalSizeClass:UIUserInterfaceSizeClassRegular];

    imageAsset = [UIImageAsset new];
    [imageAsset registerImage:[UIImage imageNamed:@"SmallDog"]
        withTraitCollection:compactHeight];
    [imageAsset registerImage:[UIImage imageNamed:@"LargeDog"]
        withTraitCollection:regularHeight];

    imageView.image =
        [imageAsset imageWithTraitCollection:self.traitCollection];
}
```

Building Images from PDFs

As this chapter has discussed, new PDF support in asset catalogs doesn't really do what you might expect—namely, offer resizable vector assets. To make up for that, Listing 9-2 provides a class that loads images from PDF files directly, building them to whatever UIImage size you need. Supply a path to the image and a target size, height, or width. If using a size, the functions scale-aspect-fit to that target. With width or height, they use the built-in aspect and build an appropriately sized partner dimension.

Listing 9-2   **PDF Rendering**

```
// First, a few utility functions

// Scale a size to a destination rectangle
static CGFloat AspectScaleFit(CGSize sourceSize, CGRect destRect)
{
    CGSize destSize = destRect.size;
    CGFloat scaleW = destSize.width / sourceSize.width;
    CGFloat scaleH = destSize.height / sourceSize.height;
    return fmin(scaleW, scaleH);
}

// Center a rectangle around a point
static CGRect RectAroundCenter(CGPoint center, CGSize size)
{
    CGFloat halfWidth = size.width / 2.0;
    CGFloat halfHeight = size.height / 2.0;

    return CGRectMake(center.x - halfWidth, center.y - halfHeight,
        size.width, size.height);
}

// Fit rectangle into destination rectangle
static CGRect RectByFittingRect(CGRect sourceRect, CGRect destinationRect)
{
    CGFloat aspect = AspectScaleFit(sourceRect.size, destinationRect);
    CGSize targetSize = CGSizeMake(sourceRect.size.width * aspect,
        sourceRect.size.height * aspect);
    CGPoint center = CGPointMake(CGRectGetMidX(destinationRect),
        CGRectGetMidY(destinationRect));
    return RectAroundCenter(center, targetSize);
}

// PDF drawing

// Draw a single PDF page into Quartz destination rectangle
// For more information about this, see my iOS Drawing book
// iOS Drawing: Practical UIKit Solutions
void DrawPDFPageInRect(CGPDFPageRef pageRef, CGRect destinationRect)
{
    CGContextRef context = UIGraphicsGetCurrentContext();
    if (context == NULL)
```

```
    {
        NSLog(@"Error: No context to draw to");
        return;
    }

    CGContextSaveGState(context);
    UIImage *image = UIGraphicsGetImageFromCurrentImageContext();

    // Flip the context to Quartz space
    CGAffineTransform transform = CGAffineTransformIdentity;
    transform = CGAffineTransformScale(transform, 1.0, -1.0);
    transform = CGAffineTransformTranslate(transform, 0.0, -image.size.height);
    CGContextConcatCTM(context, transform);

    // Flip the rect, which remains in UIKit space
    CGRect d = CGRectApplyAffineTransform(destinationRect, transform);

    // Calculate a rectangle to draw to
    CGRect pageRect = CGPDFPageGetBoxRect(pageRef, kCGPDFCropBox);
    CGFloat drawingAspect = AspectScaleFit(pageRect.size, d);
    CGRect drawingRect = RectByFittingRect(pageRect, d);

    // Adjust the context
    CGContextTranslateCTM(context, drawingRect.origin.x, drawingRect.origin.y);
    CGContextScaleCTM(context, drawingAspect, drawingAspect);

    // Draw the page
    CGContextDrawPDFPage(context, pageRef);
    CGContextRestoreGState(context);
}

// Create a UIImage instance from a PDF file
UIImage *ImageFromPDFFile(NSString *pdfPath, CGSize targetSize)
{
    CGPDFDocumentRef pdfRef = CGPDFDocumentCreateWithURL(
        (__bridge CFURLRef)[NSURL fileURLWithPath:pdfPath]);
    if (pdfRef == NULL)
    {
        NSLog(@"Error loading PDF");
        return nil;
    }

    UIGraphicsBeginImageContextWithOptions(targetSize, NO, 0);
    CGPDFPageRef pageRef = CGPDFDocumentGetPage(pdfRef, 1);
    DrawPDFPageInRect(pageRef, (CGRect){.size = targetSize});
    UIImage *image = UIGraphicsGetImageFromCurrentImageContext();
    UIGraphicsEndImageContext();
```

```
        CGPDFDocumentRelease(pdfRef);
        return image;
}


// Determine the native PDF aspect
CGFloat GetPDFFileAspect(NSString *pdfPath)
{
        CGPDFDocumentRef pdfRef = CGPDFDocumentCreateWithURL(
            (__bridge CFURLRef)[NSURL fileURLWithPath:pdfPath]);
        if (pdfRef == NULL)
        {
            NSLog(@"Error loading PDF");
            return 0.0;
        }

        CGPDFPageRef pageRef = CGPDFDocumentGetPage(pdfRef, 1);
        CGRect pageRect = CGPDFPageGetBoxRect(pageRef, kCGPDFCropBox);
        CGPDFDocumentRelease(pdfRef);
        return pageRect.size.width / pageRect.size.height;
}


// Create the image using a target width in points
UIImage *ImageFromPDFFileWithWidth(NSString *pdfPath, CGFloat targetWidth)
{
        CGFloat aspect = GetPDFFileAspect(pdfPath);
        if (aspect == 0.0) return nil;
        return ImageFromPDFFile(pdfPath,
            CGSizeMake(targetWidth, targetWidth / aspect));
}


// Create the image using a target height in points
UIImage *ImageFromPDFFileWithHeight(NSString *pdfPath, CGFloat targetHeight)
{
        CGFloat aspect = GetPDFFileAspect(pdfPath);
        if (aspect == 0.0) return nil;
        return ImageFromPDFFile(pdfPath,
            CGSizeMake(targetHeight * aspect, targetHeight));
}
```

Overriding Trait Collections

In iOS 8, split view controllers have become universal. Instances now run on both tablet and phone targets. How they're expressed depends on the trait environment they're presented in. In horizontally compact environments, the split view controller looks like a navigation controller.

Figure 9-5 shows a split view controller in its default compact presentation. Items tapped in the master table present as pushed detail controllers.

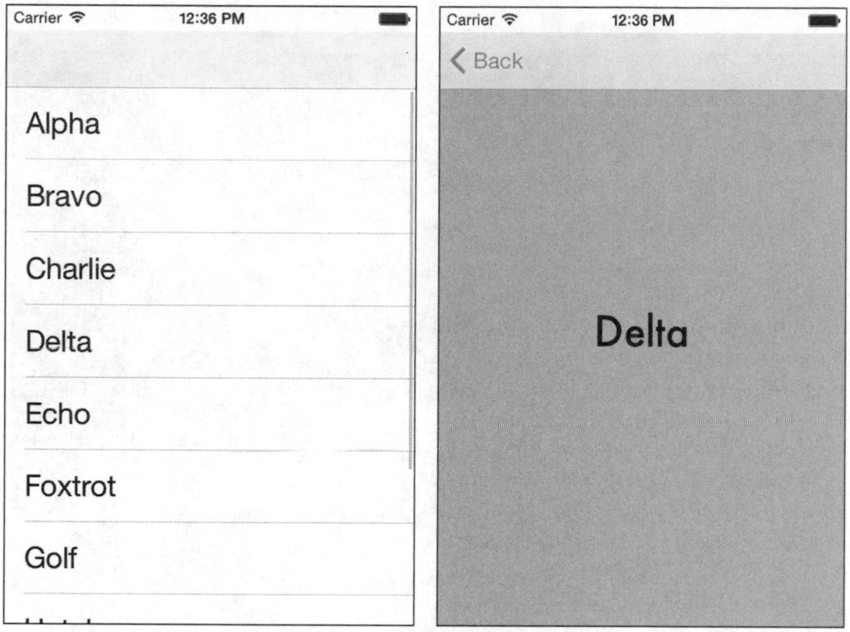

Figure 9-5   These screen shots were created from a simple split view controller, presented in a horizontally compact environment. Although the results superficially look like a navigation controller, the actual container is a `UISplitViewController`.

Here is the code that creates this example. It consists of a simple split view controller with two children—a table-based master and a detail controller that shows a label:

```
split = [UISplitViewController new];
split.viewControllers = @[masterNav, detailNav];
split.preferredDisplayMode = UISplitViewControllerDisplayModeAllVisible;
split.delegate = self;
```

When executed on an iPad, this application produces the results shown in Figure 9-6. The code base uses the same split view controller, with identical master and detail components. What changes here is the trait environment. In this case, that environment defaults from the running hardware. On the iPad, the horizontal and vertical size classes are regular and not compact.

Building Side-by-Side iPhone Split Views

As Apple's `UISplitViewController` documents state, "In a horizontally regular environment, the split view controller presents its view controllers side-by-side whenever possible." The default *horizontal* trait environment for iPad targets is always regular. For iPhone targets, it is always compact, except for the iPhone 6 Plus. To achieve side-by-side presentation on phones, establish a prevailing regular horizontal trait to override that normally compact behavior.

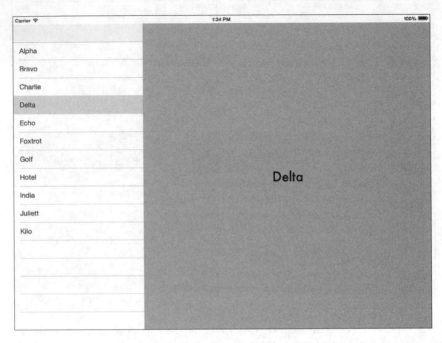

Figure 9-6   When run on an iPad, the application from Figure 9-5 appears in a more traditional split view controller configuration.

You establish a child split view controller as you would any other child controller. To parent the controller, as in the following example, you add it to a container as a new child view controller. You then place its view into the parent's hierarchy and call the did-move update:

```
[self addChildViewController:split];
// ... layout the view here ...
[split didMoveToParentViewController:self];
```

Once you've done this, you're ready to leverage a new iOS 8 view controller feature that enables containers to override the trait environment of their child controller.

A trait environment is automatically inherited from device characteristics. A parent view controller can also set it for its children. To automatically create a side-by-side split view controller layout on compact phone targets, you must override the child's default trait environment. The following call universally overrides the split view controller's traits so they always feature a horizontally regular size trait. This results in the presentation in Figure 9-7.

```
[self setOverrideTraitCollection:[UITraitCollection
    traitCollectionWithHorizontalSizeClass:UIUserInterfaceSizeClassRegular]
    forChildViewController:split];
```

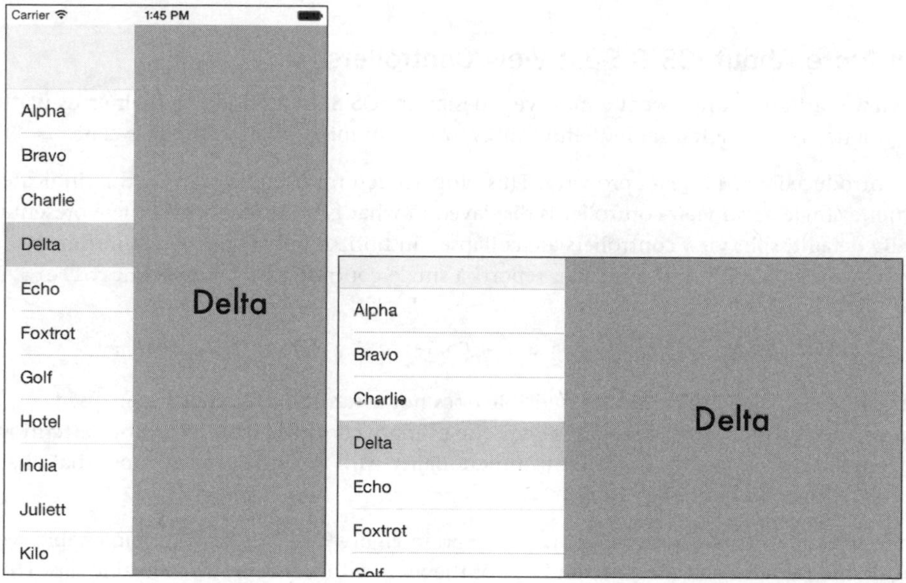

Figure 9-7   This split view controller's display mode is set to `UISplitViewController-DisplayModeAllVisible`. By overriding the presentation environment to a regular horizontal size, you produce the side-by-side layout you see here. Both screen shots are taken from an iPhone 5s destination.

For finer control, implement the `overrideTraitCollectionForChildViewController:` method in the parent view controller. Return any override traits you want the child to operate with. This method is called each time the parent controller's trait environment updates. It enables you to catch those changes and return override specific to the current device configuration. The following method implementation trivially mimics the assignment used to create Figure 9-7. In it, a phone's horizontal trait is overridden to always return a regular size class:

```
- (UITraitCollection *)overrideTraitCollectionForChildViewController:
    (UIViewController *)childViewController
{
    // No changes on iPad
    if (self.traitCollection.userInterfaceIdiom == UIUserInterfaceIdiomPad)
        return nil;
```

```
    // Use split for both orientations.
    return [UITraitCollection traitCollectionWithHorizontalSizeClass:
        UIUserInterfaceSizeClassRegular];
}
```

A Bit More About iOS 8 Split View Controllers

Split view controllers underwent a massive redesign in iOS 8. In addition to their cross-platform deployment, here are a few more useful things to keep in mind when using this class.

iOS 8 introduced a `collapsed` property. This property returns a Boolean value that indicates whether a single *detail* view controller is displayed in what is otherwise a split view presentation. By default, split view controllers are collapsed in horizontally compact environments. When collapsed, a split view controller reports a single controller in its `viewControllers` array:

```
NSLog(@"Split is %@", split.collapsed ? @"Collapsed" : @"Not Collapsed");
```

Just because a single view controller is visible does not mean the split view is collapsed. Gestures and orientation enable you to hide the primary controller and focus your attention on the detail controller. Do not confuse this functionality with the structural collapse that changes the underlying view controller array.

You see the split view's `displayModeButtonItem` in Figure 9-8. This button item enables you to toggle the master controller into and out of the view with a simple, discoverable tap. This is one of my favorite iOS 8 features.

Assign this button item property to the navigation item in your detail controller:

```
detail.navigationItem.rightBarButtonItem = split.displayModeButtonItem;
```

The split view controller takes over and manages it on your behalf.

The display mode button item appears as a double-arrowed expand button when the master view controller is visible. It presents the name of the master controller when not. Make sure to name your master controller so the button has text to present when the detail view controller is full screen.

To use this new feature most effectively, embed your detail controller into a navigation controller container. Make sure you pass the navigation controller to any calls of `showDetailView-Controller:sender:`. If you "lose" your navigation bar with its display mode button, most likely you're passing the detail controller directly.

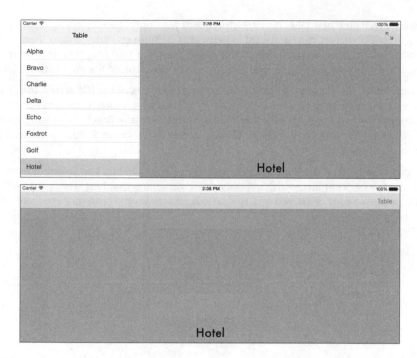

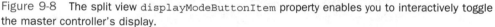

Figure 9-8   The split view `displayModeButtonItem` property enables you to interactively toggle the master controller's display.

Wrap-up

Here are a few final points to wrap up what you've read in this chapter:

- While the trait system still has room to grow, it provides a profound philosophical change for immediate use. Traits enable you to stop thinking of your apps as "iPhone apps" and "iPad apps" and to start treating them solely as "iOS apps." Allow your code base to transition to traits and prepare your apps to run on all future iOS platforms.

- Adaptation isn't just about hardware or apps running on phone or tablet destinations. Adaptation enables views and view controllers to adjust their presentation with respect to the space they have been allotted. For example, a split view controller creates new trait environments for its child view controllers, each living in a subdivided space on the screen. When you work with containers, it's trait collections all the way down.

- Before the iPhone 6 Plus debuted, apps could generally target either tablet or phone deployment. The iPhone 6 Plus, with its Retina HD display and large size, is a new hybrid target. Unlike tablets, which always default to regular trait environments, and phones, which always default to horizontally compact, the landscape 6 Plus presents a horizontally regular default target. The 6 Plus presents an excellent case for considering traits instead of idioms for adjusting interfaces.

- Xcode's welcome new launch image storyboard feature (`UILaunchStoryboardName` in Info.plist) enables you to discard expansive launch images and replace them with a simple, adaptive universal design. While some complain that they've lost their splash screens, I welcome the quieter and less intrusive beginning of the application lifetime.

- Reachability, the feature that enables users to move parts of the iOS screen into reach, doesn't affect the way you construct your apps. The screen moves, but your frames don't change. Don't confuse this new user-facing feature with the Reachability samples Apple provides for network access checks. Users enable this option in Settings > General > Accessibility > Reachability.

- Be practical when it comes to images. Although Xcode enables you to add dozens of images to connect traits to art, add only those variations that best serve your application. Just because Xcode offers you an asset catalog slot doesn't mean you have to fill it.

Development Helpers

At times, it helps to have methods, functions, and techniques to help you through the development process and support you when building apps. For example, you may lay views onscreen and need placeholder content. You may want to randomize view locations to simulate user interaction. You may need some fake user data. Or you may want to add to-do list types of warnings to your build. The solutions in this chapter enable you to speed through your development day to better arrive at the app you're working on.

All the Lorems

As you assemble applications, placeholder resources enable you to test layouts and functionality with better content. I rely on a number of APIs that produce text, image, and user placeholders and content feeds. This section reviews some of those services and how you access their content from your apps.

Placeholder Text

Text filler services are often named with some variant of "Lorem Ipsum." Interestingly, this *lorem ipsum* phrase derives from graphic design history. Wikipedia (http://en.wikipedia.org/wiki/Lorem_ipsum) writes,

> The lorem ipsum text is typically a scrambled section of *De finibus bonorum et malorum*, a 1st-century BC Latin text by Cicero, with words altered, added, and removed to make it nonsensical, improper Latin....A variation of the ordinary lorem ipsum text has been used in typesetting since the 1960s or earlier, when it was popularized by advertisements for Letraset transfer sheets. It was introduced to the Information Age in the mid-1980s by Aldus Corporation, which employed it in graphics and word processing templates for its desktop publishing program, PageMaker, for the Apple Macintosh.

Searching the web for either *lorem* or *ipsum* returns any number of generator sites. Add the phrase *api* to uncover services that offer developer-specific calls for returning placeholder text.

These APIs enable you to retrieve paragraphs of Lorem Ipsum–style text at a time, using REST requests. RESTful APIs provide simple and scalable web service access (see http://en.wikipedia.org/wiki/Representational_state_transfer).

I particularly like the loripsum site (http://loripsum.net) as it provides a flexible set of parameters like prude (family-friendly content only) and paragraph-length hints like short, medium, and verylong. The API also supports requests to incorporate HTML elements (such as ordered and unordered lists, as well as block quotes) and code samples.

Listing 10-1 uses loripsum to request shorts paragraphs, which it then trims to 20 words max, using prudish plain text content. I find that limited paragraph snippets work well with many iOS apps, although you can tweak this limit as desired or eliminate it entirely.

This implementation is blocking. Control doesn't return to the app until the request completes or fails, and requests can take a noticeable amount of time to complete. This shouldn't be a problem when building basic tests and samples, but it is something you want to be aware of for Listing 10-1 and the other service examples that follow. You can choose to wait (slow startup), to convert these examples to dispatched items (results appear after delays), or preload and cache your data (you lose their random nature). Always avoid blocking the main thread in production code.

> **Note**
>
> GitHub hosts a number of *lorem ipsum* projects, some specific to Cocoa and Objective-C, which can offload your random text requests to built-in libraries or local servers.

Listing 10-1   Requesting Lorem Ipsum Text

```
// Trim each paragraph to a maximum word count
NSString *TrimParas(NSString *string, NSUInteger numberOfWords)
{
    NSMutableArray *trimmed = [NSMutableArray array];
    NSArray *paras = [string componentsSeparatedByString:@"\n\n"];
    for (NSString *p in paras)
        [trimmed addObject:TrimWords(p, numberOfWords)];
    return [trimmed componentsJoinedByString:@"\n\n"];
}


// Return a string of Lorem Ipsum text with the specified number
// of paragraphs of content
NSString *Lorem(NSUInteger numberOfParagraphs)
{
    NSString *urlString = [NSString stringWithFormat:
        @"http://loripsum.net/api/%0ld/short/prude/plaintext",
      (long) numberOfParagraphs];
```

```
NSError *error;
NSString *string = [NSString stringWithContentsOfURL:
    [NSURL URLWithString:urlString] encoding:NSUTF8StringEncoding
    error:&error];
if (!string)
{
    NSLog(@"Error: %@", error.localizedDescription);
    return nil;
}
return TrimParas(string, 20);
}
```

In addition to sites providing standard *lorem ipsum* text, a number of specialty sites provide amusing placeholder material. Bacon Ipsum (http://baconipsum.com) creates text that's "a little meatier," and Cupcake Ipsum (http://www.cupcakeipsum.com) is "sugar-coated." Swearem Ipsum (http://www.swearemipsum.com) produces family-unfriendly material, and Beer Ipsum (http://beeripsum.com) adds liquid refreshment to your placeholders. Search the web for *alternative ipsum* to uncover text source APIs from pasta to cats to pirate themed.

Image Ipsums

When it comes to pictures, you can't get any simpler than PlaceHold.it, whose images are shown in Figure 10-1. This site returns results based on a super-basic API: http://placehold.it/*WidthxHeight* (for example, http://placehold.it/350x150). All items are gray and have the requested dimensions superimposed on them.

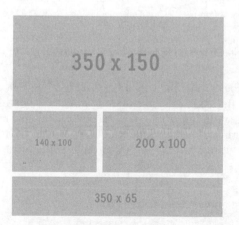

Figure 10-1   The PlaceHold.it API creates placeholder images based on the size you pass in the URL.

You might prefer the more traditional creative-commons licensed content offered by Lorem Pixel (http://lorempixel.com). This site enables you to choose a topic (such as sports, fashion, food, or business) and returns a full-color or grayscale image, using the size and theme you request. Figure 10-2 offers some examples of the site's content. Working with topics leads to more meaningful content placeholders, which is valuable when creating demos and presentations.

Figure 10-2   Lorem Pixel (http://lorempixel.com) offers a topic-driven image API. This screen shot shows four random color images from the service.

Sample layout images courtesy of Lorem Pixel and Frawemedia (http://www.flickr.com/photos/frawemedia/), Joiseyshowaa (http://www.flickr.com/photos/joiseyshowaa/), Pedro Simoes (http://www.flickr.com/photos/pedrosimoes7/), Ed Yourdon (http://www.flickr.com/photos/yourdon/) used under a Creative Commons Attribution ShareAlike license (http://creativecommons.org/licenses/by-sa/3.0/).

Listing 10-2 shows how you can use the Lorem Pixel API to retrieve UIImage instances. Add each parameter after the sizes with a forward slash. All the Lorem Pixel categories are plain text words that do not require URL encoding. This enables Listing 10-2 to skip any further processing. When working with more complex APIs, encode your request parameters before using the URL—for example, by using the NSString method stringByAddingPercentEscapesUsingEncoding:.

Listing 10-2   **Requesting Images from Lorem Pixel**

```
UIImage *LoremPixel(CGSize size, NSString *category, BOOL gray)
{
    /*
    e.g. http://lorempixel.com/400/200/sports/1/Dummy-Text
    abstract animals business cats city food nightlife fashion
    people nature sports technics transport
```

```
    */
    NSMutableString *string = [NSMutableString stringWithFormat:
        @"http://lorempixel.com%@/%0.0f/%0.0f", gray ? @"/g/" : @"",
        floorf(size.width), floorf(size.height)];
    if (category)
        [string appendFormat:@"/%@", category];
    NSData *data = [NSData dataWithContentsOfURL:[NSURL URLWithString:string]];
    return [UIImage imageWithData:data];
}
```

> **Note**
>
> For those who are into "the cute," services like Place Kitten (http://placekitten.com) offer a creative take on layout items.

Generating Random User Data

Whether you're working with contacts or just want to simulate user registration, it helps to have access to a service that establishes user data on your behalf. In the past, I've primarily used the Fake Name Generator (http://fakenamegenerator.com) but I've recently started using the Random User Generator (http://randomuser.me) site as well. This section and the one that follows discuss these services.

The Random User Generator site describes itself as being "Like Lorem Ipsum, but for people." The results include gender, name, address, e-mail address, user name, password, and other details. The site also provides a link to portraits of your fake user at large, medium, and thumbnail scales, as shown in the example in Figure 10-3. Full API details can be found at https://randomuser.me/documentation. The fields chosen for user records are simple but well chosen. For basic content, Random User Generator is an excellent choice.

Random User Generator offers JSON results, which makes it friendly for modern implementations. You request a user by calling http://api.randomuser.me. Unregistered users can generate up to 100 identities at a time. Those registered at RandomAPI (http://randomapi.com), including free tier users) can access up to 500 identities per request, according to the documentation at https://randomuser.me/documentation. Here's how you request 100 fake user identities:

```
http://api.randomuser.me/?results=100
```

Bulk Names

The Fake Name Generator site enables you to download bulk identity files without individual API calls. You can place an order for up to 50,000 identities at once at www.fakenamegenerator. com/order.php. These items are free, and you can customize which fields to include and not include in your order (see Figure 10-4). Download formats include comma-separated values (CSV) and SQLite, among others.

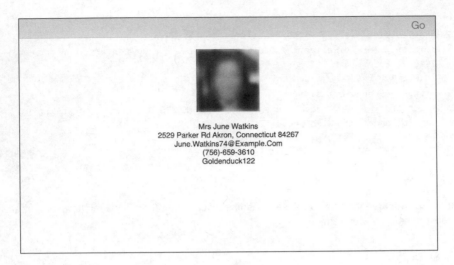

Figure 10-3   The Random User Generator (http://api.randomuser.me) generates placeholder users on demand.

The randomuser.me photo assets are released under a non-commercial license and cannot be used directly in this book. The actual photographs returned by the API are normal in appearance.

Step 3 - Choose name sets, countries, gender, and age

Name set

American
Arabic
Australian
Brazil
Chechen (Latin)

Country

Australia
Austria
Belgium
Brazil
Canada

Gender

Male: 50%   Female: 50%

Age

19 - 85 years old

Step 4 - Choose fields to include

Fields in the box on the right will be included with your order. Use the Up/Down buttons to choose which order you want the fields in.

Not all fields are available for every country. Please use the homepage to determine what information is available for the countries you have chosen.

Don't include these:

Incrementing number
Gender
Name set
Title
Given name
Middle Initial
Surname
Street address
City
State abbreviation

>>

All >>

<<

All <<

Include these:

Up

Down

Figure 10-4   The Fake Name Generator site enables you to custom order bulk identities for development and testing.

The Fake Name Generator site is international aware, so you can pick culture-specific names and country-specific contact details, as shown in Figure 10-4. You can choose many personal data fields for your fake users. Standouts include commerce, shipping, and health information, which may be suitable for specialized apps. This set expands well beyond the Random User Generator API and provides a valuable resource for developing specialty apps.

Generating Random Feeds

Fake feed data APIs are pretty scarce on the ground. One live resource, the JSON placeholder website (http://jsonplaceholder.typicode.com), enables you to access minimal fake feeds for posts, comments, albums, photos, to-do items, and users, all in a handy JSON format. For example, the following request:

```
http://jsonplaceholder.typicode.com/todos/1
```

returns a simple JSON-encoded to-do item:

```
{
  "userId": 1,
  "id": 1,
  "title": "delectus aut autem",
  "completed": false
}
```

The number passed at the end refers to a source index. Calls to the same number always return the same value. You can randomize by checking the latest source release and choosing a value between 1 and the highest number.

Because this is an open source project (https://github.com/typicode/jsonplaceholder), if the site eventually goes down, you can still run the service from your own computer. The site and feeds are pretty basic but handy for testing. A related project, JSON Server (https://github.com/typicode/json-server), promises to provide simple back-end prototyping.

Other JSON

Other mildly interesting prototyping JSON feed resources include:

- The Metallizer site (metallizer.dk) provides a JSON-encoded random heavy metal album at every request of http://metallizer.dk/api/json/0.

- Grab a random JSON-formatted Chuck Norris joke from http://api.icndb.com/jokes/random.

- Look up an acronym from the UK's National Centre for Text Mining's JSON-powered API: www.nactem.ac.uk/software/acromine/dictionary.py?sf=SMH.

XML

When you want to grab a live sample XML feed to parse and work with, check out the BBC. For example, you can fetch science headlines from http://feeds.bbci.co.uk/news/science_and_environment/rss.xml. The feeds offer plenty of XML material to work with, including summaries, links to stories, images, and publication dates.

Random Everything

Whether placing a view randomly onto a superview or coloring it with a random hue to differentiate it from other test views, a basic random generation suite helps a lot, especially for early development. The random value functions in Listing 10-3 help you avoid implementing the same number-juggling over and over again by providing a basic suite of common utilities. These elements—for example, a random value between 0 and 1 or a random item in an array— pop up on such a regular basis that it helps to know you've already gotten these covered and they're ready to use.

The random color generator in particular makes it easy to add placeholder views before apps evolve to more content-specific refinement. It's probably my most-used item in Listing 10-3, with the floating-point Random01() following as a close second.

Listing 10-3 **Random Utilities**

```
// Return a positive random integer between 0 and (max - 1)
NSUInteger RandomInteger(NSUInteger max)
{
    return arc4random_uniform((unsigned int) max);
}


// Return a floating point number between 0 and 1
CGFloat Random01()
{
    return ((CGFloat) arc4random() / (CGFloat) UINT_MAX);
}


// Return a random truth value by flipping a virtual coin
BOOL RandomBool()
{
    return (BOOL)arc4random_uniform(2);
}


// Return a random point located within a rectangle
CGPoint RandomPointInRect(CGRect rect)
{
    CGFloat x = rect.origin.x + Random01() * rect.size.width;
    CGFloat y = rect.origin.y + Random01() * rect.size.height;
    return CGPointMake(x, y);
}
```

```
// Return a random item within the supplied array
id RandomItemInArray(NSArray *array)
{
    NSUInteger index = RandomInteger(array.count);
    return array[index];
}

// Underscore prevents issues when combined with color pack
Color *Random_Color()
{
    return [UIColor colorWithRed:Random01()
                           green:Random01()
                            blue:Random01()
                           alpha:1.0];
}
```

Directives

The first half of this chapter explores resources that enable you to better prototype, grow, and demonstrate your app. Beginning with this section, the chapter switches gears and explores directives. Directives provide ways to communicate with the compiler and its preprocessor. They are language add-ons that specify how the compiler processes its input. The Clang compiler offers a rich suite of possibilities.

Although many Objective-C compiler directives exist in the Xcode wild, many developers rarely move past #define (to create macros) or #pragma mark (to add bookmarks). There's so much more you can do. This quick section introduces a few of these directives and describes how they enable you to harness warnings and errors for the greatest information impact.

Converting Comments to Warnings

Perhaps you've been envious of Swift's new TODO:, MARK:, and FIXME: comments. Build phases enable you to convert similar comment prefixes to automatically built compiler warnings. They accomplish this feat via regular expression matching, which means the solution you're about to read through is simple and expandable.

Build phases describe tasks that Xcode executes during a build. In Figure 10-5, a custom build phase enables Xcode to automatically insert a #warning directive whenever it finds to-do and fix-me comment patterns. These items transform into compile-time issues.

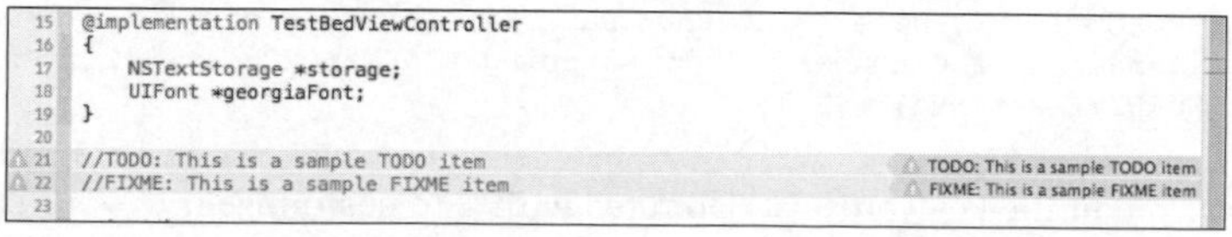

Figure 10-5   A build phase script converts comments to warnings.

The great advantage of this tweak is that it automatically centralizes project status items to your Xcode issue navigator, where you can inspect an overview throughout your project. Warnings and errors are listed on a file-by-file basis, so you can keep track of open issues you still need to address, as shown in Figure 10-6.

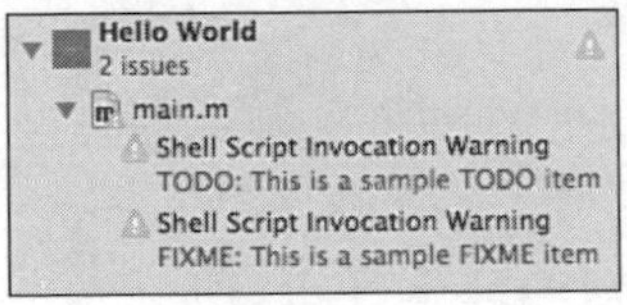

Figure 10-6   The issue navigator collects the converted warnings.

Implementing this effect takes just a few steps:

1. Customize your project by adding a build phase. Select Editor > Add Build Phase > Add Run Script Build Phase.

2. Open Run Script and locate the section that says "Type a script or drag a script file from your workspace to insert its path," as shown in Figure 10-7.

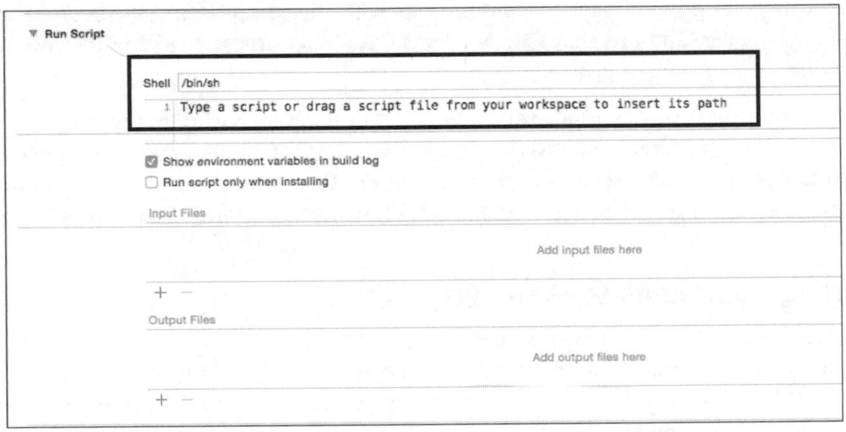

Figure 10-7   A run script build phase enables you to script changes to your build.

3. Paste in the following script:

```
KEYWORDS="TODO:|FIXME:|\?\?\?:|\!\!\!:"
find "${SRCROOT}" \( -name "*.h" -or -name "*.m" \) -print0 | xargs -0 egrep
--with-filename --line-number --only-matching "($KEYWORDS).*\$" | perl -p -e
"s/($KEYWORDS)/ warning: \$1/"
```

If you want, edit the keywords list delimited with | to customize it to your particular documentation needs. This example supports TODO:, FIXME:, ???:, and !!!: styles.

4. Compile. Your annotated comments automatically upgrade to warnings, enabling you to track to-do items throughout your project from a single navigator. Third-party code using these keywords in your project will also be flagged, so be prepared for potentially interesting insights into the status of those libraries.

Warnings

If you'd rather not tie yourself to specific comment patterns like the ones you just read about, consider using the Clang #warning directive directly. The following sequence tests for an iOS compilation target and generates a warning accordingly, as shown in Figure 10-8:

```
#if TARGET_OS_IPHONE
#warning This class is not meant for iOS deployment
#endif
```

Figure 10-8   The #warning directive produces a compiler warning. When working with deployment mismatches, you may want to escalate this to an error.

This next example uses a target test, only showing the warning for iOS builds. I've been writing a lot of cross-platform code recently for constraint utilities. Because TARGET_OS_MAC returns true for both iOS and OS X targets, you'll always want to test for TARGET_OS_IPHONE instead:

```
#ifndef  COMPATIBILITY_ALIASES_DEFINED
#if TARGET_OS_IPHONE
    @compatibility_alias View UIView;
    @compatibility_alias Color UIColor;
#else
    @compatibility_alias View NSView;
    @compatibility_alias Color NSColor;
#endif
#endif
#define COMPATIBILITY_ALIASES_DEFINED
```

You can use the same approach in Swift, although the implementation details differ slightly:

```
#if os(iOS)
    typealias View = UIView
    typealias Color = UIColor
    #else
    typealias View = NSView
    typealias Color = NSColor
#endif
```

The @compatibility_alias keyword used in the Objective-C example enables you to map an alias (like View or Color) to platform-specific classes (like UIView or NSView, or UIColor or NSColor). Guarding this code with the definition declaration ensures that these aliases are defined just once in the project, avoiding compilation errors.

Testing for the Simulator

Some classes don't work properly on the iOS simulator. Use tests for TARGET_IPHONE_SIMULATOR when developing simulator-sensitive Objective-C code. Swift checks require a slightly different approach, as shown in the following function:

```
func RunTargetTests() {
    // x86_64, arm, arm64, i386
    #if os(iOS)
        println("iOS")
        #if arch(i386) || arch(x86_64)
            println("Simulator")
            #else
            #if arch(arm)
            println("Device (arm)")
            #else
            println("Device (arm64)")
            #endif
        #endif
        #else
        println("OS X")
    #endif
}
```

Errors

The #error directive works in a similar fashion to the #warning one. The following example checks that a required include file was added in the project and produces a compiler error if it's missing:

```
#if !__has_include("Utility-Compatibility.h")
#error! Required Cross Compatibility include file not found!
#endif
```

On compile, the error produces red-circled exclamation point error feedback (as shown in Figure 10-9) instead of the yellow triangle. Use this directive when you detect inconsistent compilation conditions (for example, missing include files) or unsupported compiler targets (for example, when you know a class will not compile properly for iOS or OS X).

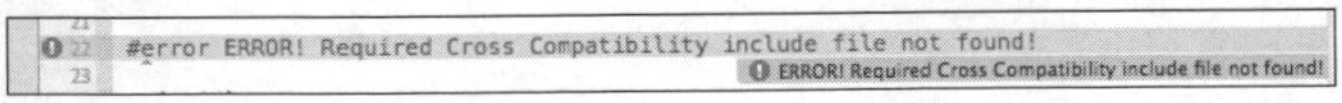

Figure 10-9   Error directives produce a red-highlighted fatal error.

> **Note**
>
> When you enable Treat Errors as Warnings in your project's Warning Policies build settings, any items you add using a `#warning` directive produce red-colored errors. Many developers enable this option to ensure that their code passes the most exhaustive scrutiny.

Errors also prevent compilation and deployment to unsupported platforms. In the following example, error directives ensure that the app builds for iOS 8 and later or OS X 10.10 and later:

```
#if TARGET_OS_IPHONE
    // iOS 8 or later only
    #if __IPHONE_OS_VERSION_MIN_REQUIRED < 80000
    #error "For iOS 8 or later deployment"
    #endif
#else
    // OS X 10.10 or later only
    #import <Availability.h>
    #ifdef __MAC_OS_X_VERSION_MIN_REQUIRED
        #if __MAC_OS_X_VERSION_MIN_REQUIRED < 101000
        #error "For OSX 10.10 or later deployment"
        #endif
    #else
        #warning "Unable to test against OS X Minimum Version"
    #endif
#endif
```

Testing for Inclusion

A simple tweak enables you to include library packs—but only when they're currently added to the project. The Essentials.h file used throughout this book's sample code contains the following tests. They include the same `__has_include` test used to create Figure 10-9. In this case, instead of triggering a warning when the file is not found, they act by including a header file if the file *is* found:

```
#if __has_include("ConstraintPack.h")
#import "ConstraintPack.h"
#endif

#if __has_include("HandyPack.h")
#import "HandyPack.h"
#endif

#if __has_include("Utility.h")
#import "Utility.h"
#endif
```

This approach enables you to lazily add library material to projects, ensuring that they're automatically available for use. This solution is Swift inspired. Swift does not require explicit include statements for files you add to your projects.

> **Note**
>
> Read more about feature-checking macros at the Clang Language Extensions website: http://clang.llvm.org/docs/LanguageExtensions.html.

Messages

Message pragmas are directives that, as their name suggests, produce messages. The messages don't convert to an error, regardless of compiler settings. Here's an example of a message that reminds you about some to-do item:

```
#pragma message ("To Do: Extend this to include Feature A")
```

Like #warning and #error directives, messages show up in your issues navigator and with inline highlighting, as shown in Figure 10-10. They are informational only. The Clang compiler basically ignores them, even when you've switched on Treat Errors as Warnings.

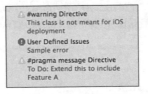

Figure 10-10   The issue navigator aggregates compilation warnings and errors in Objective-C code.

Wrapping Pragmas

Diagnostic messages can be wrapped into macros to produce standardized output. This is a handy trick, one that enables you to wrap message requests into reusable components. Here are a couple macros that combine to create to-do items:

```
#define DO_PRAGMA(_ARG_) _Pragma (#_ARG_)
#define TODO(_ITEM_) DO_PRAGMA(message ("To Do: " #_ITEM_))
```

When you invoke the TODO macro, it builds the same results as the message directive you just saw. It supplies a message argument to the _Pragma operator and adds the "To Do: " prefix to the message it builds:

```
TODO(Extend this to include Feature A)
```

If you want, you can incorporate standard compiler-supplied macros like __FILE__, __LINE__, __DATE__, and __TIME__ with message directives. For example, you might add the following message (see Figure 10-11), which uses the __FILE__ macro, to an implementation file:

```
#pragma message "Compiling " __FILE__.
```

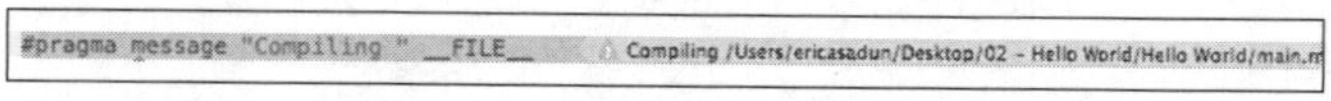

Figure 10-11   Compiler-supplied macros provide information about the items being processed.

Overriding Diagnostics

You override diagnostics with the diagnostic ignored pragma. The following example temporarily disables warnings about undeclared selectors and their leaks:

```
#pragma clang diagnostic push
#pragma clang diagnostic ignored "-Wundeclared-selector"
#pragma clang diagnostic ignored "-Warc-performSelector-leaks"
void SafePerform(id target, SEL selector, NSObject *object)
{
    if ([target respondsToSelector:selector])
        [target performSelector:selector withObject:object];
}
#pragma clang diagnostic pop
```

By surrounding these items with push and pop directives, you localize those overrides to just this section. The compiler continues to tag undeclared selector usage in the rest of your project.

Unused Variable Warnings

Unused variable warnings often crop up in development, especially as you're framing new classes and methods before filling in details and expanding functionality. They provide a good example of how you can solve a problem using any number of directives (see Figure 10-12).

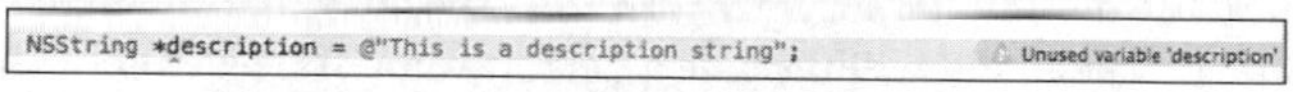

Figure 10-12   Clang warns when it encounters unused variables.

As with selector issues, you can use a diagnostic ignored pragma like the following to suppress the compiler warning:

```
#pragma clang diagnostic ignored "-Wunused-variable"
```

Or you can mark the variable with an attribute:

```
NSString *description __attribute__ ((unused));
```

Or use the __unused keyword:

```
NSInteger __unused index;
```

There's also a specific unused pragma available:

```
#pragma unused (description)
```

You can also wrap this pragma into its own macro if you're so inclined:

```
// Create "unused" macro
#define UNUSED(_ITEM_) DO_PRAGMA(unused(_ITEM_))

// Use the macro in-line with the declaration
NSString *description; UNUSED(description);
```

Marking Non-null and Nullable Items

You can require a non-null (that is, not nil) parameter in Objective-C by referencing a nonnull attribute. When this is used, the method or function expects that its parameter is not a null pointer. The following example specifies that the first parameter (the count starting with 1 and not 0) should never be nil:

```
- (BOOL) createAtPath: (NSString *) path __attribute__ ((nonnull (1)))
```

This example corresponds directly to a non-optional Swift item. Its opposite, a nullable attribute, which was just recently added to Objective-C, refers to any item that can be set to nil, and it works the same as a Swift optional, such as NSString?. Apple also added the null_unspecified keyword to support Objective-C versions of Swift's implicitly unwrapped optionals.

For most iOS development in Objective-C, the nonnull attribute suffices to indicate "this parameter must not be nil." The other two attributes were added to provide support for Swift idioms and warnings. A final keyword, null_resettable, is available for properties and also helps support Swift interchange:

```
@property (nonatomic, null_resettable) NSString *string;
```

When used in a property definition, null_resettable specifies that the item's getter will never return a non-nil value (and will provide a default value if needed) but that the property itself can be *set* to nil by the developer to reset it to that default.

Developer Tweaks

This chapter has covered two major topics: placeholders and directives. Before wrapping up, this section offers a couple of final developer tweaks. These items may seem obvious to some readers, but you'd be surprised at how often I get responses like "oh, I didn't think of doing that" when I bring these up.

Saving Files from the Simulator

It's not always clear, but your iOS simulator operates in your Mac's file system. For example, try logging the value of NSHomeDirectory() to your console. You'll see that the results are with respect to your home computer and not with respect to any application's iOS sandbox:

```
2015-02-09 11:48:21.094 Hello World[19977:1725860] /Users/ericasadun/Library/
Developer/CoreSimulator/Devices/D25F6113-075D-4169-9EB6-49890A835584/data/
Containers/Data/Application/A567D62B-4869-40E9-9F37-CA81EDF3C870
```

This is a very useful quirk. It enables you to save files from simulator apps to your desktop—a feature many developers do not consider when developing for iOS. Writing to the desktop is particularly useful. When you work with items that cannot be displayed onscreen or at the console, you can simply write them to desktop files. Don't underestimate the utility of saving test material to an easy location for inspection and review.

Listing 10-4 defines a pair of utilities that accomplishes this. The first of the two simply writes the contents of any NSData you pass as a parameter. You supply a name for the file (be sure to use a reasonable extension), and it writes it to your desktop. Make sure you edit this material so you use your own user name and not mine. The second example first extracts an image's PNG representation and then redirects to the more general implementation.

Although Listing 10-4 focuses on data and images, you can use this same idea to write to a text file. That's handy when normal logging and debugging is disabled due to early beta deployment, such as with extensions. It's a reliable way to get information out of your app.

Listing 10-4   **Saving to Your Mac's Desktop**

```
// Save data file to the desktop. The name should include
// the file extension to save to
void SaveDebugData(NSData *data, NSString *name)
{
    // This is my desktop. Change this to point to your desktop.
    NSString *desktopPath = @"/Users/ericasadun/Desktop";
    NSString *targetPath =
        [desktopPath stringByAppendingPathComponent:name];
    [data writeToFile:targetPath atomically:YES];
}


// This function automatically performs the conversion from
// a UIImage instance to its PNG representation before saving
void SaveDebugImage(UIImage *image, NSString *name)
{
    SaveDebugData(UIImagePNGRepresentation(image),
        [[name lastPathComponent] stringByAppendingPathExtension:@"png"]);
}
```

Tighter Logging

When you need to copy and share the output of your logged material, you may not want all the prefix information (things that look like 2015-02-09 11:48:21.094 Hello World[19977:1725860]) to appear with your output. In these circumstances, I use a logging function that I shamelessly adapted from master developer Landon Fuller:

```
void Log(NSString *formatString,...)
{
    va_list arglist;
    if (formatString)
    {
        va_start(arglist, formatString);
        NSString *outstring = [[NSString alloc]
            initWithFormat:formatString arguments:arglist];
        fprintf(stderr, "%s\n", [outstring UTF8String]);
        va_end(arglist);
    }
}
```

This function works just like NSLog but uses the C-language fprintf function to skip introductory material before the output. You can easily copy it, paste it, and share it with less visual clutter.

As an alternative, when you have just a few lines of debugger console output to share, hold down the Option key before selecting. This enables you to select a rectangle of text instead of lines of text. You can effectively select what you want from each line, leaving the debugger prefix behind.

Wrap-up

Here are a few final points to wrap up what you've read in this chapter:

- Whether you're working with words, pictures, contacts, or views, a solid source of dummy content can help during the early development process.

- Avoid being a bad API citizen. Don't abuse free APIs. These resources aren't meant for constant calls in production code. If you need source content for apps, grab a copy of Cicero's *De finibus bonorum et malorum* (or similar public domain incomprehensible Latinate text). Pre-fetching and caching content helps reduce the load on placeholder servers.

- Even as Apple continues to grow Swift, it hasn't neglected Objective-C. There are still great things to learn and experience in Objective-C. Apple only recently added the new nullable and null_unspecified attributes to Objective-C to enable better Swift/Objective-C co-existence.

A Taste of Swift

Apple introduced the Swift programming language at the June 2014 WWDC Keynote. Swift offers a performance-tuned type-safe modern programming language. The initial release was a beta, but by that autumn, Swift 1.0 was officially adopted for app development and submission. Even at 1.0, the language remained in flux. When Swift 1.2 arrived in 2015, many development fundamentals had coalesced, although the language and toolset were continuing to evolve.

If this sounds like a nearly impossible target to write about, well it is—at least to a point. Today, you can pick up Swift basics and be more or less assured that the floor isn't going to shift under you—or your code—for many essential tasks. The code you write today will probably look fundamentally similar to the code you write a year from now, even if the nitty-gritty specifics have shifted a little. The Xcode tools you use to construct your apps, too, will be similar, although it's a fair bet that details will evolve between the time this chapter is being prepared and the moment you read it.

Given all this, this chapter surveys the bare essentials of Swift development, providing a taste of this new technology. You won't learn the language in this chapter; that's better done by downloading a copy of Apple's *Swift Programming Language* from iBooks. What you see in your IDE may not exactly match these figures and code samples as Apple updates its tools and the language. Instead, you'll explore concepts and development issues that affect you as an iOS developer to get a sense of where this important technology is going.

Swift Versus Objective-C

Swift is an exciting language that shows great promise for the future. Its release has not caused iOS developers to abandon Objective-C. While some developers, especially larger development houses, are testing out the waters with pure Swift projects, many independent developers have invested too much in Objective-C libraries and toolsets to walk away for a completely fresh start. These developers will continue with either pure Objective-C projects or hybrid solutions that balance their current libraries with new Swift code.

While you can build an entire app today in Swift, many developers will choose not to, especially for any app more complicated than a basic to-do list or Flappy Bird clone (see http://en.wikipedia.org/wiki/Flappy_Bird). Groups with greater personnel resources that can dedicate people to building libraries and frameworks can more easily invest in large Swift projects. Smaller outfits may find themselves building Swift code bases that parallel their apps, planning for a more gradual transition.

Apple guarantees only binary compatibility for release versions of its language. Apps compiled for a specific firmware target continue to work in binary form going forward, even as the language evolves. On the developer forums site, Apple's Chris Lattner wrote,

> Our goal for Swift 1.0 is for *apps* to be binary compatible with the OS, not for Swift 1.0 frameworks to be compatible with Swift 2.0 frameworks. The formal goal (what we're shooting for) is relatively straight-forward, because apps are hemispherically sealed, and there is almost no dependence of Swift 1.0 apps on the OS.

This policy makes Objective-C an attractive target for immediate development. The Objective-C code you write today will continue to work without updates and refactoring for the immediate future.

Swift components and Objective-C can coexist in a single project. You're much more likely to see marriages of the two over the next few years than an abrupt transition from one to the other. Developers don't forsake time-tested routines they've invested time and energy in, to plunge fully into a new language when there's no compelling reason to do so. Tight deadlines and strict work schedules dictate the realities of Swift migration.

Swift programming remains an important skill to pick up over the near term. Expect to see more emphasis on Swift in sample code, in technical talks, and so forth. Developers are still good with Objective-C and will continue to be for some time to come, but they should strategize about transition plans for their applications now. Some products will live out their lives in Objective-C. Others will require modernization and refactoring to fit into the development environment of the next few years.

Time scales are going to be an intensely individual decision. When starting a new project today with a short-term delivery, you might stick with Objective-C. The tools are solid, tested, reliable, and unlikely to shift too much. At the same time, invest time in building Swift libraries and pushing boundaries. I'm not sure when I'll be ready to make a permanent jump to a stable Swift-primary development commitment, but as the language and my skills grow, I can see that transition coming closer and closer.

Building iOS Apps in Swift

To Objective-C eyes, the Swift language may look a bit foreign, but there's actually much that is familiar to grab onto. Listing 11-1 presents a compact Swift 1.2 source for a basic "Hello World" app. This standard iOS app is trimmed down to its essentials. The application delegate creates a window. It then builds a custom view controller, installs it to a navigation controller, and sets it as the window's root view controller before making the window key and visible.

> **Note**
>
> Normally this material would appear in separate view controller and application delegate source files: ViewController.swift and AppDelegate.swift. They've been merged here to create a single file app to showcase how a complete app works.

Listing 11-1   **Hello Swift**

```swift
import UIKit

class ViewController: UIViewController {
    override func viewDidLoad() {
        super.viewDidLoad()
        view.backgroundColor = UIColor.whiteColor()
        title = "Hello Swift"
    }
}

@UIApplicationMain class AppDelegate: UIResponder, UIApplicationDelegate {
    var window: UIWindow?

    func application(application: UIApplication,
        didFinishLaunchingWithOptions launchOptions:
            [NSObject: AnyObject]?) -> Bool {
        window = UIWindow(frame: UIScreen.mainScreen().bounds)
        if let window = self.window {
            let vc = ViewController(nibName: nil, bundle: nil)
            let nav = UINavigationController(rootViewController: vc);
            window.rootViewController = nav
            window.makeKeyAndVisible()
        }
        return true
    }
}
```

Figure 11-1 shows the application created by Listing 11-1 compiled and run. It consists of a simple navigation controller that presents an empty view controller. The view controller's title is assigned a "Hello Swift" text string and displays in the top navigation bar.

As you look at the code in Listing 11-1 and compare it to Objective-C, you discover numerous changes. Swift does away with square brackets. Parameters appear within parentheses, and the method signature that used to be interspersed with parameters now starts after a period. Instead of method calls that look like this in Objective-C:

```objc
[instance method:parameter1 signature:parameter2];
```

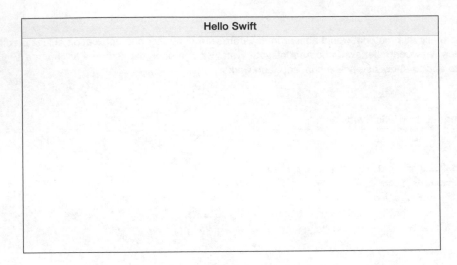

Figure 11-1   When run, Listing 11-1 essentially displays a blank view controller.

In Swift, you work with calls that look like this:

```
instance.method(parameter1, signature:parameter2)
```

Here's what the delegate class created in Listing 11-1 would look like in Objective-C:

```
@interface AppDelegate : UIResponder <UIApplicationDelegate>
@property (nonatomic, strong) UIWindow *window;
@end

@implementation AppDelegate
// . . .
@end
```

Swift drops these separate interface headers and implementation declarations, combining them into a single class definition.

In Listing 11-1, the delegate class establishes a `window` property as a variable. In Objective-C, this would use `@property` notation. In Swift, the `UIApplicationDelegate` protocol conformance declaration is separated by a comma and does not appear between angle brackets, as it does in Objective-C. In an Objective-C application, an app delegate is instantiated in `main()` by calling `UIApplicationMain()`. In Listing 11-1, the `UIApplicationMain` attribute establishes the application delegate class. If you skip this attribute, you must create a main.swift file and call `UIApplicationMain()`, as you would from Objective-C.

In Listing 11-1, you see two question marks within the Swift code. One appears in the `window` property declaration, and the other is part of the launch options parameter. In Swift, a question mark indicates a nullable, or "optional," parameter. These elements can be set to a value or to `nil`. In Swift, `nil` means "a missing value" or "no value has been assigned." The concept of optional and non-optional types plays a big role in Swift, and you read about them in the next section.

A few more points about this code before moving on:

- Swift is full of specialty keywords that indicate roles and usage. In Listing 11-1, the `override` keyword used with the `viewDidLoad()` method is required because the subclass overrides a parent method. If it is omitted, the compiler flags an error. Other common keywords include access modifiers (like `public` and `private`), reference strengths (like `weak`), and mutability indicators (like `mutating` and `nonmutating`).

- Swift variables are declared using `var` for an item whose value may change over time or `let` for an item that will not ever change once it is set. Always prefer `let` over `var`. This enables the compiler to optimize your code. Of course, if the value will be changing, you must use `var`.

- In Swift, class-based functions are still called methods.

- Swift native types like integers (`Int`) and strings (`String`) can be bridged to Cocoa types like `NSNumber` and `NSString`.

- Statement-ending semicolons can be omitted entirely except when two statements appear on the same line of code. A semicolon makes clear to the compiler that the two statements should not be combined into a single one.

- String literals in Swift do not use the `@` sign. Use double quotes to delimit your strings, as in the line that sets the Hello Swift title (`title = "Hello Swift"`) for this app.

- The `if let` construct you see in the delegate is a common Swift pattern. It says "assign a value to a local variable, and if the value is non-`nil`, execute the command that follows within the braces."

Optionals

Optional values are a foundational Swift concept, and one that's central to Cocoa Touch development. Therefore, this section dives into this one language feature in a little depth. Optionals are a part of Swift that enables you to respond to the success/fail situations you encounter when calling established framework APIs.

Any variable marked with `?` may—or may not—contain a valid value. To get a sense of this feature, look at the following code, which establishes a Swift dictionary and then looks up two items. As you see, square brackets haven't entirely disappeared from the language but are used for dictionaries and arrays:

```
let soundDictionary = ["cow":"moo", "dog":"bark", "pig":"squeal"]
println(soundDictionary["cow"]) // prints moo
println(soundDictionary["fox"]) // what does the fox say?
```

What sound does the fox say? In Swift (not to be confused with Ylvis's implementation), the answer is nil. In Swift, nil indicates "no value." Unlike in Objective-C, in Swift nil is not a pointer. Swift nil indicates a semantic missing non-existence: a Count of Monte Cristo, a cup of "not tea," or an honest politician. A nil item means "nothing to see here, move along, move along, move along." In Swift, even variables of primitive types like integers are nil before assignment.

Inferred Types

This soundDictionary example is a string dictionary. Swift infers this from assignment in the first line. Swift uses the most restrictive interpretation of the data it assigns. Keys are strings, and values are strings, so the dictionary is a string dictionary. You check this declaration by Option-clicking soundDictionary, as in Figure 11-2. If you want Swift to use a particular type instead of inferring it from assigned data, specify the type (for example, [String : String] for this dictionary) after a colon and before the = assignment operator:

```
let soundDictionary : [String : String] =
    ["cow":"moo", "dog":"bark", "pig":"squeal"]
```

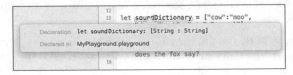

Figure 11-2   Swift infers the [String:String] type from the data assigned to the soundDictionary variable. Alt-click (or Option-click) any item in your source code to examine its inferred or declared type.

The example in Figure 11-2 is run in a Swift playground. A playground is an interactive, interpreted environment you use for prototyping Swift routines and for learning Swift. It enables you to type in code and instantly see whether it executes as expected.

When you look up any item in soundDictionary, as in Figure 11-3, the value returned is not a String. Instead of returning "moo" for "cow" and nil for "fox", this example actually returns a special *optional* form of "moo" and the nil value. In this example, these optionals are typed String?. This question mark is important and always indicates an optional type. How these results appear (whether as Optional("moo"), {Some "moo"}, etc.) will vary as Apple figures out how it wants to convey this important syntax. In Figure 11-3, Apple shows "moo" as the return value in line 14, but when you print it (see line 15 in the figure), you expose the underlying optional wrapping.

```
13   let soundDictionary = ["cow":"moo",          ["pig":"squeal", "cow": "moo", "dog": "bark"]
         "dog":"bark", "pig":"squeal"]
14   soundDictionary["cow"]                        "moo"
15   println(soundDictionary["cow"])              "Optional("moo")"
16   println(soundDictionary["fox"])              "nil"
17
18   let optionalResult =                          nil
         soundDictionary["Something"]
```

Figure 11-3   An optional value *wraps* the result of a successful dictionary lookup.

The Optional Enumeration

Optional types return either a wrapped value (the bit with the word `Optional` or braces or whatever the wrapping flavor of the week is) or `nil`. Wrapping means the actual value is stored in a logical outer structure. You cannot get to that value (in this case, `"moo"`) without unwrapping it. In Swift World, it is always Christmas, and there are always presents—or at least variables—to unwrap.

In technical terms, an optional is an enumeration. A Swift enumeration is a very different beast from the Objective-C one. While Objective-C enumerations are basically limited to declaring word-based integer sequences or flags values, Swift enumerations declare both member names and optionally associated values. In this example, the `Optional` enumeration stores either nothing (`nil`) or something (any data type you pass). Here's what that enumeration declaration looks like in Swift:

```
enum Optional<T> {
    case None
    case Some(T)
}
```

This ability to store any type is part of Swift's *generics* support. A generic item enables you to work with any data type you encounter rather than a specific class. As the name suggests, you implement generic functionality that works across specific types. In this `Optional` case, the generic support lets you store any kind of data inside the optional wrapper. The angle brackets with the `T` inside indicate a generic type for this enumeration. (There is nothing magical about the letter *T*. It's just a convenient convention for an arbitrary type.)

Some generics specify commonalities, called *requirements*. For example, a generic can be a countable item, a sequence, an item that can be compared, or, in the most general case, any kind of class at all. With generics, you can write code that appends new elements to any kind of list or counts items in any kind of collection.

Dictionary lookups always return optional types. So a `[String : String]` dictionary returns a `String?` result, as you see in Figure 11-4. Dictionaries may or may not contain a specific keyword or key object, so returning an optional enables them to fail at lookup or to succeed. The success case is encapsulated in a wrapper, which involves an extra handling step you don't encounter in Objective-C.

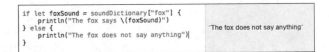

Figure 11-4   Using Option-click reveals that the dictionary lookup return type is `String?`. The question mark is part of the type.

The `String?` type in the following snippet means that `animalSound` stores either `nil` or a wrapped string value—for example, {Some "Narf!"} or Optional("Narf!")—assuming that your test sounds come from a Steven Spielberg cartoon:

```
let animalSound : String? = soundDictionary[searchString]
```

Unwrapping Optionals

You unwrap values either by adding exclamation points or by using the `if-let` construction you saw in Listing 11-1. If the value is wrapped (the `"Some"` or `"Optional()"` result you just saw), you extract the value stored within the wrapped element. If the value is `nil` and you unwrap your optional with `!`, you encounter a fatal runtime error—which is not nearly as fun or gratifying. The `nil` value is the Swift equivalent of your aunt's home-crocheted vest. It's critically important to always check whether an item is `nil` before unwrapping it. Figure 11-5 shows the safer `if-let` approach.

```
if let foxSound = soundDictionary["fox"] {
    println("The fox says \(foxSound)")
} else {
    println("The fox does not say anything")|
}
```
"The fox does not say anything"

Figure 11-5   Use `if-let` to safely unwrap optionals.

The `if-let` syntax performs a conditional assignment to an unwrapped variable. It executes the functionality that follows based on whether it could or could not complete that assignment. In this example, if the result is non-`nil`, the example uses the (unwrapped) sound variable to print out the animal-sound fact. If `nil`, it branches to the second half, where there's no valid value for a sound.

Swift also provides a feature called *implicitly unwrapped optionals*. You declare these optionals with an exclamation point at the end of the type. Figure 11-6 offers examples of first a wrapped assignment and then an implicitly unwrapped one. Both are assigned to the same value (`soundDictionary["cow"]`), but one automatically extracts the internal value, and the other retains the optional enumeration.

With unwrapped optional variables, the result is not {Some "moo"} or Optional("moo"). It is `"moo"`, a simple string. Implicit unwrapping extracts the value inside an optional item and uses the data type you'd expect from the dictionary lookup. Once it is unwrapped, use the variable directly. You don't have to add that "unwrap this variable" exclamation point.

```
let wrappedSound = soundDictionary["cow"]                              {Some "moo"}
let unwrappedSound : String! = soundDictionary["cow"]                  "moo"


wrappedSound                                                          {Some "moo"}
wrappedSound!                                                          "moo"
unwrappedSound                                                         "moo"
```

Figure 11-6   Implicitly unwrapped variables extract values on assignment. Only use these when it's clear that an optional variable will always have a value after a certain point in the program execution.

Use implicit unwrapping when you know in advance that a variable will always have a value after some logical point. For example, if you're responding to button taps or menu clicks, you probably don't have to wonder whether a particular button or menu item exists. It does. Because if it didn't, you would never have reached your callback.

Unwrapped optionals enable you to access values directly, without having to test and annotate them at each use. With great unwrapping, however, comes great responsibility. You must take care that you properly guard these items to ensure that you don't attempt to unwrap nil:

```
// This generates a nasty error
let unwrappedSound2 : String! = soundDictionary["error"]
```

When using implicit unwrapping with possible failure points, check for nil before your first variable access or you may crash your application. Here's what this approach looks like in pseudocode:

```
var variable : Type! = APIThatMightFail(arguments)
if variable == nil {...handle failure case..., return}
...now safely use implicitly unwrapped variable...
```

This approach is dangerous because the compiler won't warn you about missing nil checks. A wordier solution may better help catch errors:

```
var variable_ : Type = APIThatMightFail(arguments)
if variable_ == nil {...handle failure case..., return}
let variable = variable_!
...now safely use manually unwrapped variable...
```

The recommended solution, however, is to use an if-let construct wherever possible to ensure variable safety:

```
if let variable = APIThatMightFail(arguments) {
    ... safely use unwrapped variable...
}
```

While this approach is always safety-optimal, it can introduce the dreaded Swift "pyramid of doom," where multiple levels of nested if checks cause unsightly code structuring.

Assigning Values to Non-optionals

Swift lets you annotate variable declarations with ! and ? in addition to the mutable (`var`) and immutable (`let`) keywords. If you declare a variable without ! or ?, Swift expects you to assign a non-optional value, like this:

```
var nonOptional : String = "Hello" // This works
```

When you assign an optional result (`String?`) to a non-optional, use ! to unwrap it:

```
nonOptional = soundDictionary["cow"]! // moo
```

Better yet, test before you unwrap:

```
if let sound = soundDictionary["cow"] {
    nonOptional = sound
}
```

There are things you cannot do. You cannot assign `nil` to a non-optional:

```
nonOptional = nil // error
```

You cannot assign an optional enumeration to a non-optional:

```
nonOptional = soundDictionary["cow"] // error
// "value of optional type 'String?' not unwrapped;
// did you mean to use '!' or '?'?"
```

You cannot unwrap a `nil` optional, let alone assign it to a non-optional variable:

```
// nonOptional = soundDictionary["fox"]! // error
// fatal error: unexpectedly found nil while unwrapping an Optional value
```

Working with optionals is one of the biggest transitions from the Objective-C world and one that's most important for working with traditional Cocoa Touch APIs.

Cocoa Touch Patterns

Most Cocoa Touch APIs follow a common pattern that looks something like this in Objective-C:

```
result = [object call: with: parameters: error:&error];
if (!result)
{
    // handle error here
}
```

An API returns an object created using the parameters passed to the call. When the return value is `nil`, an error object passed by reference is populated with details about why the call failed. This enables you to handle the error and shortcut your execution.

Listing 11-2 shows an example of Objective-C code that follows this pattern. At each step, an operation is attempted and the results are tested, with an error generated for failed steps. A result returns only after passing each stage of calls and tests.

Listing 11-2   **Fetching a URL-Sourced String with Objective-C**

```
// Return an NSError instance
NSError *BuildError(NSInteger code, NSString *reason)
{
    NSString *errorDomain = @"com.sadun.examples";
    NSError *error = [NSError errorWithDomain:errorDomain code:code
    userInfo:@{NSLocalizedDescriptionKey:reason,
        NSLocalizedFailureReasonErrorKey:reason}];
    return error;
}


// Fetch a string from the specified URL
NSString *StringFromURL(NSURL *url, NSError **error)
{
    // Request data
    NSData *data = [NSData dataWithContentsOfURL:url options:0 error:error];
    if (!data) return nil;

    // Convert the data to a UTF-8 string
    NSString *string = [[NSString alloc] initWithData:data
        encoding:NSUTF8StringEncoding];
    if (!string) {
        if (error)
            *error = BuildError(1, @"Unable to build string from data");
        return nil;
    }

    // Return the string
    return string;
}


// And here are usage examples
NSError *error;
NSURL *url = [NSURL URLWithString:@"duck://ericasadun.com"]; // bad url
// NSURL *url = [NSURL URLWithString:@"http://ericasadun.com"]; // good url
NSString *string = StringFromURL(url, &error);
if (string)
    NSLog(@"string: %@", string);
else
    NSLog(@"error: %@", error.localizedDescription);
```

Listing 11-3 offers a Swift 1.2 equivalent to the Objective-C code in Listing 11-2. It follows the same steps and uses Swift's if-let syntax to test each success. At each step, the function attempts a standard API call. If the result succeeds, the value is passed to the next step. On failure, the error is assigned and nil returned. Other than a slight change in flow due to the if-let tests, the code is substantially similar to the Objective-C version.

Listing 11-3   **Fetching a URL-Sourced String with Swift 1.2**

```swift
// Return NSError from code and reason
func BuildError(code : Int, reason : String) -> NSError {
    let errorDomain = "com.sadun.examples"
    let error = NSError(domain: errorDomain, code: code,
        userInfo: [
            NSLocalizedDescriptionKey:reason,
            NSLocalizedFailureReasonErrorKey:reason])
    return error
}


// Fetch string using standard Swift if-let
func StringFromURL(url : NSURL, inout error : NSError?) -> (NSString?) {
    if let data = NSData(contentsOfURL:url,
        options: NSDataReadingOptions(rawValue:0), error: &error) {
        if let string =
        NSString(data: data, encoding: NSUTF8StringEncoding) {
            return string
        }
        error = BuildError(1, "Unable to build string from data")
        return nil
    }
    return nil
}


// Examples to test the implementation
var error : NSError?
let url = NSURL(string: "duck://ericasadun.com")! // bad url
//let url = NSURL(string: "http://ericasadun.com")! // good url

if let string = StringFromURL(url, error:&error) {
    println(string)
} else {
    // This unwraps the error into a new non-optional error instance.
    // This error/error looks confusing but same-named-unwrapping is
    // fast becoming the normal practice for unwrapping
    if let error = error {
        println(error.localizedDescription)
    }
}
```

Although they are built in two languages, Listings 11-2 and 11-3 are functionally identical. They use the same APIs, perform the same checks for `nil`, and handle errors in the same way. The one noticeable difference is how the checks flow. The `if-let` flow in Swift pushes the success case forward. The string is returned in the middle of the `StringFromURL` function in Swift versus at the end in Objective-C. The nested structure is called the Swift "pyramid of doom." This is not to say you cannot produce the same flow in Swift. By handling the `nil` case first and force-unwrapping optional results, you build Listing 11-4, which mirrors the Objective-C code even more closely.

Listing 11-4 **Handling Error Conditions First in Swift**

```
// Fetch string using a linear flow
func StringFromURL(url : NSURL, inout error : NSError?) -> (NSString?) {
    // Fetch data
    let data_ = NSData(contentsOfURL:url,
        options: NSDataReadingOptions(rawValue:0), error: &error)
    if (data_ == nil) {
        return nil
    }
    let data = data_!

    // Convert data to string
    let string_ = NSString(data: data, encoding: NSUTF8StringEncoding)
    if (string_ == nil) {
        error = BuildError(1, "Unable to build string from data")
        return nil
    }
    let string = string_!

    // Return string
    return string
}
```

Although Listing 11-4 is not nearly as "Swift-y" as Listing 11-3, I like its linear flow. This early-exit approach enhances readability and offers easier modification should additional steps become necessary. Your code should always serve your long-term needs for maintenance and self-documentation. Listing 11-4 is wordy and expansive but prosaic, practical, and safe.

Hybrid Language Development

Mixed-languages projects are an important step as companies and individuals transition from Objective-C to Swift. They will continue to be a reality for some time. When you're writing mixed-language projects, you need to know how to call Objective-C implementations from Swift and how to call Swift ones from Objective-C. This section introduces development in both directions, showing you how to accomplish this in your apps.

Calling Objective-C from Swift

On adding Objective-C class files to an otherwise-Swift project, Xcode invites you to create a bridging header file (see Figure 11-7). This file enables your Swift code to access your Objective-C code. With it, you can instantiate classes, call methods, and so forth. By default, this header is called *Project-Module-Name*-Bridging-Header.h. It uses the name of your project in the prefix.

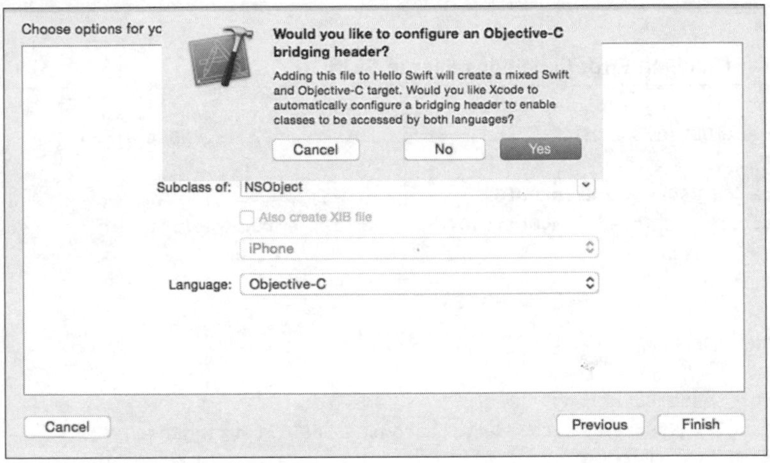

Figure 11-7   A bridging header file exposes Objective-C interfaces to Swift code. This screen shot uses the Xcode 6.3 toolset.

Edit the bridging header to include any public header you want Swift to automatically access. Make sure you add references for every Objective-C-based file you want to include:

```
// Use this file to import your target's public headers that
// you would like to expose to Swift.
```

```
#import "TestClass.h"
```

At this writing, Xcode only offers to create the bridging header when you first add Objective-C class files to your project. You can build one yourself by choosing File > New > File > iOS > Source > Header File. You can then append -Bridging-Header.h to the name of your project, but it's easier to let Xcode ensure that the file is named properly by allowing it to create the bridging header for you.

Accessing Classes

Classes included through the bridging header are accessible from Swift. Say, for example, that you have declared the following NSObject subclass:

```
@interface TestClass : NSObject
- (void) test;
@end
```

In Swift, you treat the class as if it had always been written in Swift. You construct a new instance, using a standard Swift initializer (that is, the parentheses following the class name in the following snippet). Once this is built, you can then call the test method on the new instance:

```
let myTest = TestClass()
myTest.test()
```

Calling Swift from Objective-C

It's nearly as easy to call Swift code from Objective-C as the reverse, but a few gotchas along the way may spoil your day. The first challenge is to discover an appropriate header to import. Apple's docs specify that the name of this file is your product name followed by -Swift.h.

For a project named Hello World, the Objective-C-to-swift-bridging header that is automatically created is named Hello World-Bridging-Header.h, with a space between the first two words. You might assume that the Swift import header will be named Hello World-Swift.h, but you'd be wrong. The actual name is Hello_World-Swift.h, with an underscore, not a space. Obviously, these details may change over time as Xcode is updated, so let the Xcode do as much work for you as possible.

The best way to locate the actual bridging header for your project is to perform a little file exploration. Open the Xcode Organizer (Windows > Organizer) and select your project. Click on the little arrow next to the path of your derived data. This opens a new Finder window at that path.

Next, navigate to the Build folder. Xcode 6.3 builds the Swift import header on your behalf, but it hides it. Assuming that Xcode doesn't change significantly, you need to find the DerivedSources folder for your build (somewhere deep in your Build folder, typically several levels down). At this writing, you uncover this file by descending through the following path:

- **Derived Data**—The project's derived data, for example, DerivedData/Hello_World-dfqiqgdsqctvsshpcgguyyhnyhgi
- **Build**—The folder named Build
- **Intermediates**—The folder named Intermediates
- **Build**—The Project Name build folder, for example, Hello World.build
- **Platform**—The platform folder, for example, Debug-iphonesimulator
- **Build**—Another build folder, for example, Hello World.build
- **Derived Sources**—The folder named DerivedSources

Once you confirm the name of the header file, simply import it into whatever Objective-C file needs access to the Swift-sourced code:

```
#import "Hello_World-Swift.h"
```

If you think you know the correct name, you can more or less skip this entire process. Simply add the import statement and confirm that it goes to the right place by Command-clicking the header name in any source file. If it opens up the right file in the Xcode browser, you've set up the header correctly. (See Figure 11-8.)

```
⊞ | < > | h Hello_World-Swift.h > No Selection

 1   // Generated by Apple Swift version 1.2 (swiftlang-602.0.42.4 clang-602.0.42)
 2   #pragma clang diagnostic push
 3
 4   #if defined(__has_include) && __has_include(<swift/objc-prologue.h>)
 5   # include <swift/objc-prologue.h>
 6   #endif
 7
 8   #pragma clang diagnostic ignored "-Wauto-import"
 9   #include <objc/NSObject.h>
10   #include <stdint.h>
11   #include <stddef.h>
12   #include <stdbool.h>
13
14   #if defined(__has_include) && __has_include(<uchar.h>)
15   # include <uchar.h>
16   #elif !defined(__cplusplus) || __cplusplus < 201103L
17   typedef uint_least16_t char16_t;
18   typedef uint_least32_t char32_t;
19   #endif
20
21   typedef struct _NSZone NSZone;
22
23   #if !defined(SWIFT_PASTE)
```

Figure 11-8   The -Swift.h header file includes material that enables Objective-C code to access Swift-sourced classes, methods, and protocols. This example is from Xcode 6.3 and Swift 1.2.

Preparing Swift for Objective-C

You must mark any Swift class or protocol with the `@objc` attribute before using it in Objective-C. For example, you might declare the following class skeletons in your Swift code:

```
@objc class VisibleToObjectiveC {
}

class NotVisibleToObjectiveC {
}
```

In this case, the first declaration uses the `@objc` keyword. The second does not.

In any Objective-C source file, you can reference the visible class, but if you try to use the not-visible class, you get an error (see Figure 11-9).

```
34
35       VisibleToObjectiveC *visible = nil;
36       NotVisibleToObjectiveC *invisible = nil;
37       ⊗ Unknown type name 'NotVisibleToObjectiveC'; did you mean 'VisibleToObjectiveC'?
38
```

Figure 11-9   Use the `@objc` attribute to expose classes and protocols to Objective-C.

While you can port over classes and protocols, as long as you use the @objc attribute, many Swift elements—including generics, tuples, structures, stand-alone functions, global variables, and so forth—cannot be ported at this time. The Apple docs (see "Using Swift with Cocoa and Objective-C") detail the exact restrictions involved.

Class Descent

The following Swift snippet declares two classes. Both are marked with @objc, and both can be referenced from Objective-C. The only substantial difference between the two is that the first class, MyCocoaClass, descends from NSObject and the second, MySwiftClass, does not:

```
@objc class MyCocoaClass : NSObject {
    func test() {
        println("I can call Swift from Objective-C")
    }
}

@objc class MySwiftClass {
    func test() {
        println("I can call Swift from Objective-C")
    }
}
```

You create instances of MyCocoaClass by calling new or alloc-init, as you would with any item that descends from NSObject. As Figure 11-10 shows, you cannot use standard constructors to create new MySwiftClass instances.

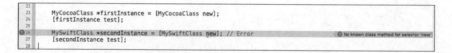

Figure 11-10   Classes that do not descend from NSObject cannot use NSObject constructors.

In Swift, you don't need Objective-C-style constructors. To build a new MySwiftClass instance, you call MySwiftClass(), with parentheses. To support Objective-C construction of your Swift class, you'll want to add a class method that instantiates and returns a new object. The following snippet adds a new method to create instances. Once added to the Swift source, as in the following example, the code in Figure 11-10 compiles without further error:

```
@objc class MySwiftClass {
    class func `new` () -> MySwiftClass {
        return MySwiftClass()
    }
}
```

```
func test() {
    println("I can call Swift from Objective-C")
}
}
```

Notice the backticks (`) in this code snippet. The word `new` is normally reserved in Swift. The backticks tell the compiler to treat this item as a normal identifier instead of as a reserved word.

Building the Basics

Playgrounds are fantastic for learning Swift development. With them, you simply type a line or two of code and see immediate results. When you're ready to dive into Swift, open your Xcode editor into the two-pane "show the assistant editor" mode. This enables you to see three critical elements at once (see Figure 11-11). On the left in the central editor pane is your code editor. Just to its right is a gray-tinted sidebar that displays code results. Further to the right, in the assistant pane, is the console output, where you can monitor print output and any compiler errors that arise.

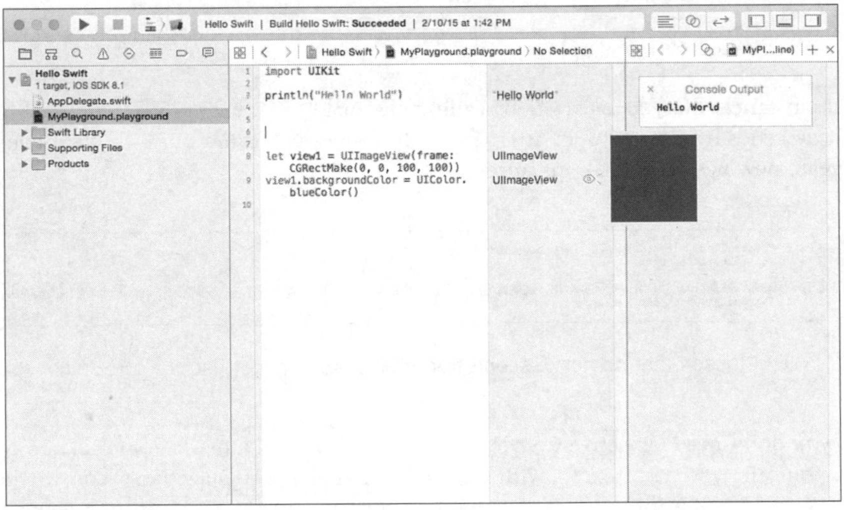

Figure 11-11   When working with playgrounds, stay in assistant mode so you can see your code and any compiler issues at the same time.

To get started, try entering a standard `println("Hello World")` line. The words Hello World appear just to the right of the print statement in the results pane and also in the console output.

Next, create a new image view:

```
let view1 = UIImageView(frame: CGRectMake(0, 0, 100, 100))
```

When you hover your mouse over the result gutter sidebar for this line, you see two items pop into view. The first is an eye-shaped Quick Look icon. If you click this, a gray pop-up appears. This is your view. It is 100×100 in size and essentially transparent. You have not associated any real properties with your image view.

The second is a value results circle. When you click it, the view presentation is integrated into the playground. Add the following lines to give the view a blue background and build an image of a circle. Then click all three value results circles. Figure 11-12 shows the results. You now monitor the view as it changes from clear to blue to containing a picture of a circle:

```
// Add a background color
view1.backgroundColor = UIColor.blueColor()

// Build an image and add it
let rect = CGRectMake(0, 0, 100, 100)
UIGraphicsBeginImageContext(rect.size)
var path = UIBezierPath(ovalInRect:rect)
UIColor.redColor().set()
path.fill()
view1.image = UIGraphicsGetImageFromCurrentImageContext();
UIGraphicsEndImageContext()
```

Watching Progress

One of the great things a playground does is let you inspect items over time. Enter the following loop and inspect the i instance in the middle of the loop:

```
let count = 400
for i in 0...count
{
    i
}
```

You can track the value as it changes over time with the handy graph shown in Figure 11-13.

Next, change that value to i*i or i*i*i. The graph becomes quadratic or cubic. Play with some other equations, as in Figure 11-14, to produce even more complex output. You can also change the number of samples to see how the results update to match the execution conditions you set:

```
for i in 0...count {
    let percent = Double(i) / Double(count)

    // Ease in-out
    let j = (percent < 0.5) ? 0.5 * pow(percent * 2, 3) :
        0.5 * (2.0 - pow((1.0 - percent) * 2, 4))

    // Damped sinusoid
```

```
    let time = percent * 3.0
    let k = 1.0 - cos(Double(M_PI) * 8.0 * percent) * exp(-1.0 * time)
}
```

```
                                Hello Swift    MyPlayground.playground
1    import UIKit
2
3    println("Hello World")                              "Hello World"
4
5    let view1 = UIImageView(frame: CGRectMake(0, 0, 100, 100))



6    view1.backgroundColor = UIColor.blueColor()


7
8
9    let rect = CGRectMake(0, 0, 100, 100)               {x 0 y 0 w 100 h 100}
10   UIGraphicsBeginImageContext(rect.size)
11   var path = UIBezierPath(ovalInRect:rect)            7 path elements
12   UIColor.redColor().set()
13   path.fill()                                         7 path elements
14   view1.image = UIGraphicsGetImageFromCurrentImageContext();



15   UIGraphicsEndImageContext()
16
                                                                    - 30 sec +
```

Figure 11-12   Swift playgrounds enable you to monitor the values assigned to items in the assistant editor.

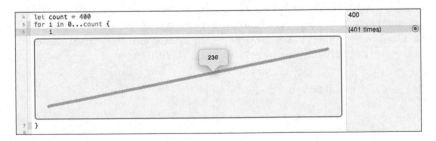

```
4    let count = 400                                     400
5    for i in 0...count {
6        i                                               (401 times)

                                236

7    }
8
```

Figure 11-13   Monitor the changes to a value over time.

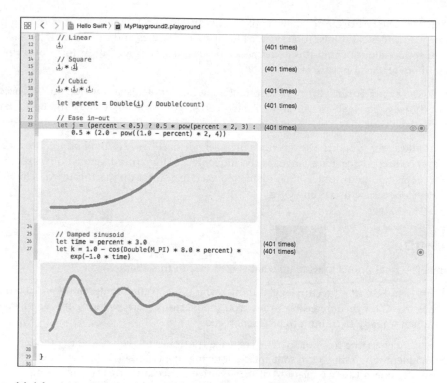

Figure 11-14   Add a little math to your playground for more exciting graphed results.

In addition to views and scalars, you can inspect sounds, colors, paths, attributed strings, common structures (rects, points, sizes, ranges), sprites (from SpriteKit), and URLs. These items are supported by the playground's Quick Look system, which continues to expand over time.

Learning Swift

While this chapter has surveyed some important Swift development topics and introduced the interactive playground, it cannot teach the language itself within the constraints of this book. To learn more about this exciting new technology, start with *The Swift Programming Language*. This is a free e-book offered by Apple on the iBooks store. Best of all, it's regularly updated as the language evolves. An extensive Revision History section lets you explore documentation and language changes by date.

A second Apple e-book, *Using Swift with Cocoa and Objective-C*, is just as essential. It provides an overview of the topics related to interoperability between languages and the details of API calls. It's a much shorter volume due to its tight focus.

The Apple Swift Blog (https://developer.apple.com/swift/blog/) is updated about once a month. Its coverage includes can't-miss topics related to language features and case studies. Its mission statement speaks about behind-the-scenes peeks into language design, but its focus over time has been more practical how-to articles.

The Apple Developer Forums (https://devforums.apple.com/index.jspa) provide the best access to Swift engineers. Navigate to Developer Tools > Language > Swift for a lively and up-to-date Swift language forum.

You're into IRC peer support? The Freenode (irc.freenode.net) `#swift-lang` room offers access to pro-level coding advice. It's a language-specific room, so if you need help with iOS-specific APIs, visit `#iphonedev` instead. A final room, `#cocoa-init`, is set up specifically to help mentor developers new to iOS and OS X.

Wrap-up

Here are a few final points to wrap up what you've read in this chapter:

- Swift is an important technology. Although you can continue to develop for iOS using Objective-C for the foreseeable future, you should really start exploring this arena even if you're not ready to commit to production code.

- Swift is a changing technology. The language continues to evolve, and the toolset is maddeningly primitive in some places. Moving to a type-safe language where the compiler doesn't fully explain what type issues it's encountering is exasperating.

- Swift is exciting. Features like generics, tuples (which enable you to return multiple values from a function), smart structs that provide class-like extensibility, and functional programming elements make this language gratifying to work with. At times, it's hard to return to Objective-C and realize how many language elements simply aren't available.

- Swift is limiting. Part of the reality of a type-safe language is that you have to play by the rules. Objective-C is relaxed and flexible in terms of meta-programming. You can build objects that build classes, you can explore the deep underbelly of your implementations from the runtime, and so forth. Swift barely and grudgingly lets you access any of these freewheeling details, so you lose out on many of the power-user development tools you may have grown used to.

- Swift is safe and powerful. When you play by the rules, you win in terms of reliable code. Swift is written to be a fast, high-performance, and trustworthy language.

Index

Symbols

#error directive, 232-233

#warning directive, 231-232

A

accessibility versions of font sizes, 27

accessing classes, 252-253

action controllers, building, 156-161

actionForKey method, 118

adaptive deployment

    rotation, 207-208

    trait collections, 201-204

        combining, 203-204

        defining, 202-203

        designing for, 204

        properties, 202

    UIScreen properties, 205-207

        application frame, 206

        coordinate spaces, 205-206

        scale, 207

        screen bounds, 206

adaptive flow, 58-60

adding

    animations to shaped views, 193-199

    behaviors to dynamic animators, 126-127

    borders to shaped views, 187-190

physics-based behaviors to collection views, 149-150

Quartz 2D contexts to UIKit context stack, 17-18

text fields to alerts, 162-163

touch to labels, 63-69

  checking for links, 67

  glyphs, 66

  implementing visual feedback, 67-69

  synchronizing Text Kit items with labels, 64-65

  translating coordinates, 65-66

adjusting

  attributes, 93-94

  pitch of voice playback, 3

alerts, 155-163

  building, 156-161

  buttons, enabling, 161

  class deprecations, 155-156

  jelly view alert, building, 150-154

    deploying jelly, 154

    drawing the view, 152-153

  text fields, adding, 162-163

angular velocity, creating the "spinner" effect, 147

angularResistance property, 138

animation, 101

  adding to shaped views, 193-199

  blocking animators, 105-106

  custom dynamic behaviors

    improving, 142-144

    secondary behaviors, 144-146

  custom dynamic items, 139-141

custom transition animations, 113-116

  building transitioning objects, 114-116

  delegation, 114

  UIViewControllerAnimated-Transitioning protocol, 113

dynamic animators, 125

  collection views, 147-150

  creating, 126-127

  detecting pauses, 127-132

  snap zones, 133-135

effect views, animating, 172-174

implicit animations, 116-124

  animating custom properties, 121-122

  animation-ready layers, building, 117-118

  completion blocks, 120-121

  coordinating, 119-120

  drawing properties, 123-124

  intercepting updates, 122

  timing, 118-119

  views, 118

keyframe animation, 101-103

  DampedSinusoid() function, 103

  scale transformation, 103-105

  shaking effect, 102-103

motion effects, 109-112

  disabling, 110

  shadow effects, 111-112

  virtual planes, 109-111

physics-based behaviors, subverting, 141-142

spring-based animation, 106-109

   damping constant, 109

   practical uses for, 108-109

system animations, 109

view animation, 101

animationKey method, 194

APIs

   Cocoa Touch, 248

   iOS dictation APIs, 5

   Swift, 249-251

   UIKit, 50-51

Apple Swift Blog, 260

application frame property, 206

applying text style ranges, 34-35

apps (iOS), building in Swift, 240-243

assets, 208-214

   overriding relationships with trait collections, 210-211

assigning values to non-optionals, 248

attachments, 77-78, 125

attributed strings

   adjusting attributes, 93-94

   attachments, 77-78

   building from HTML, 78-83

      document type dictionaries, 79-81

   converting to document data, 89-90

   converting to document representations, 81-82

   enhancing, 91-94

   fonts, updating, 35-38

      custom font faces, 36

      dynamic text views, 37-38

   initializing from a file, 84-85

   inspecting attributes, 87-88

   integrating with Dynamic Type, 31-35

      applying text style ranges, 34-35

      scanning for text style ranges, 32-34

   modifying fonts, 42

   mutable attributed strings, extending, 94

   returning copies of strings with new attributes, 92-93

   RTFD integration, 76-77

   tabular text, 76

attributedStringWithAttachment method, 78

Auto Layout, 201

AVAssetWriter class, 19

AVCaptureMetadataOutputObjectsDelegate protocol, 11

AVFoundation, movies

   building, 14-23

   pixel buffer, creating, 16-17

AVMetadataObject class, 11

AVSpeechSynthesizer class, delegate callbacks, 3-4

Aztec code, 9

B

Bacon Ipsum website, 223

barcode recognition, 1, 5-8

   CIQRCodeGenerator filter, parameters, 5-6

   enhancing recognition, 14

   extracting bounds, 13

   IOS-supported barcode formats, 8-9

   metadata, responding to, 11-13

   metadata objects, listening for, 10-11

QR codes

   building, 6-8

   disabling interpolation, 7-8

Baro, Victor, 150

beginEditing method, 56

Bezier paths

   exclusion zones, 61

   resizing, 181-183

Bezier-based shape image views, creating, 184-185

blocking animators, 105-106

blocks

   ContextDrawingBlock, drawing into the pixel buffer, 17-18

   movies, building, 15-16

blogs, Apple Swift Blog, 260

blur effect, building, 170-171

body style, 26

borders, adding to shaped views, 187-190

boundaries

   creating for gravity behavior, 138

   screen bounds, 206

bounding rectangles, 62

bounds, extracting, 13

bubbles, 176-177

building

   action controllers, 156-161

   alerts, 156-161

   animation-ready layers, 117-118

   attributed strings from HTML, 78-83

      document type dictionaries, 79-81

   AVFoundation movies, 14-23

   blur effect, 170-171

   fonts from text styles, 28

   HTML from attributed strings, 82

   images from PDFs, 211-214

iOS apps in Swift, 240-243

jelly view alert, 150-154

   deploying jelly, 154

   drawing the view, 152-153

mask views, 166-169

movies

   expressive drawing, 18-19

   from frames, 19-23

   images, adding, 23

   pixel buffer, creating, 16-17

QR codes, 6-8

shaped buttons, 190-193

side-by-side iPhone split views, 215-218

transitioning objects, 114-116

views around layers, 118

virtual planes, 110-111

buttons

   alert buttons, enabling/disabling, 161

   shaped buttons, building, 190-193

C

calculating text positions, 95

characterOffsetOfPosition:withinRange: method, 95

CIQRCodeGenerator filter, 5

circular views, creating, 180-183

Clang compiler, 229

class descent, 255-256

classes

   accessing, 252-253

   AVAssetWriter class, 19

   AVMetadataObject class, 11

   NSMutableAttributedString class, 56

   size classes, 204-205

   UIAlertController class, 155

UIBlurEffect class, 170

UIDictationController class, 5

UIDynamicAnimator class, 125-126

UIFont class, 27

UIFontDescriptor class, 40-41

UIImageAsset class, 210-211

UIImageView class, 210

UIInterpolatingMotionEffect class, 111

UIKit, enhancements to, 75-78

UITextView class, 59

UITraitCollection class, 201

UIVisualEffectView class, 169

closestPositionToPoint: method, 96

Cocoa Touch, APIs, 248

Code 39 barcode system, 9

Code 93 barcode system, 9

Code 128 barcode system, 9

collapsed property, 218

collection views

dynamic animators, 147-150

custom flow layouts, 147

returning layout attributes, 148-149

physics-based behaviors, adding, 149-150

collisions, 125

combining trait collections, 203-204

comments, converting to warnings, 229-231

comparing Objective-C and Swift, 239-240

completion blocks, 3-4

implicit completion blocks, building, 120-121

containers, 46, 57-62

adaptive flow, 58-60

bounding rectangles, 62

exclusion zones, 61

insets, 60-61

RTFD containers, 84

ContextDrawingBlock, 17-18

converting

attributed strings to document data, 89-90

attributed strings to document representations, 81-82

comments to warnings, 229-231

HTML to attributed strings, 78-83

document type dictionaries, 79-81

RTFD text to data, 85-86

coordinate spaces, 205-206

coordinating implicit animations, 119-120

Core Image filter, 5

CIQRCodeGenerator filter, parameters, 5-6

Core Motion, integrating with gravity behavior, 135-137

Core Text

glyphs, 47-50

Text Kit, ligatures, 46-47

creating

attributed strings from HTML, document type dictionaries, 79-81

boundaries for gravity behavior, 138

custom behaviors, 139-146

dynamic animators, 126-127

adding behaviors, 126-127

delegation, 126

frame-watching dynamic behaviors, 131-132

HTML from attributed strings, 82

mask views, 166-169

movies, 14-23

expressive drawing, 18-19

from frames, 19-23

images, adding, 23

PDFs, 71-73

QR codes, 6-8

views

Bezier-based shape image views, 184-185

round views, 180-183

virtual planes, 110-111

Cupcake Ipsum website, 223

custom behaviors, creating, 139-146

custom dynamic behaviors

improving, 142-144

secondary behaviors, 144-146

custom flow layouts, 147

custom properties, animating, 121-122

custom transition animations, 113-116

building transitioning objects, 114-116

delegation, 114

UIViewControllerAnimated-Transitioning protocol, 113

customAnimationForKey: method, 121

customizing font sizes, 38

D

damped harmonics, spring-based animation, 106-109

damping constant, 109

practical uses for, 108-109

DampedSinusoid() function, 103

declaring key support, 97-98

defining trait collections, 202-203

delegate callbacks for AVSpeechSynthesizer class, 3-4

delegation, 114

dynamics delegation, 126

density property, 139

designing for traits, 204

detecting

faces, 14

pauses, 127-132

diagnostics, overriding, 235

dictation, 5

directives

converting comments to warnings, 229-231

errors, 232-233

messages, 234

overriding diagnostics, 235

testing for the simulator, 232

unused variable warnings, 235-236

warnings, 231-232

wrapping pragmas, 234-235

disabling

alert buttons, 161

interpolation for QR codes, 7-8

motion effects, 110

displaying supported glyphs for fonts, 53-55

displayModeButtonItem property, 218-219

displayScale property, 202

document attribute dictionaries, establishing, 89-90

documents, creating representations from attributed strings, 81-82

draggable exclusion zones, 69-71

drawInContext:method, 123

drawing

into pixel buffer, 17-18

properties, 123-124

duration of implicit animations, 118-119

dynamic animators, 125

  collection views, 147-150

    custom flow layouts, 147

    returning layout attributes, 148-149

  creating, 126-127

    adding behaviors, 126-127

    delegation, 126

  detecting pauses, 127-132

    frame-watching dynamic behaviors, creating, 131-132

    monitoring views, 128-130

  gravity behavior

    connecting to device acceleration, 137

    creating boundaries, 138

    integrating with Core Motion, 135-137

  jelly view alert, building, 150-154

    deploying jelly, 154

    drawing the view, 152-153

  physics-based behaviors, 125-126

  snap zones, 133-135

dynamic behaviors, subverting, 141-142

Dynamic Type, 25-31

  attribute-ready dynamic elements, 35-38

    custom font faces, 36

    dynamic text views, 37-38

  font descriptors

    caveats, 40-41

    multiple font variations, 41

  font sizes, 27

    accessibility versions, 27

    customizing, 38

    user-controlled sizes, 43

  integrating with attributed strings, 31-35

    applying text style ranges, 34-35

    scanning for text style ranges, 32-34

  string attributes, modifying fonts with, 42

  styles, 26

    building fonts from, 28

  type updates, listening for, 28-31

E

EAN (European Article Number) barcode, 9

effect views, 169-174

  animating, 172-174

  blur effect, building, 170-171

  vibrancy effects, 171-172

elasticity property, 139

enabling

  alert buttons, 161

  metadata output, 11

endEditing method, 56

enhancing

  attributed strings, 91-94

  barcode recognition, 14

  view dynamics, 138-139

enumerateAttributesInRange:options: usingBlock: method, 88

enumerating

  attributes, 87-88

  optionals, 245-246

error handling in Swift, 251

"even/odd" fill rule, 186

exclusion zones, 61

  draggable exclusion zones, 69-71

expressive drawing, 18-19

extending mutable attributed strings, 94

extracting bounds, 13

F

faces, detecting, 14

fading logos, building, 122

Fake Name Generator, 225-226

files, saving from the simulator, 237

filters, Core Image filter, 5

flow layouts, 147

font descriptors, 39-42

    caveats, 40-41

    multiple font variations, 41

font sizes (Dynamic Type), 27

    accessibility versions, 27

    custom sizing, 38

    user-controlled font sizes, 43

fonts

    modifying with string attributes, 42

    with multiple variations, 41

    supported glyphs, displaying, 53-55

    updating with dynamic attributes, 35-38

        custom font faces, 36

        dynamic text views, 37-38

footnotes (Dynamic Type), 26

frames, building movies from, 19-23

frame-watching dynamic behaviors, creating, 131-132

friction property, 139

Fuller, Landon, 238

functions

    DampedSinusoid() function, 103

    UIGraphicsPopContext() function, 17

    UIGraphicsPushContext() function, 17

G

generating

    random feeds, 227

    random user data, 225-226

gestures

    draggable exclusion zones, 69-71

    taps, spring-based animation, 106-109

GitHub, xv

    lorem ipsum projects, 222

glyphs, 46-55, 66

    bounding rectangles, 62

    layout managers, 56-57

    ligatures, 46-47

    supported glyphs for fonts, displaying, 53-55

    UIKit, 51-53

gravity behavior, 125

    connecting to device acceleration, 137

    creating boundaries, 138

    integrating with Core Motion, 135-137

H

hardware key support, 97-99

    declaring, 97-98

headlines, 26

horizontalSizeClass property, 202

HTML

    converting to attributed strings, 78-83

        document type dictionaries, 79-81

    creating from attributed strings, 82

    markup initialization, 83

    writing RTFD containers from data, 86-87

hybrid language development, 252-256

    accessing classes, 252-253

    class descent, 255-256

    Objective-C, calling from Swift, 252

I

images

    adding to movies, 23

    building from PDFs, 211-214

    placeholders, 223-225

implementing snap zones, 133-135

implicit animations, 116-124

    animating custom properties, 121-122

    completion blocks, 120-121

    coordinating, 119-120

    drawing properties, 123-124

    intercepting updates, 122

    layers

        building, 117-118

        views, building, 118

    timing, 118-119

improving custom dynamic behaviors, 142-144

inferred types, 244

initializing attributed strings from a file, 84-85

inputCorrectionLevel parameter (CIQRCodeGenerator filter), 5-6

inputMessage parameter (CIQRCodeGenerator filter), 5-6

insets, 60-61

inspecting

    attributes, 87-88

    items with playgrounds, 258-259

integrating

    Dynamic Type with attributed strings, 31-35

        applying text style ranges, 34-35

        scanning for text style ranges, 32-34

    gravity behavior with Core Motion, 135-137

intercepting updates, 122

International Article Number barcode, 9

interpolation, disabling for QR codes, 7-8

iOS 8

    attributed text updates, 36

    split view controllers, 214-219

    supported barcode formats, 8-9

J-K

jelly view alert, building, 150-154

    deploying jelly, 154

    drawing the view, 152-153

JSON feed resources, 227

key support, 97-99

    declaring, 97-98

keyframe animation, 101-103

    blocking animators, 105-106

    DampedSinusoid() function, 103

    scale transformation, 103-105

    shaking effect, 102-103

L

labels, enabling touch, 63-69

    adding visual feedback, 67-69

    checking for links, 67

    glyphs, 66

synchronizing Text Kit items with labels, 64-65

translating coordinates, 65-66

layers

animation-ready layers, building, 117-118

border layers, generating, 188-190

views, building, 118

layout managers (Text Kit), 46, 56-57

layouts

attributes, returning, 148-149

Auto Layout, 201

containers, 57-62

adaptive flow, 58-60

exclusion zones, 61

insets, 60-61

custom flow layouts, 147

document attribute dictionaries, 89-90

draggable exclusion zones, 69-71

side-by-side iPhone split views, building, 215-218

learning Swift, 259

ligatures, 46-47

listening

for metadata objects, 10-11

for type updates, 28-31

logging, 238

lorem ipsum text, 221-223

requesting, 222-223

Lorem Pixel website, 224

M

Markdown, 83

marking non-null and nullable items, 236

mask views, 164-169

building, 166-169

shape layer masking, 164-166

media

barcodes, 5-8

enhancing recognition, 14

extracting bounds, 13

iOS-supported barcode formats, 8-9

listening for metadata objects, 10-11

QR codes, building, 6-8

responding to metadata, 11-13

dictation, 5

movies

adding images, 23

building, 16-17

creating from frames, 19-23

expressive drawing, 18-19

TTS, 1-4

completion blocks, 3-4

utterances, 2

messages, 234

metadata

enabling output, 11

objects, listening for, 10-11

responding to, 11-13

methods

actionForKey method, 118

animationKey method, 194

attributedStringWithAttachment method, 78

characterOffsetOfPosition:withinRange: method, 95

closestPositionToPoint: method, 96

customAnimationForKey: method, 121

drawInContext: method, 123

enumerateAttributesInRange:options: usingBlock: method, 88

needsDisplayForKey: method, 122

setAnimation: method, 194

transformedMetadataObjectFor-
MetadataObject method, 13

viewWillTransitionToSize:with-
TransitionCoordinator: method, 207

modifying

attributed strings, 93-94

fonts with string attributes, 42

monitoring

items with playgrounds, 258-259

views, 128-130

motion effects, 109-112

disabling, 110

shadow effects, 111-112

virtual planes, 109-110

building, 110-111

movies

building, 14-23

expressive drawing, 18-19

pixel buffer, creating, 16-17

images, adding, 23

pixel buffer

creating, 16-17

drawing into, 17-18

multiple snap zones, handling, 133-135

mutable attributed strings, extending, 94

N

needsDisplayForKey: method, 122

NeXTSTEP, 83

non-null items, marking, 236

NSAttributedString

class convenience methods, 91-92

integrating with Dynamic Type, 31-35

applying text style ranges, 34-35

scanning for text style ranges, 32-34

NSMutableAttributedString class, 56

nullable items, marking, 236

O

Objective-C

calling from Swift, 252

comparing to Swift, 239-240

preparing Swift for, 254-255

objects

text ranges, 95-97

transitioning objects, building, 114-116

optionals, 243-248

enumeration, 245-246

inferred types, 244

unwrapping, 246-247

overriding

relationships between trait collections and assets, 210-211

trait collections, 214-219

P

parameters for CIQRCodeGenerator filter, 5-6

pauses, detecting, 127-132

PDF417 standard, 9

PDFs

building, 71-73

creating images from, 211-214

printing, 74

physics-based behaviors, 125-126

adding to collection views, 149-150

custom behaviors, creating, 139-146

frame-watching dynamic behaviors, creating, 131-132

gravity
  connecting to device acceleration, 137
  creating boundaries, 138
  integrating with Core Motion, 135-137
  improving, 142-144
  pauses, detecting, 127-132
  properties, 138-139
  secondary behaviors, 144-146
  subverting, 141-142
pitch of voice playback, adjusting, 3
pixel buffer
  creating, 16-17
  drawing into, 17-18
placeholders
  for images, 223-225
  lorem ipsum text, 221-223
playgrounds, 256-258
popovers, 175-177
  supporting bubbles, 176-177
positions, text positions
  calculating, 95
  geometry, 95-96
  updating selection points, 97
pragmas, wrapping, 234-235
presentations, 155
  alerts, 155-163
    building, 156-161
    buttons, enabling, 161
    class deprecations, 155-156
    text fields, adding, 162-163
  effect views, 169-174
    animating, 172-174
    blur effect, 170-171
    vibrancy effects, 171-172

  mask views, 164-169
    building, 166-169
    shape layer masking, 164-166
  popovers, 175-177
    supporting bubbles, 176-177
printing text views, 73-74
properties
  of dynamic behaviors, 138-139
  of trait collections, 202
  UIScreen properties, 205-207
    application frame, 206
    coordinate spaces, 205-206
    scale, 207
    screen bounds, 206
pushes, 125

Q-R

QR (Quick Response) codes, 5
  building, 6-8
Quartz 2D contexts, adding to UIKit context stack, 17-18

random feeds, generating, 227
random generation suite, 228-229
Random User Generator, 225
range dictionaries
  applying text style ranges, 34-35
  scanning for text style ranges, 32-34
reading barcodes
  enhancing recognition, 14
  extracting bounds, 13
  iOS-supported barcode formats, 8-9
  listening for metadata objects, 10-11
  responding to metadata, 11-13
repairing attributes for text storage, 56
requesting lorem ipsum text, 222-223

resistance property, 139

resizing Bezier paths, 181-183

responding to metadata, 11-13

Retina display scales, 202

retrieving sample code, xv

returning copies of strings with new attributes, 92-93

rotation property, 138

"spinner" effect, creating, 147

round views, creating, 180-183

RTF, 83

RTFD containers

converting text to data, 85-86

writing from data, 86-87

S

sample code, retrieving, xv

saving files from the simulator, 237

scale property, 207

scanning for text style ranges, 32-34

screen bounds, 206

setAnimation: method, 194

shadow effects, 111-112

shake keyframe animation, 102-103

shape layer masking, 164-166

shaped buttons, building, 190-193

shaped views

animations, adding, 193-199

borders, adding, 187-190

creating, 179-187

Bezier-based shape image views, 184-185

round views, 180-183

shapes, unclosed shapes, 185-187

side-by-side iPhone split views, building, 215-218

simulator, saving files from, 237

size classes, 204-205

snap zones, 133-135

multiple snap zones, handling, 133-135

snaps, 125

speech generation, 1

completion blocks, 3-4

TTS, utterances, 2

"spinner" effect, creating, 147

split view controllers, 214-219

side-by-side iPhone split views, building, 215-218

spring-based animation, 106-109

damping constant, 109

practical uses for, 108-109

string attributes, modifying fonts with, 42

structs, UIEdgeInsets struct, 60

styles

building fonts from, 28

Dynamic Type, 26

layout managers, 56-57

subheadlines, 26

subverting dynamic behaviors, 141-142

supported barcode formats, 8-9

Swift, 239

APIs, 249-251

calling from Objective-C, 253-254

error handling, 251

iOS apps, building, 240-243

learning, 259-260

non-optionals, assigning values to, 248

versus Objective-C, 239-240

optionals, 243-248

  enumeration, 245-246

  inferred types, 244

  unwrapping, 246-247

playgrounds, 256-258

preparing for Objective-C, 254-255

The Swift Programming Language, **259**

system animations, 109

T

tabular text, 76

tap gestures, spring-based animation, 106-109

  damping constant, 109

  practical uses for, 108-109

text. *See also* Dynamic Type

  RTFD text, converting to data, 85-86

text fields, adding to alerts, 162-163

Text Kit, 43

  containers, 46, 57-62

    adaptive flow, 58-60

    bounding rectangles, 62

    exclusion zones, 61

    insets, 60-61

  exclusion zones, draggable exclusion zones, 69-71

  glyphs, 46-55

    ligatures, 46-47

  layout managers, 46, 56-57

  PDFs

    building, 71-73

    printing, 74

  text storage, 46, 55-56

    objects, 55

    repairing attributes, 56

  text views, printing, 73-74

touch-enabled labels, 63-69

  adding visual feedback, 67-69

  checking for links, 67

  glyphs, 66

  synchronizing Text Kit items with labels, 64-65

  translating coordinates, 65-66

text ranges, **95-97**

  text positions

    calculating, 95

    geometry, 95-96

    updating selection points, 97

text storage (Text Kit), **46, 55-56**

  objects, 55

  repairing attributes, 56

text style ranges

  applying, 34-35

  scanning for, 32-34

text views

  dynamic text views, 37-38

  printing, 73-74

touch-enabled labels, **63-69**

  adding visual feedback, 67-69

  checking for links, 67

  glyphs, 66

  synchronizing Text Kit items with labels, 64-65

  translating coordinates, 65-66

trait collections, **201-204**

  combining, 203-204

  defining, 202-203

  designing for, 204

  overriding relationships with assets, 210-211

  properties, 202

  split view controllers, 214-219

transformedMetadataObjectForMetadata-
Object method, 13

TTS (text-to-speech), 1-4. *See also* dictation

utterances, 2

completion blocks, 3-4

pitchMultiplier, 3

type updates, listening for, 28-31

typography

Dynamic Type, 25-31

font sizes, 27

integrating with attributed strings,
31-35

styles, 26

type updates, listening for, 28-31

glyphs

ligatures, 46-47

supported glyphs for fonts,
displaying, 53-55

U

UIAlertController class, 155

UIBlurEffect class, 170

UIDictationController class, 5

UIDynamicAnimator class, 125-126

UIDynamicItem protocol, 139

UIEdgeInsets struct, 60

UIFont class, 27

UIFontDescriptor class, 40-41

UIGraphicsPopContext() function, 17

UIGraphicsPushContext() function, 17

UIImageAsset class, 210-211

UIImageView class, 210

UIInterpolatingMotionEffect class, 111

UIKit

adding Quartz 2D contexts, 17-18

APIs, 50-51

classes, enhancements to, 75-78

dynamic behaviors, 125-126

font descriptors, 39-42

glyphs, 51-53

spring-based animation, 106-109

UINavigationControllerDelegate
protocol, 114

UIScreen properties, 205-207

application frame, 206

coordinate spaces, 205-206

scale, 207

screen bounds, 206

UISystemAnimationDelete animation, 109

UITabBarControllerDelegate protocol, 114

UITextInput protocol, text ranges

geometry, 95-96

positions, calculating, 95

updating selection points, 97

UITextView class, 59

UITraitCollection class, 201

UIViewControllerAnimatedTransitioning
protocol, 113-114

UIVisualEffectView class, 169

unclosed shapes, 185-187

unused variable warnings, 235-236

unwrapping optionals, 246-247

UPC (Universal Product Code) standard, 9

updating fonts, 35-38

custom font faces, 36

dynamic text views, 37-38

user interface idioms, 202

user-controlled font sizes, 43
*Using Swift with Cocoa and
Objective-C*, 259
utterances, 2
    completion blocks, 3-4

V

verticalSizeClass property, 202
vibrancy effects, 171-172
view animation, 101
view controllers,
UIViewControllerAnimatedTransitioning
protocol, 113
views
    Bezier-based shape image views,
        creating, 184-185
    building around layers, 118
    collection views
        dynamic animators, 147-150
        physics-based behaviors, adding,
            149-150
    dynamics, enhancing, 138-139
    effect views, 169-174
        animating, 172-174
        vibrancy effects, 171-172
    jelly view alert, building, 150-154
        deploying jelly, 154
        drawing the view, 152-153
    mask views, 164-169
        building, 166-169
        shape layer masking, 164-166

monitoring, 128-130
round views, creating, 180-183
shaped views
    animations, adding, 193-199
    borders, adding, 187-190
text views, printing, 73-74
viewWillTransitionToSize:
withTransitionCoordinator: method, 207
virtual planes, 109-110
    building, 110-111
visual feedback, adding to touch-enabled
labels, 67-69
voice playback, adjusting pitch, 3

W

warnings, 231-232
    unused variable warnings, 235-236
websites
    Bacon Ipsum, 223
    Clang Language Extensions, 234
    Cupcake Ipsum, 223
    Lorem Pixel, 224
wrapping pragmas, 234-235
writing RTFD containers from data, 86-87

X-Y-Z

XML feed resources, 228

yaw, 14

informIT.com
THE TRUSTED TECHNOLOGY LEARNING SOURCE

PEARSON

InformIT is a brand of Pearson and the online presence for the world's leading technology publishers. It's your source for reliable and qualified content and knowledge, providing access to the top brands, authors, and contributors from the tech community.

Addison-Wesley | Cisco Press | EXAM/CRAM | IBM Press. | QUE | PRENTICE HALL | SAMS | Safari Books Online

LearnIT at InformIT

Looking for a book, eBook, or training video on a new technology? Seeking timely and relevant information and tutorials? Looking for expert opinions, advice, and tips? **InformIT has the solution.**

- Learn about new releases and special promotions by subscribing to a wide variety of newsletters.
  Visit **informit.com/newsletters**.

- Access FREE podcasts from experts at **informit.com/podcasts**.

- Read the latest author articles and sample chapters at **informit.com/articles**.

- Access thousands of books and videos in the Safari Books Online digital library at **safari.informit.com**.

- Get tips from expert blogs at **informit.com/blogs**.

Visit **informit.com/learn** to discover all the ways you can access the hottest technology content.

Are You Part of the IT Crowd?

Connect with Pearson authors and editors via RSS feeds, Facebook, Twitter, YouTube, and more! Visit **informit.com/socialconnect**.

informIT.com THE TRUSTED TECHNOLOGY LEARNING SOURCE   PEARSON

Addison-Wesley | Cisco Press | EXAM/CRAM | IBM Press. | QUE | PRENTICE HALL | SAMS | Safari Books Online